Televising Democracies

Televising Democracies is the first book to assess the impact of television broadcasting on the House of Commons and its Members' behaviour. It looks at the implications for political journalism as well as broader questions concerning the role of media in a democracy. It also examines the lessons to be learned from the experience of televising the American Congress, the German Bundestag and the European Parliament.

Bringing together contributions from senior broadcasters, politicians from various parties and academics and researchers, the book approaches the issues from a range of different perspectives. The first section of the book focuses on broadcasters' accounts of the difficulties involved in establishing the structure and organisation of Parliamentary broadcasting, while the second section gives politicians' own assessments of the consequences of the admission of cameras to the House. The third section looks at the findings of research studies assessing the type of materials broadcast, the impact on political journalism, and audience responses. The fourth section draws comparison with the American, German and European experience of televising democracy.

Televising Democracies

Edited by Bob Franklin

London and New York

First published 1992
by Routledge
11 New Fetter Lane, London EC4P 4EE

Simultaneously published in the USA and Canada
by Routledge
a division of Routledge, Chapman and Hall Inc.
29 West 35th Street, New York, NY 10001

Set in 10/12pt Times by Selectmove
Printed and bound in Great Britain by T J Press (Padstow) Ltd,
Padstow, Cornwall

British Library Cataloguing in Publication Data
Televising democracies.
1. Politics. Effects of television
I. Franklin, Bob
320

Library of Congress Cataloguing in Publication Data
Televising democracies/edited by Bob Franklin.
    p.   cm.
Includes bibliographical references and index.
1. Great Britain. Parliament. House of Commons – Television
broadcasting of proceedings. 2. Legislative bodies – Television
broadcasting of proceedings. I. Franklin, Bob, 1949–.
JN611.T45 1992
328.41'0068 – dc20   91–16157

ISBN 0–415–07021–X
ISBN 0–415–07022–8 pbk

Contents

Tables

Contributors

Moira Bovill, Researcher, BBC Broadcasting Research Department

Brian Brown, Researcher, Broadcasting Research Unit, University of Aston

Caroline Culey, Secretary to the Liberal Democrat Parliamentary Party and Assistant to the Chief Whip

Guy Cumberbatch, Head of the Broadcasting Research Unit at the University of Aston

Bob Franklin, Lecturer in Politics, University of Keele

Roger Gale MP, member of the Select Committee on Televising of Proceedings of the House of Commons

James Leaton Gray, programme editor with BBC Westminster and BBC Television's Committee Co-ordinator during the experimental period; he is Robert T. McKenzie Fellow at the London School of Economics and Social Science

John Grist, Supervisor of Broadcasting, House of Commons

Alastair Hetherington, Emeritus Professor of Media Studies, University of Stirling

Charles Kennedy MP, President of the Liberal Democrat Party, member of the Select Committee on Televising of Proceedings of the House of Commons

Brian P. Lamb, Chief Executive, C-SPAN

Robin McGregor, Head of Special Projects, BBC Broadcasting Research Department

Glyn Mathias, Assistant Editor, ITN

Austin Mitchell, MP and broadcaster

Tony O'Donnell, Head of Production, Audio-Visual Division, European Parliament

Heribert Schatz, Professor of Political Science, University of Duisberg

Julia Skelton, Researcher, Broadcasting Research Unit, University of Aston

Brian Tutt, member of the Parliamentary Research Group, University of Leeds (1989–90); currently a doctoral student at the London School of Economics

Kay Weaver, Department of Media Studies, University of Stirling

Mallory Wober, Deputy Head of Research, IBA

Acknowledgements

Edited books are necessarily a collective and co-operative enterprise and I would like to acknowledge my gratitude to the contributors who have written about their perceptions, experiences and studies of the experiment in televising the Commons for this book. Broadcasters, politicians and academics typically work under pressure and I was, on occasion, very conscious that people were making considerable efforts to find time for 'one more' commitment in an already hectic schedule. Christine Bailey, of the Institute of Communication Studies at the University of Leeds, has, as always, been greatly supportive in the book's production. Thanks also to Brian Tutt and David Mercer, who were excellent colleagues, good friends and fellow members of the Parliamentary Research Group at the University of Leeds. Many others are owed thanks for their contribution to the book, including Ruth Battye and Pauline Weston from the Department of Politics, University of Keele, Barbara Edmundson and Paul Nicholson from Computing Services at the University of Leeds, Peter Humphries from the Department of Government, University of Manchester, Roger Bufton and John Conway from BBC Regional Programming, News and Current Affairs, and Michael Fay, IBA Regional Officer for Yorkshire. Many thanks also to Margaret Douglas, Chief Adviser on Policy and Planning at the BBC.

Special thanks are due to Jay Blumler and Tom Nossiter, who were my colleagues at the Centre for Television Research from 1985 to 1990. They supported and guided my early work in the field of political communications, infused me with some of their energy and enthusiasm for the enterprise, but, most importantly, introduced me to the delights as well as frustrations involved in conducting serious social science research. The centre was not always an easy place in which to work, especially when the workload was punitive, but it was never dull. I feel I was very lucky to have the opportunity to work closely with two such distinguished scholars and, more importantly, demanding teachers.

The final but most important acknowledgement is for the support offered over many years by my father Arthur Franklin, until his death in January 1988. As with so many people of his generation and class, the educational system denied him any opportunities to develop his undoubted skills, intellect and abilities. He was a gentle man, with a great gift for telling stories. He was rarely quiet. I doubt that he really understood what was involved in being a student, much less a teacher, in a university. But he was immensely proud of me, always supported me and read, conscientiously and with great relish, everything I published. He would have been very proud of his son's involvement in this book and told his mates at work all about it. It is dedicated to his memory.

Bob Franklin

Foreword

I am grateful for this opportunity to offer a few words of introduction to this interesting and lively collection of essays on the recent experiment in the televising of proceedings of the House of Commons. The editor, Dr Bob Franklin of the Department of Politics at Keele University, is already well known to many Members through his leading role in the detailed study commissioned by the Select Committee on Televising of Proceedings of the House on the use made by the broadcasters of the signals from the Chamber and committees. I pay tribute to his achievement in bringing together within a single volume such a distinguished and disparate set of authors.

The common thread running through all these contributions is the feeling that, while the task of televising the work of the House was in many ways, not least technically, something of a leap in the dark, the resulting success of the operation has surprised even the most dedicated and persistent champions of the cause. Perhaps more significant is the extent to which those who initially harboured some misgivings (among whom I cautiously number myself) have been won over – albeit with varying degrees of enthusiasm – by the practical realities of televising. Indeed, so far has the issue now been anaesthetized as a source of controversy that in July 1990 only 32 Members voted against the motion approving the Select Committee's recommendation that televising be made permanent, compared with 264 who had opposed the holding of an experiment in 1988.

I believe that a number of factors have contributed to this development – the scale of which few would have predicted when the experiment began in November 1989. Chief among these have undoubtedly been the rules of coverage, drawn up by the Select Committee and agreed by the House, which govern the television director's choice of shots. Although it is often claimed that Members watch very little television themselves, I am sure none the less that most of my parliamentary colleagues will have formed their judgement on the basis of how the House was actually portrayed on the screen. A clear set of guidelines was therefore necessary to provide reassurance to the many Members worried about the risk of trivialization and sensationalism, while at the same time striking a fair balance with the broadcasters' natural desire to show the House 'warts and all'. The other important aspect, it seems to me, has been the existence of a Select Committee, and an officer of the House in the form of the Supervisor of Broadcasting directly answerable to it, which have been able to protect the interests both of the House generally and of individual Members. By this means, it has proved possible to contain at a remarkably low level the volume of complaints about such matters as the intensity of the lighting in the Chamber and the intrusiveness of camera crews in committee rooms. (The question of the sound system in the Chamber, though not related in a technical sense to the televising of proceedings, has given rise to increasing complaints since the start of the experiment. This is not the place to go into further detail on that subject which, in any case, is receiving urgent attention from the Select Committee.)

Perhaps I might, however, offer some observations of my own from the particular vantage-point of the Chair, whose occupants, after all, appear 'in shot' more often than any other Members. I referred earlier to the considerable apprehensiveness felt by many Members over the way in which the broadcasters might exploit their access to a new source of political reporting. But many Members were equally, if not more, concerned about how the House itself might react to the presence of the cameras. It would certainly have required a touching faith in human nature to have expected no changes at all, but looking back at the experience so far what strikes me most forcibly is how *little* impact televising has had on the way in which the House goes about its business.

It is true that on Tuesdays and Thursdays after Question Time, when proceedings are transmitted live, there has been a tendency for points of order of a more or less bogus nature to compete with Government statements, the latter often on subjects whose importance or urgency has not been immediately apparent. My deputies and I have also noticed an increased anxiety on the part of Members generally to be called at Question Time and in debates in 'prime time'. The phenomenon known as 'doughnutting' (i.e. clustering around the Member speaking) has certainly been in evidence but not on nearly so widespread a scale as had been predicted, possibly because the director's occasional use of a wide-angle shot shows up the practice in all its artificiality.

Nor have fears that televising would encourage some Members to 'play to the gallery', or even that it would have an adverse impact on their conduct in the Chamber, been borne out. I judge that there is a reluctance on the part of Members to be suspended or named for defying the chair and for this to be seen by their constituents on TV. As for what is usually described as 'rowdiness', I cannot honestly say that I have detected any significant deterioration during the last two sessions.

Interestingly, my postbag, which has been greatly swollen by the introduction of televising, has been overwhelmingly supportive. I have no doubt that one reason for this is that viewers can now see for themselves, on the screen, the context in which noisy exchanges take place. Another intriguing feature of my correspondence is that, contrary to a widespread belief initially, the viewing public does not for the most part seem to have found our often somewhat arcane procedures unduly confusing or difficult to follow. I suspect that this is because the broadcasters have gone to considerable lengths to provide explanatory commentary – to the point, indeed, where some people have complained about its intrusiveness. Most of the letters I receive on this subject are actually more concerned to find out the reasons for particular aspects of the House's practice and to seek explanations for the historical origins of some of our quainter rituals.

If I have one specific regret about the way in which televising has developed so far, it is the lack of a channel devoted to continuous coverage of the House's proceedings and of the important work done by its Select and Standing committees. At present, our constituents – in whose name, after all, we take decisions and debate the issues of the day – receive a very untypical picture of the House's work. Brief snippets on news programmes, concentrated heavily on Prime Minister's Question Time, plus occasional live broadcasts of set-piece occasions like the Budget, are really no substitute for comprehensive coverage of our proceedings. Of course, we should not delude ourselves that all our constituents, or even perhaps a majority of them, would wish to spend a much greater part of their spare time watching a parliamentary channel. But the crucial point is that the very *existence* of such a channel would enable the individual elector to make his or her choice of what was worth following, rather than leaving this important decision to the editorial judgement of the broadcasters – however responsibly they may have exercised it so far. I am therefore glad that the Select Committee on Broadcasting, as it is now known, is to take further evidence on this subject, though I recognize that the House's own powers of initiative are fairly limited in what is, in the absence of public funding, essentially a commercial matter.

To conclude on a more positive note, however, I believe that the televising of the House's proceedings has proved a considerable triumph, to the extent that it is already virtually taken for granted by the vast majority of Members, not to mention the public at large. The test of this success was surely most aptly illustrated by the coverage of the two-day debate on the Gulf crisis for which the House was recalled from its summer recess in 1990. It is a fair bet that, had our constituents not been able to follow on television this debate on a subject of vital national and international importance, the floods of protest would have matched any representations about the merits of the issues themselves. Many people, including Members of all parties, must now be asking themselves: why did it take us so long?

Rt Hon. Bernard Weatherill MP
Speaker of the House of Commons

Part I

Televising the Commons

Chapter 1

Televising the British House of Commons: issues and developments

Bob Franklin

Mr Bernard Weatherill, the Speaker of the House of Commons, in an interview for *The New Yorker*, described the televising of the House's proceedings as 'the best show in town'. The theatrical metaphor is perhaps appropriate, since one of the most forceful and persistent objections offered by opponents of the cameras has been that television would trivialize the Commons' proceedings by incorporating Parliament into the entertainment industry. MPTV, as Roger Gale alleges, might become mere 'info-tainment' (chapter 6). A similar reluctance had, of course, characterized politicians' attitudes to radio and press reporting of parliamentary affairs. When journalists were initially allowed into the Chamber, they could not take their pens with them – which made a good memory a prerequisite for a career in journalism. The parliamentary reporters on *The Times* were legendary for their powers of recall.

But television, more than other media, has prompted particularly strong suspicions among politicians, reflecting perhaps their beliefs concerning its potential for influencing the opinions of a mass audience. Churchill, for example, was highly sceptical about the new medium, believing television to be nothing less than 'a red conspiracy' (Hood 1980:63). His support for the Fourteen-Day Rule, a censorial mechanism which, until the mid-1950s, prohibited television discussion of any topic likely to occur in Parliament in the subsequent fortnight, was unequivocal. In the House debate on the rule, Churchill argued that 'it would be a shocking thing to have the debates of Parliament forestalled by this new robot organization of television and BBC broadcasting'. The rights of MPs must be protected 'against the mass and against the machine' (Cockerell 1988:41). This belief that television might in some way subvert the role of politicians received a strikingly similar endorsement from Tony Benn during the 19 July 1990 debate on the report of the Select Committee on Televising of Proceedings of the House. Benn claimed:

> The media, the pollsters, the people who hype it up and the public relations people who engage in politics have taken the democratic process away from us and made it something that highly paid experts want to manage for us. This House is made up of people whose commitment to politics is real because we are answerable to our constituents.
>
> (HC Debs 1990: col. 1264)

Given this analysis, the task of politicians is to 'recover democracy for the people from the media' (HC Debs 1990: col. 1263). The concern expressed here is not merely that the media might constitute a fourth estate, critical and watchful of government, but that they might become an independent but unaccountable force in British politics. It is interesting to hear Benn update, but essentially echo, Baldwin's rebuke of Beaverbrook and Rothermere in 1931, that they were out for 'power without responsibility, the prerogative of the harlot throughout the ages'.

But most politicians have long since come to accept television's pervasive involvement in British political life. Many have adapted their politial style accordingly in an effort to manipulate the medium to their advantage. The major political parties, at both local and national levels, employ media advisers, marketing, advertising and public relations specialists to develop strategies for promoting positive media images for their leaders, senior politicians and key policies. Partly conferences, local and general elections are the foci of sustained media attentions, which politicians are pleased to receive and enthusiastic to promote. As Martin Harrop observed, media involvement in the political and electoral processes is so extensive that 'in elections especially the media do not cover the campaign: they are the campaign. We must ask how, not whether, the media matter' (Seaton and Pimlott 1987:45).

It is perhaps surprising, then, that television should, until recently, have been excluded from the very heart of British political life: the British Parliament and the British House of Commons. The House eventually agreed, on 9 February 1988, to an experiment in television broadcasting of its proceedings.

A Select Committee was established to make the necessary arrangements for the arrival of the cameras and to oversee the conduct of the experiment. The first pictures of the British House of Commons were broadcast live on 21 November 1989 to coincide with the state opening of the new parliamentary session.

This chapter explores central features of the experiment in television broadcasting from the Commons by addressing three key questions. First, what objections to televising House proceedings have been expressed by parliamentarians in the various debates on this issue across a quarter of a century? Second, how have the structure and organization of parliamentary broadcasting developed and been informed both by the outcome of these debates and by changes in the broader political and media environments? Finally, can the tardiness which has characterized the admission of the cameras into the House – when compared with the United States, Germany or the European Parliament (chapters 13, 14 and 15) – be explained by politicians' adversarial and sceptical attitudes towards the media or does this 'model' of politician–broadcaster relations require redefinition?

TELEVISING THE COMMONS: THE DEBATE

Since May 1985 there have been twelve parliamentary debates concerning the televising of the House. On two occasions prior to 1988, bills have achieved a slender majority in favour, although later they have been lost because of lack of parliamentary time. The question, which has always been decided on a free vote, has always split the House closely but never wholly on party lines, with advocates and opponents being drawn from both sides.

The substantive arguments in favour of televising the Commons have tended to be constitutional in character, stressing the democratic benefits which might accrue from broadcasting proceedings. Televising the House would make it more accountable to the public, enhance public participation in the political process, albeit vicariously, as well as performing an important educational function in revealing to the public the procedures and conventions of the House and, by reporting debates, the key policy issues of the day. Television might also serve to halt the twentieth-century decline of Parliament by publicizing, and thereby bolstering, its effectiveness as a checking mechanism on the executive during a period when it had become commonplace for Governments to enjoy a large majority in the House. Kennedy and Culey express the matter succinctly: 'As a party firmly committed to the principle of open government, we believe that the public have a right to see their elected representatives at work' (chapter 7).

The admission of cameras to the Commons has also been advocated on two additional grounds. First, the House's reluctance to allow the televising of its affairs seemed to express a peculiarly British reserve. Fifty-eight countries, including most West European democracies, some East European countries and the Soviet Union, currently televise their Parliaments, although the extent of coverage, its use by broadcasters and the degree of editorial control exercised by the legislature varies considerably. In the context of such widespread legislative broadcasting, the absence of cameras in the Commons seemed anomalous.

Second, near-universal television ownership guarantees that increasingly news, current affairs and political debate reach the majority of the public via television. Television's ability to 'reach' a mass audience, moreover, would assist the Commons in the accomplishment of one of its key functions which, Mitchell suggests, 'is to dramatize and educate. The purpose of debate is to put the case for and against what the Government is doing. It is intended for the electorate, to give them the raw material with which to decide their vote. That role is futile if it doesn't reach the people' (chapter 5).

Many of the arguments raised by opponents of televising have been similarly constitutional. A review of the numerous debates since 1965 reveals that the same arguments have been marshalled persistently against the proposal. They can be classified into four broad categories which may be labelled technical, reputational, party political and procedural.

Technical objections emphasize the difficulties arising from the introduction of cameras and lighting equipment necessary to broadcast from the House. Particular grievances have concerned the number of microphones which might be necessary, where to site them and whether or not they would transmit the level of annoying and intrusive background noise which has characterized sound broadcasting (HC Debs 1985: col. 281). Members' fears that cameras in the Chamber would be intrusive have been allayed by the installation of remote-control cameras under the public galleries, but concern continues about the use of bulky and invasive camera equipment in the committee rooms (Cumberbatch, Brown and Skelton, chapter 12). Undoubtedly the most frequently voiced technical objection has been to the powerful lighting necessary for broadcasting, which, it was alleged prior to the experiment, would generate an oppressive and unacceptable degree of heat. After a number of attempts to modify the system these difficulties appear to have been largely resolved, although 'A few Members still find the glare a little trying' (Grist, chapter 2). Few technical difficulties remain unresolved. Indeed, Roger Gale, a long-term opponent of televising the House, confirms that many of his 'technical reservations have been allayed. There are few who would now quarrel with the technical quality of the pictures leaving the Chamber' (Gale, chapter 6).

Reputational objections are less readily dispelled. The argument typically offered here has been that edited television coverage of the Commons proceedings would undermine the reputation and stature of the House and, by featuring only selected aspects of the House's activities, would misrepresent the House's work. Some Members have expressed their misgivings in more forceful rhetoric. James Kilfedder, for example, argued that 'people outside see on their television screens only what the television producers and editors permit them to see and that is contrary to the democratic principle. Why should we permit the media manipulators to censor the televising of our proceedings?' (HC Debs 1990: col. 1265).

Members' doubts about the accuracy of television coverage of Parliament reflect what they consider to be the incompatibility of the two institutions, expressed by the antithetical objectives which they pursue and the values which motivate them. The ultimate telos of television is judged to be entertainment, which is most readily achieved by stressing the trivial and the sensational. By contrast, the Commons is concerned with informed and rational debate, based on the forceful presentation of a particular case. Some Members believe that in any encounter between television and Parliament the interests and purposes of the latter will necessarily prevail. Consequently, Marion Roe declared the experiment to have been 'a television success but a political failure . . . televising has provided entertainment at low cost for the television stations. Edited highlights appear on the evening news bulletins enabling the political correspondents to spice up their coverage of the proceedings of the House' (HC Debs 1990: col. 1258). Roger

Gale's assessment is broadly similar and attributes a decisive role to journalists' news values in the selection of material for broadcast. 'What we were offered . . . by the BBC and ITV', he suggests, 'was *Match of the Day* and edited highlights used to tart up the *Nine O'Clock News* and *News at Ten* with occasional "live" coverage of the "sexy bits" – such as Prime Minister's Question Time and the Budget – and selective forays on to the committee floors' (chapter 6).

A third set of objections has articulated worries that the presence of television cameras might promote the interests of political parties inequitably. This might involve not only the misrepresentation of levels of support for the different parties, but the very nature of the party conflict within the Chamber. It is the minority parties that have tended to express such concerns. Kennedy and Culey confirm that the Liberal Democrats' 'enthusiastic support for the principle of televising' has been 'tinged with concern that, as the "third party", televising the House's proceedings would in practice prove to be to our disadvantage' (chapter 7). Alan Beith has expressed similar reservations, alleging that television would disadvantage smaller parties by reinforcing public perceptions of an adversarial two-party contest in the House. If, moreover, politicians' suspicions proved correct and broadcasters were attracted to personalities rather than policies and preferred conflict to consensus, then the Prime Minister, the Leader of the Opposition and the two parties they lead are likely to enjoy disproportionate broadcast attentions (HC Debs 1985: cols. 291–2). This tendency, as Kennedy and Culey note, has, during the experimental period, been exacerbated by the very procedures of the House which are based on the 'politics of confrontation between two parties' (chapter 7).

Procedural objections range from the relatively minor to the highly significant – from predictions that MPs' behaviour might change (and for the worse), through more substantive concerns that specific procedures of the House might be altered, to yet more worrying and general forecasts that televising the House would change, if not destroy, its essential character. The experiment in broadcasting has done little to settle these contentious matters, with both advocates and opponents of the cameras claiming endorsement for their position.

Some MPs believe that the cameras have prompted more theatrical behaviour. One Member claimed:

the arrival of television has had a strange and unforeseeable effect on the behaviour of many hon. Members. . . . Television has brought out the worst in us . . . it is a sad fact that hon. Members check up on who is asking the Prime Minister questions beforehand so that they can sit next to the questioner and be guaranteed to appear on television screens in millions of homes . . . the sight of hon. Members scrambling to sit within camera shot reminds me of those outside broadcasts in which an interviewer speaks to camera with a couple of young children bouncing up and down pulling faces in the background. Who after all can resist the lure of publicity.

(HC Debs 1990: cols 1258–60)

Roger Gale endorses this view (chapter 6), while Mitchell denies anything more than marginal changes in behaviour and rejects the issue as largely irrelevant (chapter 5). The findings of the Aston University research group suggest that few MPs believed Members' behaviour in the Chamber had been influenced by the admission of cameras, but, significantly, where changes were observed they were judged to have led to an improvement (chapter 12).

Both opponents and advocates of the television cameras claim changes in House procedures as a consequence of televising. Gale (chapter 6) notes the growing practice of 'doughnutting', while Kennedy and Culey record four changes subsequent to the introduction of the cameras, each with significant implications for minority parties: frontbench speeches have increased in length; an increased use of the ten-minute time limit on backbench speeches is apparent; Opposition spokespersons are tending to make longer responses to Government statements; and growing pressure at Question Time has tended to 'squeeze out' minor parties (chapter 7).

Lamb (chapter 13) and O'Donnell (chapter 15) report little evidence of procedural change following the admission of the cameras to the American Congress and the European Parliament, while Schatz notes substantial changes which he interprets as products of the broader phenomenon of 'television democracy' rather than televising the Bundestag (chapter 14).

In the Commons, the major procedural objection has been that relatively minor changes in behaviour and procedure, if aggregated, might culminate in a serious threat to the essential character of the House. The clearest statement of this position has been by Quintin Hogg (Lord Hailsham). 'Parliament', he claimed, 'is a wonderful and unique institution and I want to keep it as it is . . . it is different in character after television is brought in. That is what I am afraid of' (HC Debs 1965: col. 1065). In a more recent debate, David Amess echoed Hogg's sentiments closely. 'We have allowed ourselves to be seduced by the media,' he claimed. 'Increasingly the House seems to be more media driven than the other way round and I regret that. . . . We have trivialized our proceedings and Members of future Parliaments will never know how this place used to be' (HC Debs 1990: cols 1268–9).

These four types of argument – technical, reputational, party political and procedural – have until quite recently proved extremely effective in denying television cameras access to the House. But on 9 February 1988, by a majority of 54, Members voted in favour of an experiment in television broadcasting from the Commons. It seemed as if the Commons' suspicions had given way to at least a cautious approval of the cameras. The motion included provision for a Select Committee to oversee the experiment and it was envisaged that broadcasting might commence with the state opening of Parliament in autumn later that year. But the deliberations of the committee proved more protracted than many imagined, objections to the enterprise more resilient than anticipated. The debate on the Select Committee's first report on 12 June 1989, more than a year after the initial decision, confirmed that broadcasting would begin with the state opening of Parliament on 21 November 1989.

THE DEVELOPMENT AND ORGANIZATIONAL STRUCTURE OF PARLIAMENTARY BROADCASTING

The House's decision to televise its proceedings prompted great excitement in the media, with every British national newspaper carrying the story on its front page. Alastair Burnet spoke in euphuistic terms about the significance of broadcasting. 'We should have seen Suez debated and the Falklands,' he claimed. 'These are memorable debates which are important in our lives and which', he concluded in more utilitarian style, 'will get significant audiences from time to time' (Burnet 1988: 11). Within days of the Commons decision, both the BBC and the commercial networks had announced ambitious plans for programming. But broadcasters' early enthusiasms turned quickly to disappointment. By June 1988, media trade journals were lamenting the Select Committee's slow progress and alleging delaying tactics by opponents of parliamentary broadcasting.

The committee's major task was to decide who would provide the television signal from the Chamber of the House – what is known as the 'clean feed'. The 'clean feed' is the constant, uninterrupted televisual coverage of the events on the floor of the House which forms the 'raw material' that is subsequently edited and used by broadcasters, perhaps with other materials, to make programmes. It proved to be a lengthy and contentious decision, although most broadcasters and politicians have subsequently come to agree that the eventual outcome was both acceptable and workable.

The committee discussed three broad options for the provision of the signal which, as Lamb records, were very similar to those discussed by the House of Representatives when establishing congressional broadcasting. The signal should be provided jointly by the BBC and ITN; an independent company should be contracted for the service; an 'in-house' broadcasting unit should be established along the lines of the unit in the American Congress or the European Parliament (chapter 13). There was an air of novelty about these deliberations, since when the Lords was first televised in January 1985 it had been considered uncontroversial and axiomatic, as Mathias notes (chapter 3), that the BBC and ITN jointly should provide the clean feed which each should then use independently in programme production. In the Commons, however, the BBC/ITN bid was received unfavourably by the committee, even though the projected costs of £520,000, at that time, undercut by more than half the equivalent tenders from any independent company. Austin Mitchell defended the BBC/ITN bid on the grounds of cost, but also because they possessed considerable experience of broadcasting state ceremonials and affairs – not least the proceedings of the House of Lords – and both were large organizations with equipment which could be redeployed after the experiment. The BBC and ITN, moreover, would undoubtedly constitute the largest market for the clean feed and, consequently, 'to accept an independent bid will mean forcing these organizations to pay more for a service they can provide more cheaply for themselves' (Mitchell 1988: 15).

Some observers interpreted the committee's unhappiness with

the BBC/ITN proposal as an expression of a broader 'beyond Westminster' change in the relationship between politicians and broadcasters; more specifically, of the tensions between some Conservative MPs and the BBC. Conservative allegations of bias in the BBC reporting of the American bombing of Libya, journalists' unease with the decisions of BBC governors to accede to requests from the Home Secretary not to broadcast certain politically sensitive programmes, restrictions on coverage of Northern Ireland affairs since October 1988, in conjunction with the Government's more traditional levers on broadcasters via the licence fee, seem to have contributed to a growing estrangement. The rejection of the BBC/ITN bid, it was alleged, reflected these broader ideological considerations rather than any technical matters. One broadcaster suggested:

> Everyone knows that if a state occasion were held at Westminster Abbey, the BBC and ITN could, within seven days' notice or less, provide TV coverage to a high editorial standard with a technical proficiency unsurpassed throughout the world. Yet excellence of this kind will count for nothing. . . . It is a sign of the times that the most natural course [to choose the BBC/ITN bid] has become the most unthinkable.
>
> (Woffinden 1988: 13)

The choice of an independent contractor seemed, at least prima facie, to be more ideologically congruent with Conservative dispositions. The independent sector was deemed to be competitive, cost effective, reliant wholly on market forces and, perhaps significantly, capable of splintering the BBC/ITV duopoly in broadcasting. It was argued, moreover, that splitting the tasks of originating the signal and of making programmes between an independent company and the BBC/ITN respectively would guarantee greater independence of editorial control than if both tasks were allocated to either one. But advocates of televising believed that the Select Committee's decision to interview each of the eleven independent companies which had submitted bids was merely a ploy being deliberately used by opponents of television to postpone the decision.

Critics of the independents pointed to the relatively high initial cost of their proposals, while some expressed scepticism concerning their broadcast competences. Frank Dobson, then Shadow Leader of the House, claimed that he 'wouldn't have entrusted some of them with making wedding videos' (quoted in Woffinden 1988: 9). With the benefit of hindsight, neither criticism can be sustained.

A parliamentary television unit, similar to the American or European model, was undoubtedly judged by some MPs to be the ideal option. The Select Committee report confirmed that 'such a unit remains our preferred solution for the longer term' (HC Select Committee 1989: 141–I, para. 106). The unit would be owned and controlled by the Commons and placed under the direct responsibility of the Speaker. But at the time few considered the proposal a realistic policy option. Some Conservative Members opposed the expansion of the state into an area where a private company could provide an adequate service and suggested that a parliamentary unit would, at least for the period of the experiment, be too expensive in capital terms and would require considerable staffing and running costs. Additionally, some argued that such an arrangement might place too much editorial control with politicians.

The Select Committee's eventual decision, embodied in its May 1989 report and endorsed by a majority of 293 to 69 in the House debate of 12 June, proved to be as interesting as it was unpredictable; it represented a curiously British compromise. The BBC and ITN were to fund a joint subsidiary company to be called the House of Commons Broadcasting Unit Limited – HOCBUL. The board of the company was to have twelve members drawn equally from the House of Commons and the broadcasters, with an independent chair nominated by the House but acceptable to both parties. The company would provide and maintain the necessary equipment for broadcasting but the operation of the cameras and provision of the clean feed would be the responsibility of an independent company selected by competitive tender.

The House would retain copyright and thereby final authority over the signal. The financial arrangements governing the experiment were expressed in the report with an apparent and evident simplicity which was confounded by the complex reality of subsequent practice (chapter 4). But, in theory, the company would sell the signal at a price calculated on the general principle that costs should be shared equitably among the various users of the signal. Income would be used to offset the costs of the independent company originating the signal, with additional revenues divided between the broadcasters, to assist with their equipment expenditure, and the House, to help offset archive costs.

The May report also established guidelines for broadcasters which proscribed certain camera shots. The picture of Members to be portrayed on the screen was to be confined to a head-and-shoulders shot of the speaking Member. There were to be no panning shots along the benches, no reaction shots and no pictures of the clerks or other officers of the House. On occasions of disruption, the cameras must focus on Mr Speaker. In order to enforce these editorial guidelines and amend them as necessary, the House should appoint a Select Committee and a new officer of the House, the Supervisor of Broadcasting. The Supervisor of Broadcasting should, among other matters, oversee arrangements concerning the sale of the signal and arbitrate in any disputes between the company and the purchaser (see chapter 2).

The Select Committee's proposals to the House represented a skilful political compromise with many evident features to offset the concerns expressed by some Members, but they were not universally well received. At the time, the independent companies claimed the arrangement would diminish their role in parliamentary broadcasting to that of 'mere technicians'. For their part, the ITV regional companies were no happier with the formula. This prompted Robert Hargreaves, who chaired the ITV working party on televising the Commons, to suggest in a letter to the Select Committee that 'the diverse (and sometimes conflicting) interests of ITV will not be adequately represented on the board' of HOCBUL (Hargreaves 1989:3). Broadcasters as well as politicians from most parties complained about what they considered to be the over-restrictive guidelines, but, despite an amendment supported by Frank Dobson and John Biffen to 'moderate' the rules of coverage, they remained intact prior to the experiment.

The first televised broadcasts from the Commons began with the state opening of Parliament on 21 November 1989. Politically these were exciting and interesting times. Nigel Lawson, the Chancellor of the Exchequer, had resigned the previous week. The Government was under substantial challenge from a newly invigorated Opposition enjoying an upturned success in the opinion polls. Within her own party, Mrs Thatcher faced a challenge to her leadership, albeit none too serious on that occasion, from Antony Meyer. It promised to be an exciting parliamentary session, with controversial bills on broadcasting, embryology and abortion, a long-running industrial dispute in the ambulance service which seemed bound to feature in ministerial questions, and growing extra-Parliamentary opposition to the poll tax.

From the outset, the experiment in broadcasting was judged a success by a majority of broadcasters, politicians and the public. In January 1990, three months into the experiment, the Select Committee 'relaxed' the rules of coverage by allowing broadcasters to use a wider camera shot which generated televisually more interesting pictures. On 19 July 1990 the House agreed, by a majority of 99, to make permanent the televising of its proceedings.

The Select Committee report of 12 March 1991 made recommendations for the structure and financing of parliamentary television on a permanent basis (HC Select Committee 1991). The report made three recommendations for the House's consideration. First, the televising of Parliament should become an integrated operation incorporating coverage of the Commons Chamber, committees and the Lords. HOCBUL, which had been established as a transitional body to oversee the experimental period of broadcasting was to metamorphose into PARBUL, the Parliamentary Broadcasting Unit. The board of PARBUL should reflect these changes and would subsequently be composed of seven broadcasters, three Members of the Commons, three Members of the Lords and the Supervisor of Broadcasting. Second, the task of producing the signal, or clean feed, was to remain the responsibility of an independent operator, chosen by public tender, with contracts being renewable on a five-year cycle. Finally, the arrangements for meeting the costs of televising Parliament which prevailed during the experimental period should continue unchanged. Broadcasters should finance equipment and running costs, the Parliamentary Works Office should be responsible for capital expenditure within the parliamentary estate (i.e. changes to the fabric of the building to accommodate equipment), while the House of Commons Commission should fund the Select Committee and any staff, including the Supervisor of Broadcasting, associated with the management of the television operation within the House itself.

In summary, these proposals suggested minimum change from the structure of broadcasting established for the experimental period. The committees's argument against alternative proposals, which included the establishment of an in-house broadcasting unit as well as suggestions by broadcasters that the entire costs of the operation should be met from the public purse, was that while present arrangements may appear 'unnecessarily complex and cumbersome' they have 'worked remarkably well and are now accepted and understood. None of the evidence we have received suggests that there would be anything to be gained by abandoning them for the sake of some other untried formula' (HC Select Committee 1991: 11, para. 143). Not everyone was convinced, and Roger Gale (chapter 6) argues that the new arrangements may militate against the establishment of a dedicated channel for parliamentary television.

The Select Committee has, to date, received proposals to establish a dedicated channel from Commons Committee Television (CCTV, the company responsible for producing committee coverage during the first two years of broadcasting), Thames Television and United Artists Entertainment Programming (UAP). Since November 1990, UAP have been making daily recordings of proceedings between 4 and 10 p.m. (9.30 a.m. to 3 p.m. on Fridays) which are captioned and broadcast overnight, via the Intelsat satellite, for cable operators to broadcast the following morning. The committee believes the UAP scheme offers the best possibility for creating a dedicated channel but remains concerned that initially the channel would be available only to satellite subscribers.

After a decade of radio broadcasting, an experimental period of television broadcasting and twelve debates across a quarter of a century, and five years after the House of Lords had consented to the televising of its affairs, the Commons has allowed permanent entry to the cameras. If the public had missed the debate on Suez and the Falklands, they were given the opportunity to see, 'live', Geoffrey Howe's resignation statement, Mrs Thatcher's defence of the Government's record against an Opposition motion of no confidence on the day that she resigned as Prime Minister and, on 29 November 1990, the first Prime Minister's Question Time taken by John Major, the new Conservative party leader and Prime Minister. Writing in the *Guardian* on the day after Mrs Thatcher's valedictory performance as Prime Minister, Nancy Banks-Smith claimed: 'Yesterday was the ultimate justification of the televising of Parliament. It flowed in three continuous streams from BBC, ITN and Sky. Without it we [the viewers] too would have been outside on the frost-bitten grass in our thermal underwear' (*Guardian*, 23 November 1990).

POLITICIANS AND THE MEDIA

The experiment in televising the proceedings of the Commons proved successful so quickly that many observers, not to say MPs, must wonder what all the fuss was ever about. Why did televising the Commons prove such a difficult issue for the British Parliament? Some parliamentarians, of course, objected strongly to televising and their case has been reiterated in the first part of this discussion. But not everyone has been convinced that such objections constitute sufficient explanation for the tardiness which has characterized the admission of cameras to the Commons. Austin Mitchell, for example, is unhappy to accept such protestations at face value and imputes a different and more interesting motive: 'the advent of MPTV', he suggests, 'was delayed for far too long by fear, disguised as high principle' (chapter 5). This suggestion that politicians might be fearful of the media seems to rest on a view of broadcaster–politician relations as essentially adversarial. Mitchell's claim is not without precedent. Seymour-Ure, in an early essay, explained Parliament's reluctance to televise its affairs by highlighting this power relationship between politicans and broadcasters and the potential ability of each institution to influence developments in the other. 'Put briefly,' he asked 'which is "bigger", Parliament or television?' (Seymour-Ure 1974: 139).

But this view of media–politician relations needs modification on at least two counts. First, while relations between politicians and media may be characterized by conflict and possibly suspicion, they can also assume a more positive and co-operative guise. Bernard Ingham, the Prime Minister's press officer until November 1991, in a lecture entitled 'Government and media: co-existence and tension' suggested that Government and media live 'in a permanent and natural state of tension'. The relationship, he argued, 'is essentially cannibalistic. They feed off each other, but no one knows who is next on the menu' (Ingham 1990). Putting aside the graphic metaphor, this last remark is interesting and signals at least the hint of a different kind of relationship, based on a form of mutual reliance, which none the less does not deny the possibility of the adversarial component.

Second, Seymour-Ure may be correct in pointing to the potential for conflict in the relationship between politicians and broadcasters, but these two battalions do not line up as neatly and homogeneously as he suggests. Each is characterized by diversity and riven with conflicts, so far as the enterprise of televising Parliament is concerned, creating a complex amalgam of shifting alliances and allegiances which confounds any Manichaeistic perception of 'politicians versus broadcasters'. Let me elaborate briefly on each of these concerns.

Seaton and Pimlott identify two broad traditions in the analysis of media–politician relations, differentiated according to whether media are judged to be 'the masters or the servants of politicians' (Seaton and Pimlott 1987: ix). The former tradition, which is closely associated with liberal or pluralist theorizing, considers media to be a fourth estate, critical and watchful of Governments and a key mechanism for securing their accountability to the public. The latter tradition, which is associated with Marxism in its different guises, suggests that media do not challenge politicians but, in various ways, sustain them in power. On this account, media are the agents of consensus, encouraging the acquiescence of the masses by serving as mere conduits for politicians' messages and propaganda.

Each tradition can generate prima-facie evidence sufficient both to support its own and to undermine its opponents' position. Media can, of course, prove forceful critics of politicians' explanations of events and policies. Media may even, on occasion, play a central role in the downfall of politicians, as some observers believe was the case with Mrs Thatcher's resignation. But equally the problem of increasingly scarce resources which media confront, combined with politicians' continuing tendency to hire ever growing numbers of press and public relations advisers, creates enhanced possibilities for politicians to influence media news agendas.

What is required is an account of politician–broadcaster relations which combines elements of both traditions and thereby achieves a greater power to explain the realities of that relationship. A closer examination reveals that the relationship between politicians and broadcasters is less adversarial than may appear at first glance. Both groups have objectives, interests and needs which can be achieved most readily when they can solicit and acquire the co-operation of the other group; a process described as 'mutual adaptation' (Blumler and Gurevitch 1981: 472). Politicians, of course, remain wary of broadcasters, but without prejudice to their understanding of the potential opportunities which media can provide. For their part, broadcasters appreciate that without at least a minimal co-operation from politicians the enterprise of political journalism is doomed to failure if not rendered wholly impossible. Recognition of this mutuality of interest has drawn the two groups closer together to the point where some observers have described them as 'inextricably linked' (Blumler and Gurevitch 1981: 473). Consequently, political news and current affairs have come to be understood not as the outcome of any adversarial encounter but as the product of a process of negotiation between, and mutual construction by, journalists and politicians.

Media can perform invaluable functions for politicians, although not all politicians are aware of these opportunities or convinced about the media's ability to achieve them. Politicians may, for example, wish to use media to promote themselves with their local community and constituency, especially where they occupy a marginal seat; to stimulate public awareness and support for particular policy initiatives; to inform the public about the progress of policy implementation in different areas of government policy and service provision; to assess public reaction to innovative policy proposals; to create a favourable climate of opinion about particular issues, perhaps of policy; to promote a favourable image of party or government; to communicate messages 'indirectly' to political friends, but mainly opponents in opposition parties as well as their own; to offset a political opponent's propaganda efforts; to enhance their political careers; to assist them in their efforts to secure re-election. The list is almost endless.

Television may, on occasion, be judged capable of fulfilling substantially more significant functions for politicians. Schatz, for example, argues that much of the impetus behind televising the German Parliament, following the collapse of the Nazi regime in 1945, reflected the belief of politicians of all parties in the need to 'popularize' the Bundestag and re-establish a democratic way of life in Germany. Television was considered central to this process (chapter 14). Similarly, O'Donnell confirms that the admission of the cameras early in the life of the European Parliament was part of a strategy by politicians intended to enhance 'public perceptions of both the European Community and its Parliament' (chapter 15). In both settings, politicians identified television as an influential factor in establishing the legitimacy of the new Parliaments.

Politicians fulfil a smaller but no less important range of functions for broadcasters and broadcast media. Politicians' activities consti- tute broadcasters' largest and major source of stories – significant for both their number and their news value; they act routinely as informants about political affairs; they appear regularly as 'performers' filling interview seats on news programmes and being panel members in current affairs discussions; they provide background and contextualizing information about political affairs; they offer authoritative comment on political matters; they consti- tute a very knowledgeable section of the media audience, providing feedback and comment on content.

This mutuality of interests and concerns, this 'occupational complementarity', suggests that it would be inappropriate and misleading to characterize media as either watchdogs or lapdogs, since, depending on circumstances, they may be either. On occasion broadcasters can find their 'teeth' and reproach politicians for inefficiency or good old-fashioned incompetence, but at other times they can help to support or promote particular politicians or policies. The popular tabloid press, perhaps above other media, exemplifies this Janus-like ability to support and promote politicians or to cajole them.

But perceptions of the relationship between politicians and broadcasters require revision not simply because they are too frequently considered only in their adversarial aspects, but also because both groups lack the homogeneity so often and misleadingly attributed to them. To claim that politicians are a heterogeneous group, separated by conflicting interests, is uncontentious and may even be considered to be stating the obvious, but broadcasters are also characterized by a diversity of possibly conflicting interests which make it unlikely that they would respond uniformly to given circumstances. Such differences were certainly evident in the case of televising the Commons.

Politicians are divided, perhaps most obviously, by party. De- bates on the issue of televising the Commons have always been decided on a free vote, but a growing influence of party has been evident on recent occasions. In the 1988 vote which established the experiment in television broadcasting, Labour divided 176 (86 per cent) in favour with only 28 (14 per cent) against, while the Conservative vote split 116 (33 per cent) in favour with 264 (67 per cent) against. What shifted dramatically between the vote of November 1985 and that of February 1988, however, was the Conservative proportion of the 'No' lobby: 231 (88 per cent) of the 264 Members in the 'No' lobby were Conservative compared with 28 (11 per cent) Labour. In the debate on 19 July 1990 to determine whether the cameras should be allowed permanent access to the

House, only a single Labour Member, voted against the proposal. For their part, the Liberal Democrats have voted overwhelmingly in favour of televising proceedings.

This leads to a second area of potential division between politicians. The minority parties have always believed that they would be relatively disadvantaged by television coverage of the House, with the two major parties being the beneficiaries of the greater part of coverage. Kennedy and Culey, for example, believe that the arrival of the cameras has prompted a number of changes to the procedures of the House which are 'damaging to the Liberal Democrats as the third party, to the minority parties in the House and to backbenchers from all parties' (chapter 7). James Kilfedder of the Ulster Popular Unionist Party raised similar objections, alleging broadcasters' apparent neglect of Northern Ireland Members and parties in their coverage (HC Debs 1990: col. 1265). Tutt's analysis of broadcasters' attention to the different parties confirms minority-party suspicions. But there is no allegation of broadcaster partisanship here; the predominance of Conservative and Labour over other parties is explained as 'perhaps inevitable given the nature of both parliamentary procedure and journalistic attitudes' (chapter 8).

A third division between politicians reflects their status as members of the front or back benches. The suspicions of some backbenchers concerning the cameras were expressed forcefully by Sir Antony Grant, who claimed that they would be 'yet another weapon in the hands of what is loosely called the "establishment front bench" to put itself over compared with backbenchers' (HC Select Committee 1990: 265–IV, para. 267). Broadcasters seem to have been conscious of these anxieties and arranged a series of meetings with backbenchers to persuade them of the potential opportunities which the cameras might provide for increased television exposure in their constituencies (chapter 3). Analysis of television coverage reveals that the Prime Minister, Leader of the Opposition, cabinet and shadow cabinet appeared regularly in programming but did not overwhelm the appearances by other parliamentarians (chapter 8). Indeed, Franklin's analysis of regional broadcasting shows that appearances by backbenchers accounted for as much as 60 per cent of all parliamentarians featured in regional television coverage (chapter 11).

There is, of course, nothing sinister about a certain predominance of the front bench (especially on the Government side) over the back bench. Frontbench politicians are typically better known and more public figures and, as members of the Government or senior Opposition figures, are the authoritative decision makers whose views and opinions are judged newsworthy. The predominance of the front bench in certain news programmes need not necessarily reflect the 'publicity hierarchy' identified by Schatz (chapter 14) but simply the procedures of the House which ensure prominence for ministers and Opposition spokespersons when making or replying to statements, at Question Time and in debates. But Kennedy and Culey claim that the cameras have enhanced the prominence of the front bench; consequently the Government front bench tends to make longer statements while Opposition spokespersons tend to make longer replies.

A fourth division between politicians, which might prompt a different attitude towards televising proceedings, is between those Members who work primarily in the Chamber and those whose major focus of work is the committees. Leaton Gray notes that prior to the experiment the majority of those who chaired committees were against the admission of the cameras because they were concerned that 'the ground that the departmental Select Committees had gained, in redressing the balance between the executive and the legislature, might be lost as MPs and the press turned their attention from the consensus committees to the adversarial Chamber' (chapter 4).

Two further divisions between politicians might inform Members' differing attitudes towards the cameras. First, Members in marginal seats may be more favourably disposed towards the televising of Commons proceedings because they envisage possible electoral advantage accruing from the opportunities television provides for fairly regular appearances in regional news and current affairs programmes broadcast in their constituency. Second, those MPs considered to be 'good performers' or 'telegenic' might be expected to be more favourably disposed to television, seeing personal advantage in their ability to exploit the cameras' presence. Gale cites, with alarm, a remark by the Speaker of the Canadian House that 'the televisual MPs are at the top of the whips' list . . . they choose "performers" in preference to the thoughtful' (chapter 6). In the British setting, certain backbenchers, by virtue of their status as elder statesmen or their reliability as sources of controversial comment, have attracted the attention of the cameras, but overall 'backbenchers who made telling points were likely to be featured in television reports without regard to any previous celebrity' (chapter 8).

In summary, politicians are characterized by diversity, reflecting their membership of the various political parties, their membership of a minority party or one of the two major parties, their status as a frontbench or backbench MP, the primary focus of their parliamentary work in committee or Chamber activities, their occupancy of a seat in a marginal or safe constituency and their personal qualities and competences as media 'performers'. Each of these differences might be expected to give rise to differing attitudes towards televising Parliament.

Broadcasters display an equivalent diversity. The evident divisions of interest between them, influencing their often distinctive approaches to televising the Commons, were acknowledged by the Supervisor of Broadcasting, who complained that 'It was no easy task to get competing broadcasters to . . . orchestrate an approach to the House' (Grist, chapter 2). Similarly, Glyn Mathias's observation that ITN's position on HOCBUL was 'complicated by the disparate interests of Independent Television' acknowledges the possibility of divisions between them (chapter 3). Indeed, James Leaton Gray highlights cross-media divisions by pointing to the 'growing resentment towards television on the part of the remainder of the press gallery' following the arrival of the cameras in the committee rooms (chapter 4).

A first and perhaps obvious distinction between broadcasters separates those highly committed journalists who are located in the House, and actively involved in programme making, from the more remote managers and executives who may be less committed to the enterprise of parliamentary broadcasting or whose commitments may express different priorities in which financial considerations predominate over public service concerns. For their part, 'working' broadcasters will be less preoccupied with broader issues such as the intricacies of programme budgeting or where parliamentary items might fit into the programming schedule. Consequently journalists and managers within broadcasting might be expected to adopt quite distinctive views about televising the Commons. John Grist alludes to such differences when he observes that the costs of parliamentary broadcasting will 'have to pass the eagle . . . eyes of executives who are more interested in the bottom line than their producers, news editors and journalists' (chapter 2).

Second, broadcasters working on network programming might

likewise be expected to approach parliamentary broadcasting with a distinctive set of interests and attitudes to their counterparts in the regions. In the regions, broadcasters make programmes for substantially smaller audiences, offer their viewers distinctive news agendas in which parliamentary items may rank less prominently and must compete with regional or local matters, operate with more limited budgets, have less flexibility and 'space' for new programmes in their schedules and have a much smaller 'pool' of local MPs on which to draw for programme making.

Third, divisions might be anticipated between broadcasters in the ITV and BBC sectors of the industry in the various regions (chapter 11). BBC regional coverage of the House was part of a co-ordinated response by the Corporation to the challenge of parliamentary broadcasting. Consequently, BBC regional parliamentary programming was informed by a distinctive programme philosophy which perhaps unduly constrained programme style, but programmes were undoubtedly financially resourced more fully than their ITV counterparts and enjoyed a new and distinctive slot in scheduling; in the ITV regions parliamentary materials were incorporated into extant current affairs programming. But distinctions were apparent within the ITV services with some evidence, albeit limited, that the smaller ITV companies were experiencing resource shortages, resulting in infrequent uses of actuality in news and review programmes and an inability to sustain programmes across the full parliamentary session. Programme makers in some ITV companies expressed concern about their company's ability to meet its public service commitments in a changing and deregulated broadcasting environment.

Fourth, broadcasters working on news and current affairs programming for satellite stations may come increasingly to form another group reflecting distinctive newsgathering priorities and practices and characterized by differential access to resources. Satellite coverage of the Commons during the experimental period differed in a number of ways, perhaps as a result of these variations in delivery systems and resources. The Leeds University study concluded that coverage of the Commons on Sky News was 'a little disappointing' by comparison with the network terrestrial stations, with the former reporting a 'relatively limited spectrum of Parliamentary events, Parliamentary office holders, non-Parliamentary actors and political parties compared to its terrestrial counterparts' (HC Select Committee 1990: 265–I, 27).

A final distinction may be drawn between those broadcasters from the independent sector contracted to supply the clean feed and broadcasters working in the companies of the 'old duopoly' whose task is to use the signal thus provided in programme making. These are radically different tasks which might be expected to engender divisions between the two groups. BBC and ITV broadcasters have been excluded from part of the television production process which previously they might have imagined to be unquestionably theirs. The independent broadcasters are earning valuable public service credentials for their sector of the industry and creating a new respectability for this burgeoning group within broadcasting.

In summary, the impetus behind televising Parliament reflects the interaction between an extraordinarily complex and shifting network of alliances within and between broadcasters and politicians. This account of politician–broadcaster relations undermines the notion that, in certain policy arenas, neat and orderly ranks of broadcasters and politicians confront each other in an adversarial fashion. The reality is infinitely more complex and, on occasion, more co-operative.

But this inherent complexity has undoubtedly been thrown into further flux by the broader changes in the broadcasting environment stemming from the Broadcasting Act 1990. A broadcasting system driven by consumer choice and competition between broadcasters makes the future of news and current affairs, of which parliamentary broadcasting is a significant part, uncertain. The 'quality threshold' offers critics of the legislation some guarantees that quality and range of programming will be sustained across all areas including news and current affairs. But critics suggest that the large sums of money necessary to guarantee success in the auction of franchises require both substantial staff redundancies and cuts in programme budgets. The Act, moreover, requires the current owners of ITN (the fifteen regional ITV companies) to sell a 51 per cent stake in the company. In tandem these developments do not augur well for a continued priority, measured in terms both of resources and of allocation of schedule time, for news, current affairs and parliamentary broadcasting.

Satellite broadcasting is still in its infancy. The advent of a twenty-four-hour news channel signals a growing emphasis on news and perhaps parliamentary affairs but, during the experimental period, satellite coverage of the Commons has been undistinguished. The merger of Sky with British Satellite Broadcasting may confound such pessimistic prognoses by creating a financially well-resourced satellite channel, replete with viewers and advertising revenues.

The future of parliamentary broadcasting seems unclear. Satellite technology offers broadcasters and politicians the opportunity for a channel dedicated to continuous coverage of parliamentary proceedings, but the costs, estimated at around £5.5 million per annum, combined with modest audience reach, seem to be prohibitive in the short run. Cable technology offers a lower-cost option but the audience size is even more severely restricted. Little change is envisaged in the structure and financial organization of the BBC before its charter becomes subject to renewal in 1996. Consequently the Corporation's commitments to the public service tradition of broadcasting, embracing parliamentary coverage, might be expected to continue. But Channel 3's regional companies are likely to be 'strapped for cash' following the ITC's franchise auctions. They will be eager to attract the largest possible audiences but keen to minimize their programme production costs. In this intensely competitive broadcasting climate, the commercial side of the British television divide might be less able to provide comprehensive coverage of parliamentary proceedings than it might wish.

Part II

The organization of Commons television: the broadcasters' perspectives

Chapter 2

'As long as a piece of string': the role of the Supervisor of Broadcasting

John Grist

The televising of the House of Commons was a comparatively simple technical problem. Broadcasting was to begin on 21 November 1989 at 2.30 p.m. for four and a half days a week, most weeks, until 31 July 1990. It was to come from an oddly shaped hall in south-west London, with poor lighting and acoustics, which had deteriorated markedly since its bombing in 1941. The building was elderly, protected by all the devices of conservation which the law and sentiment could devise. There were to be eight cameras; the sound was provided. It had been a long time coming.

My first memory of televising the House of Commons was when Aneurin Bevan suggested, on 9 November 1959 just before his death, that the House should open its doors to cameras. About the same time, Robin Day wrote a pamphlet (Day 1963), and it appeared to those of us involved in political broadcasting that the television cameras would probably move into the Chamber in the foreseeable future. In the early 1960s Martin Redmayne, as he was then, Chief Whip in Harold Macmillan's Government, took me into the Chamber and I showed him where the cameras would hang under the gallery. Even thirty years ago it was recognized that camera operators would not be allowed into the Chamber on a regular basis and remotely controlled cameras, which were just coming into use at the time, would have to be the solution.

My next involvement came when Richard Crossman MP, at that time Lord President of the Council, asked me privately whether I would advise him about the televising of the House. This was quite satisfactory until the Director General of the BBC came to hear that I was assisting the Lord President. The Director-General thought that I should not be dealing with a senior member of the cabinet without his knowledge or permission, so on that rather sour note ended my connection with the televising of Parliament. As debate followed debate across almost two decades, it began to look as if something else useful had joined that list of 'not in my time'. Then, in May 1988, out of the blue I was asked to become a specialist adviser to the Select Committee on Televising of Proceedings of the House, with Jay Blumler, Emeritus Professor at Leeds University. Later we were joined by Mike Reed, a distinguished lighting cameraman, and Robert Longman OBE, formerly Chief Engineer of the BBC Television Service.

It was fascinating for someone who had been involved in political journalism for many years to see a Select Committee working from the inside. But the published record tells nothing of the private discussions of a Select Committee; it merely records, 'The Committee deliberated'.

A Select Committee presents a formidable aspect to a witness. This particular Select Committee had twenty members with an extremely high attendance record. In public sessions there is normally an opening set of questions, but after that, individual members follow their own line of questioning. The large number of sessions and the range and the interest of the participating members meant that a considerable amount of information and ideas crossed the committee floor. It was not, however, until the Select Committee went to Canada in the summer of 1988 that the ideas began to be clothed in reality. One of the most useful questions in television has always been 'What will I see on the screen?' The Select Committee's Canadian experience in Ottawa and Toronto focused attention on that question when they returned for the 1988–9 session.

TECHNICAL PROBLEMS

Before the experiment in television broadcasting, the Chamber of the House was dimly lit and, even the most sensitive cameras with the stops wide open would require additional lighting. Luckily the strip lighting under the galleries was old and inefficient and was due to be replaced. This solved one of the problems and unexpectedly transformed the back benches into quite an attractive background for Members, who could be seen by the cameras without having to share the picture with portions of the anatomies of other Members. But lighting is not only a question of the quantity of illumination; it is important and necessary to 'model' the face. The lighting adviser,

Mike Reed, was only too conscious that when extracts from the Commons were shown on a news programme the appearance of the Members would be compared with that of newsreaders and presenters who blossom under the personal attention of a lighting engineer. In addition, he was handicapped by the fact that the cameras, being mounted under the galleries, were well above the eyeline of Members, particularly on the front benches, and thus not at the best angle for good pictures.

The original lighting in the House was in the high ceiling, and however much it was increased it would still have created unfortunate portraiture. Light therefore had to be provided at a lower level. There were several painful experiments when Members, who may have to sit in the Chamber for many hours waiting to speak, rejected the various technical remedies offered. The eventual solution was the eight space lights which now hang in the Chamber – a temporary form of illumination which will probably be turned into chandeliers suitably designed for Sir Gilbert Scott's Chamber. A few Members still find the glare a little trying, but many more seem pleased that overall the lighting has improved.

The cameras were selected to work successfully at low levels of lighting but it was inherent in their construction that they created soft pictures without the pitiless clarity of some studio cameras. These portraits, coupled with the green of the benches and the wooden panelling, and with the addition of the intricate design of the Speaker's Chair and the canopy, the layout of the table and the wigged clerks, created at once a more attractive picture than one might have expected from the poorly lit past.

THE RULES OF COVERAGE

The quality of the pictures was one of the factors that defused the public argument concerning the rules of coverage, about which there was always a touch of nonsense. The House of Commons over the years had shown perhaps an unnecessary fear of television; but the feelings were strong. There is a special and unique character in a place where 650 elected Members go about their legislative duties on a site that has seen parliamentary activities for more than 600 years. The fear, rightly or wrongly, was that television would represent this without understanding. More importantly it was suggested that the very presence of television would distort the essential style and spirit of the place. The Chamber of the House of Commons has always been noted for its peculiarly club-like atmosphere, albeit a volatile one, but there was a fear that this would become another victim of television and that it would not be the same Chamber that Members had known in the past. Some Members, to be frank, were afraid of a minority of their own colleagues and what they might get up to. They were also apprehensive about the television directors, who over the years had been painted in lurid colours as potential despoilers. There was a fear that they would take the 'St Michael' out of the House.

The original rules laid down in the Select Committee report were predicated on the assumption that it was sensible to start with explicit rules which could be revised later rather than to start with a so-called 'liberal' regime which might subsequently, but with difficulty, have to be tightened. The publication of the rules in May 1989, essentially dealing with the type of shot of a speaking Member, cutaways, panning cameras and rules about disorder, was greeted with criticism from the press, the television industry and some Members. Channel 4, which had previously announced that they would cover the House 'live' at certain times, withdrew that commitment. Parliament was accused of censorship and various other social and political crimes. The arguments rumbled on throughout the summer and created an assumption that television was going to be pretty much of a yawn. With the benefit of hindsight this was the best thing that could have happened. A low level of expectation is a healthy starting-point for a programme that has to run and run.

The controversy was based, as were the rules, on a lack of understanding about the limitations of the camera operation. A Member speaks standing in the Chamber, whereas in a studio a participant is anchored to a chair. A standing speaker does not normally stand still; most tend to shift their weight from one foot to another and move quite appreciably. The House of Commons is a debating chamber and, although the Members address the Speaker, in practice they turn around, talk to different parts of the House or other Members, and some positively gyrate. The camera has to allow much more space around a standing than a sitting figure, and this makes a head-and-shoulders shot an impossibility, so that the actual pictures of the Member speaking often contain substantial portions of other Members and a considerable area of the benches. One unique quality of the House of Commons as a parliamentary assembly is that any Member may be called from any seat, and Mr Speaker in Question Time chooses one Member from as many as forty or more who are trying to catch his eye by standing. There can be a delay of anything up to seven or eight seconds while the camera finds and focuses on the Member chosen by Mr Speaker. The director of the cameras has to cover this gap and uses a wide-angle shot of the whole Chamber or a portion of it. When critics – before the pictures were seen – complained about the coverage, they were assuming that head-and-shoulders pictures would follow one another, 'talking heads' in the jargon. The critics could not anticipate the liveliness, constant movement and the feeling for geography of the Chamber which would be contained in the wide-angle pictures.

As soon as the pictures were seen publicly, the previous criticism was forgotten and the House was rightly judged by what the Members did, rather than what the television director was doing. This was an important early development, with the result that the direction was never controversial during the experiment.

How far the present rules of coverage allow a true representation of the House as it is must remain a topic for argument. Even eight cameras lack the sweeping comprehension of one pair of eyes but, if well directed, the cameras can overcome the problem of distance and the limitation of a single seat in any of the galleries. The use of the group shot – initially in March 1990 – provides a helpful picture of a group of Members or a section of the benches and allows the viewer to gauge the level of interest and the feeling in the House. What the coverage lacks is the cutaway, catching the individual reaction – a visual image that is of itself a political comment. To some extent this is the sketch writer's role, and for that reason it is unlikely to find much encouragement in the House. The current brief of the director is to cover the proceedings of the House; it is not to provide a running commentary with pictures. If this changed and the director was expected to provide individual and relevant cutaways at his own discretion, it would create an extra responsibility. The director necessarily occupies a delicate position because he or she is operating as a detached observer in a confrontational atmosphere. The individual cutaway as opposed to the group cutaway, and the estimation of its political content, is open to so many interpretations that it would place an unfair burden on the director. This may be called a weasel judgement, but as there is no immediate demand for a modification of the present rules of coverage it is unlikely that the rules will be reconsidered until after the next election.

THE ROLE OF THE SUPERVISOR OF BROADCASTING

I took up the job of Supervisor of Broadcasting on 1 October 1989 – when it looked as though the enforcement of the rules of coverage would be the major problem of the post. In fact, because of the co-operation of Patrick Harpur, the Director of the Broadcast Communications team which had won the competitive tender to produce the signal, the actual rules and their implementation were never much of a problem. Patrick, who is a very experienced and talented director of news and current affairs programmes, followed the written rules with the most scrupulous care – not always the simplest task because of the way in which they were written.

Early in 1990 the broadcasters, through the Users' Group set up under the first report of the Select Committee, proposed, and the Select Committee, after discussion, agreed to some modifications in the rules of coverage. It was agreed by Patrick Harpur that the changes should not be brought in for four weeks until his other directors and crew were thoroughly familiar with the new situation. When some time in the future others come to judge the arrival of television in the House they should pay credit to the small team in the cramped control room on the committee floor. Pragmatically and quietly under the innovative senior engineer, Steve Fox, they developed a new operation and made it work in a remarkably lean and efficient manner. It was a small public exhibition of the efficiency of their industry. The Palace of Westminster – even the support services – appears to run on precedent, but there were no precedents for television. And sometimes, perhaps, the newest servants of the House appeared a little too robust, too matter of fact, to earn the total satisfaction of all their new colleagues.

There were two other main responsibilities given to the Supervisor: the co-ordination of committee coverage (dealt with elsewhere in this volume) and 'as a general point of liaison for the management of the Unit and the Operator, the Broadcasters, and Members and Officers of the House'. This part of the job description was as long as a piece of string but much more rewarding.

The arrival of television in the House was a media event and this was dangerous to the experiment. There were many Members who had voted against it on 9 February 1988 and there were more than 300 accredited journalists, so the more it became 'hyped' the greater would be the fall if it went wrong. There is an almost universal pleasure in the misfortune of those who may become puffed up – even if somebody else does the puffing.

It was essential that the Members should be thoroughly informed before the pictures were seen outside the House. After an initial closed-circuit training period for the crew, the pictures from the Chamber were shown in the lobbies. Then over 200 Members were briefed in the Chamber on the new lighting and on the capabilities and limitations of the cameras – with visits to the control room.

The press is a vital part of Parliament, not least because it is a major source of information for Members. As there is no press office at Westminster, a comprehensive press pack was prepared in the Supervisor's office by collecting contributions from broadcasters, contractors, manufacturers and the parliamentary works office. The parliamentary press were also given a full briefing in the Chamber. As a result, most newspapers carried full and very accurate descriptions of the equipment in the House and the programmes that the audience at home would see. Many newspapers carried excellent explanatory introductions to procedure. The appearance of members, their suits, ties, haircuts, and the work of 'charm schools' set up to brief Members, were given a lot of cheerful coverage. There were numerous special introductory broadcasts. Altogether the experiment got a good press.

Liaison in the House itself means opening and maintaining channels to the widest possible number of Members. The most important are of course Mr Speaker and the Leader of the House, but for a 'Johnny-come-lately' like television it was essential that the party leaders, the whips' offices and the important officers of the House and their staffs should be kept in the picture, even for the smallest change in the cameras or microphones. One group of major importance was the Select Committee members, most of whom had been with the committee for over two years and had been involved in many hours of discussion besides hearing the explanations of arcane devices and opinions by a variety of witnesses mainly from the broadcasting industry. The size of the committee was a positive advantage because it represented a wide range of views about televising, while the length and depth of the investigation gave the opportunity to explore all possibilities and created a group of well-informed MPs. This was one reason why the Leader of the House was able to say on 19 July 1990:

> As I said when the matter was last voted upon, seven of the 20 on the Committee considering the matter voted against it but, as a result of our work together over the last 12 months – all except one have concluded in favour of the words recorded in our recommendations.
>
> (HC Debs 1990: cols 1223–74)

The broadcasters, who paid for about 50 per cent of the costs of the experiment within the Palace of Westminster, had, as of right, regular access to the Select Committee and the House. This was organized through two regular committees chaired by the Supervisor of Broadcasting – one which met weekly to discuss the following week's committee coverage. This included senior officers of the House and their staffs and a wide representation from the broadcasters at producer and journalist level. Informally this was a powerful piece of machinery which kept broadcasters and the House and its officers in contact; even more so when the meeting uncovered matters of unease or potential conflict. There was also the senior or corporate monthly meeting of the Users' Group where the broadcasters were represented at a senior level to co-ordinate the approach to the House. The members of this group were largely the broadcasting people on the board of HOCBUL (the House of Commons Broadcasting Unit Ltd) which administered the coverage and marketed the signals from the House.

It was no easy task to get competing broadcasters to organize the pool operations and effectively orchestrate an approach to the House. This was a valuable and unique operation by a small group of senior executives from the major broadcasting organizations, encouraged and supported by the two chairmen of the Select Committee, the Rt Hon. John Wakeham MP and the Rt Hon. Sir Geoffrey Howe QC MP, who said to the House on 19 July 1990: 'We have been able – broadcasters alongside politicians – to develop an important interpenetrating partnership in which each has come increasingly to understand the other and in which, so far at least, we may all have some modest pride' (HC Debs 1990: cols 1223–74).

Speaking in the debate on the same day, the Rt Hon. Tony Benn MP referred to another aspect of the complicated relationship between politics and television:

We must recognize that there is a conflict between those who claim the right to speak because they work in the media and those who claim the right to speak because they have been elected. That is the essential conflict that has been tilted in our favour by the televising of Parliament.

(HC Debs 1990: cols 1223–74)

There has always been and always will be an argument about the agenda of public debate, but broadcasters are wise to acknowledge that their ability to edit speeches and to report politics by the use of the 'sound bite' does make the politicians uneasy and it is this freedom from the editor, producer, interviewer and analyst which is the reason for the intense interest by the House in a dedicated channel.

ASSESSMENT AND PROSPECTS

The provision of a dedicated channel with a service available live to everybody with a television set would be the ultimate satisfaction for television to provide, but it is highly unlikely that there can ever be a universal service provided free throughout the country. The universality of Channels 1, 2, 3 and 4 by terrestrial distribution is not now an option; a dedicated channel will have to be an adjunct to some paid-for service provided by cable or satellite or a mixture of both. This will almost certainly come about but it is not clear at the time of writing when or how it will be achieved. The transponder cost for a satellite service to the home would appear, at £5 million a year, to be prohibitive. The cable answer – delivery by low-powered satellite and then by cable – has many financial advantages but a small audience. If Her Majesty's Government will not provide substantial support – an unlikely prospect at present – finance is the key to the problem, although the way in which C-SPAN started in the United States ten years ago, with a mixture of entrepreneurial skill, flair and a shrewd estimation of present and future interest, may have lessons for Britain. What is evident is that the provision of a dedicated channel by whatever means is a very desirable target and a most important addition to the use of parliamentary material by the news and current affairs services of the present domestic networks.

It is very rare for something which includes 'political' and 'television' to merit such praise as is found in the first paragraph of the conclusions of the Parliamentary Research Group at the Institute of Communications Studies, Leeds University:

> It is difficult to resist the conclusion that British television has responded impressively to the challenge presented by its long-awaited entry to the House of Commons. Broadcast reporting of Parliamentary proceedings has evidently been extensive, serious, responsible, balanced in many respects, even at times creative. Interesting and positive divisions of labour in coverage, moreover, seem to have been forged between national and regional television broadcasters.
>
> (HC Select Committee 1990: 265–I, 47)

On 19 July 1990 only thirty-two MPs voted against the motion to have television permanently in the House. It was surprising that television should have been accepted in such a short time as part of the scenery of Westminster. The complaints that arose during the session were mainly directed at the efficiency of the sound systems in the Chamber, which was a problem long before the cameras arrived. Conditions in the committee rooms overlooking the river in hot weather are unpleasant; that they have been so for over a hundred years affords no relief. The use of the signal by the broadcasters started at a very high level, which was to be expected because of the novelty, but the high usage went on after Christmas into the spring and early summer. It might have been expected that the initial enthusiasm would die, because the wide spectrum and long history of news and current affairs broadcasting had grown up without the use of material from the Commons; but instead the news editors and producers continued to seize on the material for developing the themes of debate. It strengthened the opportunity to report, and it swung, in some measure, the balance against the analyst and commentator which many broadcasters had been suggesting for years would result from the cameras' arrival in the House.

The experimental televising of Parliament was a media event, and all those taking part were caught up in the event of which they were themselves participating. The period of the experiment was one of peculiar political and party excitement for a session in the middle of a Parliament. While dramatic political events developed almost daily in Central and Eastern Europe, political 'actors', as the Leeds University group rather disrespectfully referred to them, were consistently at the focus of media and political interest.

There is a note of caution in the last two paragraphs of the Leeds University study when it refers to the future financial pressures that might arise from the major changes taking place in British broadcasting.

It is legitimate to ask whether this great interest in Parliament will continue. How will coverage look two years after the next election? The television industry has been in a state of such constant change that it would be a brave person who would give a prognostication. Before long the recently formed satellite channel (British Sky Broadcasting) will have had time to make or break its reputation, Channel 3 will be in its new shape and the BBC will be facing yet another of its perennial decisive testing periods. Many of 'the actors' on the television stage will themselves be fighting for survival and the role of House coverage and its cost will inevitably be closely examined. Those involved in political broadcasting are in favour of coverage of the House and represent a strong vested interest, but finance has a way of overcoming every other consideration if a company is fighting for its survival.

Those people who argued for television coverage of Parliament over the years are of a generation largely devoted to the idea of public service broadcasting, and most of the present producers and reporters are of that persuasion. The televising of Parliament and the serious representation of the nation's political life to the audience would seem to be the bedrock of responsible public service broadcasting, or in fact any broadcasting in a democracy, but there is no reason to assume that this will remain and automatically permeate corporate boardrooms in the future as it did in the days of the former duopoly.

Finance has rarely been mentioned in the last two years. The Select Committee estimates £1.64 million as the cost of the ten-month experiment, divided roughly between Her Majesty's Government and the broadcasters. In addition, the cost to the broadcasters of the coverage of the House of Lords takes the total to approximately £2 million. Rightly or wrongly this is sometimes described as cheap television, but at a very rough estimate the broadcasters had additional costs of seven or eight times that amount during the experiment. It is these additional sums – the costs of staff working in central London in high-rent areas at hours set by Parliament, the heavy use of expensive equipment which lies idle when Parliament is not sitting, the cost of lines for regional companies – which in aggregate make a substantial overhead.

Coverage of Parliament will always have to compete for money with other desirable uses of the broadcasting industry. Coverage of the Chamber itself will not be a problem, but the cost of cameras in committees, especially for the smaller companies and coverage of the House of Lords, will have to pass the eagle and unpolitical eyes of executives who are more interested in the bottom line than their producers, news editors and journalists.

Television is now a permanent feature of the House of Commons and its committees. It would be a mistake, however, to assume there are no future problems. For thirty years there were arguments about the cameras moving into the House, thirty years of apprehensions dissolved in a very short time. In one session most of these fears were discovered to be groundless. There must be a lesson there.

Chapter 3

Putting the House on television

Glyn Mathias

IN THE BEGINNING THERE WAS THE HOUSE OF LORDS

It was the Leader of the House of Lords, Viscount Whitelaw, who put the argument clearly and forcibly. In a lecture in 1985, he declared his long-time support for televising proceedings in both Houses of Parliament:

> My simple reason is that TV is increasingly becoming a dominant feature of our national life. The nation's Parliament and what goes on there is also a dominant feature. But if we fail to give it the same coverage as other aspects of our life, it will inevitably become increasingly irrelevant in the minds of far too many people.
>
> (Whitelaw 1985)

It took several more years for the House of Commons to take the same view.

Lord Whitelaw, with the support of Lord Cledwyn, the Labour leader in the Lords, arranged for a debate in December 1983, on a motion calling for an experimental period of public televising of their proceedings. This was not the first time that their Lordships had debated the possibility of televising their affairs. An earlier vote in 1966 led to a brief closed-circuit experiment; the black-and-white footage shows that the Chamber has changed little in the intervening years. Nothing came of that experiment, but it served as a useful precedent for later attempts.

By comparison with the Commons Select Committee half a decade later, the Lords moved ahead with eminent dispatch. After taking evidence from the broadcasters, among others, the Lords' Sound Broadcasting Committee produced their report in July 1984.

Some of the principles enunciated were admirably clear-cut: 'The right to broadcast any part of the proceedings ought . . . to be as clear as is that of the public to watch the proceedings from the galleries and of the Press to report and comment on those proceedings.' It followed that editorial control and selection should be left to the broadcasters, subject to the ultimate control of the House (HL Select Committee 1984: para. 12). This was ground which had to be fought over all again when the issue came to the Commons.

In fact, the Lords left it to the broadcasters to choose which days they wished to televise during the experiment. This became known as the 'drive-in' system, hard to contemplate now in the days of gavel-to-gavel coverage. Either the BBC or ITN, subject to adequate notice, could move in their outside-broadcast unit, equipped usually with three manned cameras (two on the floor of the Chamber and one in the gallery). In practice, it wasn't long before coverage became more or less continuous, with ITN cameras providing the signal for the BBC and other broadcasters.

The ground rules for the coverage were, for the most part, satisfactory to the broadcasters. The cameramen in the Chamber were asked to remain as inconspicuous as possible, and always wear jackets and ties (not always easy in the more casually dressed world of television). The coverage should be limited to the 'strict confines' of the Chamber, meaning in particular no shots of the galleries even if there were interruptions or demonstrations from there. Otherwise, there was to be considerable latitude:

> The camera would concentrate on the Peer who is speaking, but not to the extent required by the Canadian House of Commons where only the head and shoulders of the Member who is speaking is televised. The Committee are conscious that this will be a matter of considerable sensitivity but they think it right to leave it to the expertise and good faith of the broadcasters.
>
> (HL Select Committee 1984: para. 40)

I interpreted this at the time as enabling us to take wide shots and reaction shots, but 'it would be unwise to use shots of peers asleep' (ITN memorandum, 11 December 1984).

There were some comments (though not from the Select Committee) about Members of the House who appeared to be asleep. Sometimes it was impossible to avoid someone apparently slumbering behind the peer who had the floor, but I don't think we ever deliberately focused on them. This small point aside, the rules were successful: the wide-angle shots allowed the viewer to understand the geography of the Chamber and the so-called 'cutaway' shots made it easier to follow the exchanges across the floor of the House. The broadcasters were strongly in favour of the Lords' rules being copied in the Commons.

The rules did give the broadcasters one major headache, which has been little commented upon. There was to be no televising of ministerial statements in the Lords, a prohibition made particularly onerous by the fact that statements were often the most topical business of the day. The reason was that most ministerial statements were repetitions of statements being made in the Commons, and their Lordships did not want to upstage or upset their Commons counterparts. (We could televise statements initiated by the small minority of cabinet ministers who were Members of the Lords). The cameras were switched off when such statements began, and this meant that live programmes covering the Lords could be interrupted for periods lasting up to forty minutes. It wasn't until the Commons was being televised that this prohibition was lifted (HL Select Committee 1990).

With the Select Committee's report approved by the House by 113 votes to 66, the experiment began on 23 January 1985. The date was chosen specifically because that day was allocated to a debate in which the Earl of Stockton, formerly Harold Macmillan, was due to speak. The rules were tested at the very outset. When the Earl of Stockton rose to make his speech, there was a demonstration from the public gallery in support of the miners' strike. However strong his native instincts, the OB director did not show one frame of the demonstration – instead the cameras showed peers looking up at the gallery. Thus the broadcasters established their bona fides at an early stage.

The huge public interest generated at the outset of the experiment helped lift the public profile of the Lords, as Lord Whitelaw had anticipated. Both the BBC and Channel 4 had transmitted live special programmes of the first day seen by millions of viewers. But news bulletins were envisaged as the vehicles for the bread-and-butter coverage, the biggest complaint being that the broadcasters were not present with their cameras often enough. An item in *The Times* headlined 'Lords May Not Extend TV Viewing' (8 March 1985) reported 'growing disillusionment among peers' who were, it was claimed, 'increasingly unlikely to renew the six-month experiment'. This came straight from the Select Committee chairman, Lord Aberdare, and as a shot across the bows it worked. In the early summer, Channel 4 pioneered a nightly fifteen-minute summary programme called *Their Lordships' House* during the turbulent passage of the bill to abolish the Greater London Council and the six metropolitan county councils. To some more cynical broadcasters it seemed a mad idea at the time: how could we possibly find enough interesting material to fill the space? But the late-night programme collected an aficionado following when it began regular transmission the following year, and the BBC also picked up considerable audiences for their weekly summary programme.

The opposition to televising in the Lords began to fade away. The original six-month period was extended, and by May 1986 the move to permanent televising was unopposed. The Select Committee in their report had concluded:

> The Committee are of the opinion that over the full period of the experimental public televising of the proceedings of the House, there can be little dissatisfaction at the standard of editing and the balance achieved within specific programmes by those responsible.
>
> (HL Select Committee 1986: para. 30)

Moreover, the committee compared the kind of camera coverage they allowed in their Chamber with the restrictions in some other televised Parliaments: 'the resulting production', they said, 'provided better viewing than it would have done if restricted (ibid., para. 32). The independent Hansard Society agreed the experiment had been a success: it had not fully lived up to the expectations of its advocates, but 'few, if any, of the critics' worst fears have been realised' (Stradling and Bennett 1986: 1).

Nobody in the House of Commons was listening. A few months previously, in November 1985, MPs had voted once again to keep the television cameras out, this time by the narrow margin of 12 votes. The prevailing view in the Commons was then, and continued to be, that the elected Chamber was so different from the unelected Chamber that few useful parallels could be drawn. The debates in the Commons barely mentioned the experiences of the Lords. But many of the issues were similar, and the arguments about the cameras changing the nature of the House, about how much the cameras should be allowed to show, about whether the broadcasters could be trusted to be fair – all these were rehearsed again as if they were all brand new.

The anxieties in the Lords were the opposite: the opponents of televising had long been suspicious, as Lord Peyton put it, that 'your Lordships' House is being used as a key to the door of another place' (HL Debs 1985: col. 994). In other words, the main prize was to televise the Commons, and the broadcasters would lose interest in the Lords as soon as that prize had been gained. In the wake of the 1985 Commons defeat, this concern showed up slightly differently – that the broadcasters would drop their coverage of the Lords because the prospect of Commons televising seemed so remote. In the event, both Channel 4 and the BBC went ahead with their programme plans (in 1988, Channel 4's nightly *Their Lordships' House* was replaced for scheduling reasons by the daily *Parliament Programme*). As the coverage in the Chamber and the programme production settled down into a regular pattern, the Select Committee was convened less frequently. There were a few grumbles, with some members of the committee suggesting the cameras were shut down too early on some nights and with the broadcasters complaining at the quality of the lighting, which at times seemed to leave their Lordships in a vestigial gloom. But relations remained harmonious, with the House satisfied with the broadcasters' role. (HC Select Committee 1988: 473–IV).

It was on the basis of their record in the Lords that the BBC and ITN approached the prospect of cameras in the Commons. They anticipated that their experience of co-operating in broadcasting from the Lords equipped them to do the same for an equivalent experiment in the Commons. This was an assumption that was to be strongly challenged.

THE CAMPAIGN IN THE COMMONS

Prior to the Commons vote in November 1985, there had been a general expectation that this time it would go in favour of televising, if only narrowly. The broadcasters sought advice from political insiders about how best to proceed. ITN received strong guidance that high-profile lobbying might prove counter-productive, and campaigning was confined to private briefings of senior MPs. The Leader of the House, John Biffen, urged MPs to make what he called 'a leap in the dark' (HC Debs 1985: col. 305), and to some extent it would have been. Prior discussions among the broadcasting organizations and with cabinet officials had failed to generate a clear line on whether to go for an early experiment with manned cameras or wait for the installation of a remote-control system. There was also little consensus on how long the experiment should be. None of that was crucial, however. In the last few days before the vote, there was a swing of opinion against televising, fuelled by growing rumours that the Prime Minister herself (contrary to previous speculation) was going to vote against, and a procedural mix-up on the night allowed many Conservative MPs advance notice of which lobby she was planning to go into. The defeat by just 12 votes meant the issue was dead until after the next general election.

But there were some who felt the case had gone by default; the supporters of televising had failed to set out their stall. Next time, the preparations were to be more thorough. In early 1987 – well before the election – the BBC and ITN sought to create a small, informal group of broadcasters and MPs to establish a better grounding for the case for televising. This developed rapidly into the parliamentary all-party group for televising the proceedings of the House.

At its first meeting on 24 March the group elected Merlyn Rees to the chair – as a former Home Secretary, he commanded widespread respect in the House (and indeed became a member of the eventual Select Committee on televising). Background papers were supplied by the BBC and ITN on televising the Lords and other Parliaments worldwide. Austin Mitchell, the group's secretary, wrote to a number of MPs asking them to support an early-day motion endorsing 'in principle' the televising of the Commons. This eventually secured about 150 signatures. The objectives of the group were to keep up the pressure for the issue of televising to be debated again and to combat some of the fears of televising expressed by opponents in the last debate.

In November 1987 the all-party group staged an exhibition in the Commons displaying the kind of cameras and lighting that would be required in the Chamber, and in particular the latest developments in remote-control systems. Up to a hundred MPs attended during the two days, including the Speaker, the Leader of the Opposition and the Leader of the House, John Wakeham. This exhibition in particular helped to put televising firmly on the parliamentary agenda. By December, Merlyn Rees was writing to John Wakeham about the terms of the motion to be put before the House.

The campaign of persuasion also saw two broadcasters, myself and John Foster of the BBC, talking to a series of backbench groups of MPs. It was our belief that too little notice had so far been taken of the use that would be made of televised material from the Commons by the regional ITV and BBC stations, and we sought to convince the regional groupings of Conservative and Labour MPs that it would be here that backbench MPs would get most coverage (a prediction that turned out to be true). The meetings, particularly with the Conservative groups, were often tough going and attendance could vary wildly. But there was some evidence that it was worth it – two MPs who had been opposed to televising ended up as key supporters on the Select Committee. In contrast, the Prime Minister turned down an offer to discuss the issue.

The general expectation remained that, because the Prime Minister was so strongly opposed, the vote was likely to be lost again. Challenged at Question Time in November, she replied: 'I do not think that televising the House would enhance its reputation' (HC Debs 1987: col. 137). But an analysis of the 1985 vote revealed one surprising fact – although the opponents were predominantly Conservative, the 'No' vote had included a total of 69 Labour MPs, and 45 of them were still in the House. Even if the Conservative vote against remained static, changing Labour minds could win the day.

The party leader, Neil Kinnock, was strongly predisposed towards televising, and concerted efforts were made on his behalf to persuade doubtful Labour troops that televising would advantage the Labour Party. During the debate on 9 February 1988, the Shadow Leader of the House, Frank Dobson, made a crude attack on the Prime Minister's television style: 'She was even taught when sitting to shift her weight from one buttock to another in order to appear more interesting on television' (HC Debs 1988a: col. 213). After the vote, Neil Kinnock wrote to me on 16 February:

> I must say I was amused by the attitude taken in the Press Gallery on Tuesday afternoon following my approach to Mrs Thatcher and Frank Dobson's lack of felicity. The Hacks didn't seem to realise that what we had to do to win was to ensure the maximum turnout from our side since the Tory vote was, in my view, more or less guaranteed.

Whether the 'lack of felicity' was justified or not, the number of Labour MPs voting against fell to 30, while the Conservative 'No' vote actually rose in a higher turnout. The Labour 'Yes' vote increased from 111 in 1985 to 178 in 1988.

Just as crucial would be the views of the 130 new MPs, elected only the previous June. The bulk of the retiring MPs they had replaced had been opposed in 1985 and the reckoning was that those new to Parliament would be more open to the innovation of television. Moreover, the election result meant there was a strong Labour representation in the new intake. The independent Hansard Society decided to carry out a survey to find out the views of the new MPs. Among those they contacted, it revealed a significant preponderance in favour of televising: 68 for the cameras compared with 16 against, with 21 'don't know' or doubtful (Hansard Society for Parliamentary Government 1988).

The result was strategically released to the press the day before the vote, inspiring some last-minute predictions that the vote might get through. But nobody had reckoned on the majority of 54 – the turnout of 582 MPs had been massive. The Conservative MP, Anthony Nelson, who moved the motion, urged the House to take 'this modest but historic step' (HC Debs 1988a: col. 201). The result was now decisive enough to put the issue of principle beyond doubt.

By the time of the vote, all MPs had been contacted several times over on the issues involved. Apart from those campaigning within the House, the main broadcasting organizations had informed MPs of their programme plans in the event of televising, stressing the increased coverage of Parliament that would result. A joint BBC/ITV paper of 20 January was circulated to MPs outlining the proposals to be put before the Select Committee that would be considering the experiment. The broadcasters proposed a six-month experiment beginning in November 1988, using remote-controlled cameras; if asked, they would conduct the experiment jointly. The arrangements for editorial control should be broadly those which operated for the radio coverage and for the House of Lords television coverage. In the event, it was to take more than a year for these questions to be settled.

THE SELECT COMMITTEE MEETS . . . AND MEETS

There was a considerable delay in setting up the Select Committee on Televising of Proceedings of the House, partly because of a dispute about the number of places to be allocated to minority parties. It wasn't until the beginning of May that the broadcasters representing the BBC, the IBA and ITN gave evidence to its first session. The BBC and ITN had already activated detailed discussions with equipment manufacturers, and devised plans for a control room where the BBC and ITN staff would rotate. But it soon became clear that the timetable (originally anticipated by the Leader of the House, John Wakeham, who now chaired the committee) for the experiment to begin with the Queen's Speech in November was going to slip. When the committee decided to take submissions from independent broadcast companies in addition to the BBC, IBA and ITN, delay became inevitable. In a submission on 21 June, Austin Mitchell, surprisingly left off the committee, accused them of wasting time. 'The Committee must get its collective finger out,' he urged.

But the broadcasters had made some tactical errors. As in the House of Lords, we were proposing to become simultaneously the providers and the consumers of the signal. There were few problems in practice with this, but it helped to confuse some important issues. In their very first paper to the committee on 12 April 1988, the IBA felt it important to stress: 'We draw a crucial distinction between the provision of the signal to be fed from the Chamber and the use made of such a signal in broadcast programmes.' The first was a matter for the House (although the broadcasters had strong views) and the second the responsibility of the broadcasting organizations (in the case of the IBA, operating under statute).

One problem was that the phrase 'editorial control' was used in both these different contexts, but gradually it was replaced in the context of the Commons signal by the phrase 'rules of coverage', and that helped to reduce the confusion. Despite the evident distrust of the broadcasters by some members of the committee (there were difficult exchanges in particular about BBC Radio's *Today in Parliament*), there was ultimately no challenge to this contention by the broadcasters:

> We would rest very strongly on the principle of editorial freedom and independence; that once the signal has left the Chamber, we should be free to use it in our programmes much as we now use material from the House of Lords or the BBC uses material from the sound broadcasting.

> (HC Select Committee 1988)

But we became much more bogged down over the issue of accommodation. Historically, space had been provided in the parliamentary estate for the press and broadcasters reporting the proceedings, and the advent of televising would clearly generate more programme coverage than hitherto. Requests for more space for programme production became hopelessly entangled with the space required for the generation of the signal from the Chamber. Thus the proposal for a small control room staffed by a maximum of twelve people became swamped in the request for some 12,500 square feet for programme production and talk of hundreds of extra staff (preponderantly for the BBC because of their wider programme commitments).

This was exploited by rival applicants and by some MPs to suggest that an independent company providing the signal would be more efficient. A Conservative member of the committee, Bob Hughes, suggested, for instance, that 'the independent companies bidding for the contract have produced new ideas, enthusiasm and technical suggestions missing from the BBC/ITN duopoly' (Hughes 1988). In fact, Austin Mitchell drew up an interesting, if controversial, comparison of the rival costings for the experiment, in which the BBC/ITN estimate of £520,000 came out the cheapest (Mitchell 1988). But that wasn't the point; the battle was for control of the signal. An independent company might be more amenable to the wishes of the House than the broadcasters. British Telecom, who by the summer were believed to be the front-runners for the contract, were quite explicit: 'We would work as servants to the House in that context. We would provide the feed in the way the Committee and the House wishes us to' (HC Select Committee 1988: 473–V).

The problem of lighting the Chamber also did not help the broadcasters at this stage. We had predicted that a modest increase in the lighting level would be necessary, despite the proposed use of the new CCD cameras. But the potential heat and glare from the lights was worrying many MPs not on the committee (HC Select Committee 1988: 473–II). In June the broadcasters staged a demonstration of cameras and lighting in the Chamber itself. I had the unique experience of addressing about sixty to eighty MPs, who were gathered on the Opposition benches, from a lectern at the bar of the House. But it was a no-win situation: Andrew Faulds, a long-time opponent of televising, said one option involved 'a long green light that made the Chamber look like a fish tank' (HC Debs 1988b: col. 590). We knew that further development work was needed.

Development work proceeded throughout the year, not least the development of a smaller and less obtrusive pan-and-tilt head for the cameras and a computerized remote-control system (in conjunction with the manufacturers Radamec-EPO). However, it was increasingly difficult to work to a target date which kept slipping. By the end of the year, the Select Committee appeared to be completely bogged down, with little prospect of an early decision. The Shadow Leader of the House, Frank Dobson, said it was taking longer to put a few cameras into one room in Westminster than it took to organize the Normandy landings. The committee had reached an apparent consensus that the contract should go to an independent company (other than British Telecom), but there were seemingly intractable problems about how such a company could finance the project over the limited period envisaged for the experiment and still keep the costs to the broadcasters at a reasonable level.

It was in this context that, at the start of the New Year, John Wakeham held meetings with the BBC and ITN (separately) to urge a consensus solution in which the broadcasters would be involved. It was not immediately clear how, but it was apparent that John Wakeham needed to get detailed negotiations going outside the forum of the committee, if any further progress was to be made. So discussions began between the BBC and ITN on the one hand and committee officials on the other. The basis was a paper of 12 January 1989 from the chairman which for the first time outlined the proposed structure: there should be an operator independent of the broadcasters and accountable to the House, with the broadcasters meeting the costs, which should be kept as low as possible.

One committee official put the proposition like this. 'The assumption is that we are all broadly on the same side, but the broadcasters won't end up with their fingers on the sensitive bits like deciding the shots.' This was swallowed with some difficulty (and, indeed, there were some in Independent Television who felt we should at that stage have left the field), but we had been called on to make something work. Just as important was who would have financial control of the project – no self-respecting company could just hand over large sums of money for others to spend for them. And so was born the consortium which eventually became known as HOCBUL (House of Commons Broadcasting Unit Ltd). The company, funded by the broadcasters, would provide and install the equipment, and contract an independent operator to originate the signal. The operator was to be selected by tender; the company board would include representatives of the broadcasting organizations and the House. It was a compromise which seemed unnecessarily complex, but it had one beneficial effect we did not anticipate at the time – it provided a cordon sanitaire between the broadcasters and the politicians which contributed significantly to the eventual smooth running of the experiment.

The February meeting of the committee did not consider this proposal in isolation. Mysteriously, the submission from British Telecom had reappeared on the committee's agenda after intense lobbying behind the scenes. But John Wakeham, backed by Frank Dobson, supported the compromise his officials had produced, and that was enough to override the powerful support for the BT proposal.

The negotiations in private on the legal and financial organization of the company now stepped up apace. These negotiations were sometimes so sticky that some of the broadcasting side were at times resigned to failure. The sessions were usually chaired by John Grist, who was to become the Supervisor of Broadcasting, with Alan Sandall, the Clerk to the Committee, providing the political input from the Select Committee. On the broadcasting side, the main protagonists were Margaret Douglas, Chief Policy Adviser to the BBC, and Paul Mathews. Deputy Chief Executive of ITN, who were later the executive officers of HOCBUL. The position of ITN was further complicated by the disparate interests of Independent Television, for all of which we could not speak. TV-am among others, had suggested the service would best be provided by an independent organization. This led later to the IBA taking over ITN's role as the principal partner of the BBC in HOCBUL.

But where lay control in this complex structure? The composition of the board was one difficulty – who should have a majority, the broadcasters or the politicians? It was finally agreed there should be equal numbers on either side with an independent chair. Ironically, after all that, the independent chair was never appointed. There was only ever one meeting of the board up to the end of the experimental period, and that was chaired by the Deputy Speaker, Harold Walker.

The broadcasting side had established the degree of control over the costs they required, but what was to be the status of the agreement between HOCBUL and the House of Commons? In a note to the committee on 23 February 1989, Speaker's counsel declared that: 'Because the House has no corporate legal personality, it cannot enter into a legally binding contract'. The 650 MPs could no more sign a binding contract than a chance group of passengers on the 8.10 from Guildford. As a sovereign body, the House could not limit its future freedom of action. This exposed the broadcasters to the possibility, however unlikely, that after a considerable financial commitment the House could unilaterally terminate the agreement, leaving the broadcasters no legal redress.

But the real concern here was that the broadcasting negotiators did not yet know what the rules of coverage were going to be – whether the restrictions on what the cameras could show might seriously erode the value of establishing HOCBUL in the first place. In fact, the Select Committee were only just beginning to address their attention to this issue (a year after the vote!), and the indications – such as they were – pointed to rules almost as relaxed as in the House of Lords. The broadcasters had no intention of entering into any binding commitment before the rules were specified, but what if the rules were tightened up during the course of the experiment in a fashion unacceptable to the broadcasters?

We fought to the last against a blanket obligation for the company to require the operator to comply with any rules laid down by the House, without any provision for the broadcasters to have a say in the rules or any changes to them. John Wakeham insisted, however, that the rules of coverage were a matter for the House and not for the broadcasters, who had no right even to be consulted. The best we achieved was a paragraph inserted in the Select Committee report which said:

> We believe the broadcasters are entitled, once they are financially committed, to rely on the House not to impose any changes in the ground rules for the experiment, particularly the rules of coverage, which are manifestly unreasonable . . . The House, if it approves this paragraph of our report, will associate itself with that undertaking.
>
> (HC Select Committee 1989: 141–I, para. 71)

THE RULES OF COVERAGE

However, all this was overtaken when the broadcasters got wind of the restrictions the committee now favoured. Paul Mathews, in a letter of 6 April 1989 to the committee, spelt out the principle we felt should apply:

> The rules should enable the coverage to provide the public with a fair, balanced and impartial view of the proceedings of the House of Commons. Fundamental to this is that the rules should not restrict the coverage in any way which would distort the public's view of the proceedings. The guiding principle should be that a television viewer should be able to follow the proceedings of the House in the same way as a spectator in the Public Gallery.

The draft rules we received in mid-April hardly fulfilled this principle (they were broadly as subsequently approved in the report): 'The standard format . . . should be a head and shoulders shot, not a close-up; wide-angle shots of the Chamber may be used from time to time.' So far so good. But then:

> As a matter of general practice, the director should switch to a picture of the occupant of the Chair whenever he or she rises; this principle should be applied all the more strictly during incidents of disorder or altercations between the Chair and other Members . . . the camera should normally remain on the Member speaking until he has finished; and during questions (including private notice questions and questions arising out of ministerial statements) the director should only show the Member asking a question and the Minister replying to it. At other times, cut-away shots are not normally to be allowed, except to show a Member who has been referred to by the Member speaking.
>
> (HC Select Committee 1989: 141–I, para. 39)

There were additional restrictions. notably on panning shots, and the broadcasters felt the cumulative effect was to allow the television audience only the most formalized view of events – only a part of what could be seen from the public gallery. With no chance to see the reaction of individual MPs or groups of MPs (except a Member specifically referred to), the viewers' ability to follow and comprehend everyday parliamentary exchanges would inevitably be limited.

It seems that an earlier draft of the rules was rewritten by the committee chairman. His logic was that the MPs he had to win over in the debate were the doubters, not the supporters of televising, and beginning the experiment with more restrictive rules would help to reassure them. It was argued that it would be easier to relax the rules during the course of the experiment than it would be to tighten them up. Indeed, the report emphasized that the rules 'might be modified in the light of experience during the course of the trial period' (HC Select Committee 1989: 141–I, para. 37). In political terms, this may have made sense, but it caused consternation for the broadcasters. In Independent Television there was a strong feeling that they could not abdicate normal editorial responsibilities in this way; they were funding and organizing a form of television coverage which they would not transmit themselves. One prominent figure said it amounted to a Commons corporate video. For a period, it looked as if some broadcasting organizations might pull out of the experiment.

It was made clear on behalf of John Wakeham that he had no intention of altering the proposed rules to suit the broadcasters (and their vocal objections might help carry the report through the House). Most of the participants from Independent Television consequently sought a more arms-length relationship with the system being created; they did not want to be answerable to the Select Committee for rules with which they fundamentally disagreed. The suggestion was revived that the broadcasters should instead just subscribe to a signal produced by an independent operator on behalf of the House.

This confrontation reached a climax at a meeting in the Commons with committee officials, who made it crystal clear that changing the structure at the last moment would serve only to delay and possibly torpedo the whole experiment. The Select Committee had already reached agreement on the structure of HOCBUL, and the draft report was about to be considered. The risk for the broadcasters was blame for the possible collapse of the experiment. It was ITN's view that, despite our grave disquiet about the rules of coverage, it was vital that the experiment go ahead.

Some modifications were made to the planned arrangements: the right to choose the operator was transferred from HOCBUL to the Select Committee, and Channel 4 declined to join the board of HOCBUL. (Channel 4 subsequently took their objections to the rules much further and dropped their earlier plans for regular live coverage of the proceedings.) Otherwise, the broadcasting organizations swallowed their reservations and allowed the proposed structure to go ahead. The BBC, ITN, the IBA and other broadcasters issued strongly worded press statements to coincide with the publication of the report on 17 May 1989. The resulting headlines talked of 'tough curbs' (*Guardian*), 'Outrage as MPs prove the TV camera can lie' (*Today*) and 'MPs tune in for Commons TV show – but you won't see the naughty bits' (*Sun*).

ON AIR AT LAST . . .

This perception coloured public expectations about what they would see when the experiment actually began in November 1989, but the result was livelier and more interesting than we had predicted. This was in part because the rules were interpreted as flexibly as possible under the aegis of the Supervisor of Broadcasting, John Grist, and operated intelligently by Broadcast Communications and their director, Patrick Harpur (Broadcast Communications having emerged the winners from a quartet of applicants for the operator's contract). It was also in part because the live coverage that most people saw focused on Question Time, which was faster paced than other proceedings and allowed the wide-angle shot to be used as a constant bridge between question and response. Gradually a greater variety of camera angles was developed, still within the rules laid down. So had the broadcasting organizations made an unnecessary fuss?

On the point of principle, the broadcasters were bound to be unhappy at funding a signal, the content of which they could not control. And in practice, too, there remained crucial limitations on what the viewer could see. During the closed-circuit rehearsal period, prior to the broadcasting of the Commons to the public, Nigel Lawson spoke to the House to explain his resignation as Chancellor. One of the cameras on the Government side picked out an emphatic profile of the Prime Minister turned to look intently at him. It was a shot the director was unable to select because it was against the rules, and there were other examples during the opening weeks.

Consequently, only two months after the experimental period had begun, the broadcaster users of the signal made further representations to the Select Committee. The smooth running of the experiment had led to indications that there was now a fair wind behind moves to relax the rules a little (and there was a new committee chairman, Sir Geoffrey Howe). In a submission to the committee on 23 January 1990, the broadcasters asked for

> a greater range of reaction shots which are relevant and appropriate to the proceedings . . . it is not our wish to feature casual and arbitrary cutaways of individual backbenchers, but to convey the mood of the House as it would be apparent to someone present in the Chamber. This facility is most needed during debates and statements:

In addition, it was proving difficult at times to edit the single mixed feed for news and other programmes because of the shortage of alternative contemporaneous shots. The broadcasters asked for access to an isolated feed of the wide-angle camera for editing purposes.

The Select Committee granted much of what we wanted, most importantly on reaction shots.

> A group shot – mid way between the standard head and shoulders shot and the wide-angle shot – will be permitted; such shots may be used either for the purposes of showing the reaction of a group of Members or in order to establish the geography of a particular part of the Chamber.
>
> (Written Commons Answer, 31 January 1990)

This now permitted viewers to see the Labour benchers jeering at the Government (or vice versa), to see the reaction of an MP's colleagues to his or her speech, and to see the Chamber from a much greater variety of angles. In addition, the committee relaxed the rule on individual cutaways, and granted the isolated feed of the wide-angle camera.

So, after all the fierce debate, most broadcasters are now 'reasonably content that the rules allow them to give an accurate representation of the House's proceedings' (HC Select Committee 1990: 265–I, para. 81). The remaining restrictions affecting the floor of the Chamber are regarded as unnecessary, and it is true that the restrictions relating to disorder in the Chamber have yet to be seriously tested (the cameras had not, as opponents had predicted, worsened standards of behaviour, ibid., para. 144). But the rules are no longer a point of contention.

HE WHO PAYS THE PIPER . . .

Other contributors will discuss the progress of the experiment, and the technical details of the arrangements. In particular, the coverage of committees was as successful as that of the Chamber (some said more so); but was funded and organized entirely separately (see chapter 4). The broadcasting organizations pooled resources to contract an operator to provide the coverage – but there all similarity ended. The service to be provided was infinitely more complex: committees were to be covered on demand, with differing payments depending on the number of broadcasters involved. A large proportion of the time of broadcasters, Commons Committee Television (the contracted operator) and House officials was taken up during the experiment with the organizational, procedural, technical and financial problems generated by committee coverage.

By comparison, that Byzantine animal, HOCBUL, proved well suited to life in the parliamentary undergrowth. It provided a vehicle for the contractual relationship, both financial and organizational, between the broadcasters and the politicians which proved difficult to replace. The BBC and the IBA were each 50 per cent shareholders in the company and jointly underwrote the financial risks. The aim was to recover the outlay (eventually costed at £595,000 for the experiment) from subscriptions, so as to recover it by the end of the experimental period in July 1990. The subscriptions were levied on a 'per channel' basis – in other words, according to the number of channels on which the broadcasting organization was likely to make use of the signal. Thus the BBC subscribed for two channels, ITV and Channel 4 for one each. Sky Television, not a formal part of HOCBUL, nevertheless subscribed on the same basis. Elaborate arrangements had been devised in the event of a dispute about the level of pricing of the signal, but arbitration under the aegis of the Select Committee was never necessary. In the event, there were few problems about access to the signal from the Chamber (HC Select Committee 1990: 265–I, para. 9).

It had been the intention of the broadcasters that HOCBUL should only last for the period of the experiment (particularly in the light of some of the doubts described earlier), and the planned 'zero-financing' by July 1990 was achieved. But the

Select Committee needed more time to decide on the nature of any permanent arrangement in the light of the success of the experiment. So HOCBUL was rolled on for another year on the same basis, with the end of its life planned for July 1991.

HOCBUL has been superseded by PARBUL but, since the start of the experiment, it has been the intention of the broadcasters, certainly in Independent Television, to stand back from the process of generating the Commons signal and act instead just as customers of it. The advent of PARBUL means that ITN cameras will cease to televise the House of Lords and makes possible the integrated televising of the Commons, Lords and committees in a single system. A prime requirement of the broadcasters, however, must be a mechanism for setting a fair price for the signal, since effectively we shall all be customers of a monopoly supplier. And in the increasingly competitive world of television the downward pressure on costs can only intensify. Indeed, the Government's own broadcasting legislation has served to destabilize the financial basis of ITV, and this could well be reflected in the coming years in the degree of willingness to pay for something which in other countries, such as the United States and Canada, is funded by the parliamentary authorities themselves.

But I don't want to lose sight of what the televising is all about – making Parliament more available and understandable to the voters. In that, the broadcasters have been judged to have acquitted themselves well; a Hansard Society report in April said 'the experiment has been a greater success than seemed possible beforehand' (Hetherington, Weaver and Ryle 1990: 3). It pointed to the increased reporting of Commons affairs on national news programmes: it also noted the 'outstanding quality' of Channel 4's specialist programmes such as *The Parliament Programme* (produced by ITN) and *The Week in Politics*. The Select Committee's report in July 1990 said 'the broadcasters can legitimately claim to have made a praiseworthy attempt to deliver what they promised' (HC Select Committee 1990: 265–I, para. 94). Considering the fierce debate which had surrounded the introduction of televising, that was quite an accolade.

Chapter 4

The committees and the cameras: Romeo and Juliet or Cinderella and Prince Charming?

James Leaton Gray

It is worth remembering that, although the vote which instigated
the experiment in televising the Commons was taken on the
floor of the House, most of the effort in realizing that decision
took place on the Committee Corridor. The original report
of the Select Committee on Televising of Proceedings of the
House (henceforth referred to in this chapter as the Televising
Committee) reflected this reality in the section which dealt with
coverage of committees:

> The work of Committees is an essential part of the House's
> functions to which many members devote long hours, both
> at formal meetings and in background preparation. The
> experiment in televising proceedings would therefore be
> seriously incomplete without a significant measure of Committee
> coverage.
>
> (HC Select Committee 1989: 141–I, para. 72)

But was this the conclusion of most politicians or simply of those
who because of their very service on a committee demonstrated
that they liked them? How important to the experiment was
coverage of the committees going to be? The answer is provided
in evidence given to the Televising Committee by one of their
own advisers. Professor Jay Blumler analysed letters received by
the committee from MPs and found that twice as many wrote
emphasizing the coverage of committees than on any other subject.
'It is striking and remarkable that as many as 31 MPs (one-
third of the sample) spontaneously stressed the need to ensure
television coverage of Select and Standing Committees' (HC Select
Committee 1989: 141–V, para. 8.1). This being so, it would seem
that the love affair between the committees and the cameras was set

fair from the very beginning, but here life reflects romantic fiction
– it ain't that easy!

THE COURTSHIP

After the vote on the principle of televising the House, an analysis
of the views of those chairmen of Select Committees who voted
would have revealed a majority against the introduction of the
cameras. Obviously they were not just expressing their opinions
as committee chairmen; some voted on 'party' lines, while others
were in favour of the committees being covered rather than the
Chamber. For many, though, there was the fear that the ground
that the departmental Select Committees had gained, in redressing
the balance between the executive and the legislature, might
be lost as MPs and the press turned their attention from the
consensus committees to the adversarial Chamber. Another fear
was expressed by Sir Hugh Rossi, speaking as a member of
the Liaison Committee (which comprises all Select Committee
chairmen), when their representatives gave evidence before the
experiment began.

> They do not object to the idea of appearing in public and,
> indeed, they would value the work of their Committees being
> more widely known to the general public, but there is a worry
> that we could create conditions that would make it very, very
> difficult for us to carry on the work we are doing at the
> moment.
>
> (HC Select Committee 1989: 141–II–iv, para. 1114)

This statement by one of the minority of chairmen who voted in
favour of the experiment underlined the feelings of nervousness
that inhabited the Committee Corridor in the aftermath of the
initial vote, with some members worried that the committees would
not get sufficient coverage, others concerned that they would get
too much and therefore change, a few even holding both views
simultaneously. But what practical problems faced the members
of the Televising Committee as they began their deliberations over
the coverage of committees?

The deliberations

Select Committees

To understand some of the difficulties that the Televising Committee had to tackle, it is necessary to have some knowledge of the differences between the Chamber and the committees, indeed between the two main types of committee. Select Committees are first recorded in the third Parliament of Elizabeth I in 1571 and have operated intermittently since then, as, for example, during the Crimean War. Subsequently they became a regular feature of parliamentary life, with some, such as the Public Accounts Committee, enjoying considerable political clout. Yet the coverage of the available committees was patchy, with many areas of government left unscrutinized, and consequently the system of Select Committees was revamped dramatically as well as enlarged in 1979. In the debate that led to these new bodies the then Leader of the House, Norman St John Stevas, trumpeted their arrival. 'We are embarking on a series of changes which could constitute the most important parliamentary reforms of the century.'

The system approved on that day allowed for the continuation of the Public Accounts Committee and the creation of fourteen new departmental Select Committees, one to shadow each department of state. They were to be cross-party but with a Government majority on each, although it was agreed that a set proportion of the chairmanships would go to the Opposition. They were to be made up of backbenchers, and their brief was to scrutinize 'their' department on behalf of Parliament as a whole. To this end the House would delegate to them powers to call for 'persons and papers' and to cross-examine any witnesses thus called. They could choose any subject for examination that fell within the remit of their department, investigate it, produce a report, offer 'recommendations' to the House and Government. The members would be selected to serve on each particular committee for a complete Parliament, allowing them to build up a store of knowledge on their subject areas. The depth and length of any inquiry would also be left to them, ranging from single-session snap inspections to lengthy investigations of almost Royal Commission proportions. They would meet in the House in the rooms along the Committee Corridor, or they could at their own volition take evidence away from the Palace of Westminster in either formal or informal sessions. Many of the restrictive procedures of the Chamber were not adopted; most important, members could carry on asking questions, even the same question, for as long as they had the indulgence of the chairman. Yet, despite all these differences from the procedures in the Chamber, it is perhaps the layout of Select Committee rooms that sets them aside from the confrontational Chamber. The committees sit around a horseshoe-shaped table, with the chairman at its toe and the witnesses at a table opposite him. In one or two of the committees, members of different parties sit on opposite arms of the table, but in the vast majority the members of all parties sit mixed up next to one another. This break with the strict segregation of the two rows of benches opposite each other has an immediate effect on both the eye of the observer and the reactions of the members to each other. Indeed, it may well be no coincidence that the press often use hunting-pack analogies when referring to these committees, and that they reach consensus conclusions on some quite controversial political subjects.

Standing Committees

Like that of the smaller Select Committees, the purpose of the Standing Committees is also scrutiny, but of individual pieces of legislation rather than the work of a Government department. As each bill progresses through the House, it arrives at its committee stage. A Standing Committee is then convened to examine it, but, unlike the Select Committees, the Standing Committees exist only for the period of time when the bill is under scrutiny 'in committee'. The membership reflects the numbers of seats each party has in the House, with each side being led by the relevant departmental minister and the Opposition shadow. The committee's constitutional purpose is to undertake the line-by-line scrutiny of the bill which the House as a whole does not have time to pursue. Each Standing Committee is chaired by one of a group of senior backbenchers, collectively known as the Chairmen's Panel, and members sit with the parties ranged against each other, as in a mini-Chamber. Although there are exceptions, these committees tend to do worthy rather than exciting work. Occasionally the shadow spokesperson will try to undertake an elongated second-reading debate rather than detailed deliberation, but this rarely engenders much interest from either the press or the

Government. Indeed, it is often the case that committee members on the Government benches are regarded in this context as little more than lobby fodder and are to be seen dealing with their correspondence rather than intervening in the debate, which might slow down the progress of a Government bill and gain the unwelcome attention of the Whips' Office.

Grand Committees

The Scottish and Welsh Grand Committees consist of all the MPs from their respective countries. They act like Standing Committees in that they are chaired by members of the Chairmen's Panel, sit in smaller versions of the Chamber and are adversarial in nature. Obviously, by contrast with the Standing Committees, their composition does not vary between Parliaments (excluding changes because of by-elections). They meet on an irregular basis and discuss matters relating to the specific needs of their countries. They have no legislative powers, but are prized by the Opposition, since they are in the majority on both, and these committees provide a better opportunity to quiz Scottish and Welsh Office ministers than Question Time does.

The obstacles to coverage

One problem in televising the committees was immediately obvious – the sheer volume of committee work. On a Wednesday there might be as many as fifteen Select Committees meeting, while on Tuesdays and Thursdays as many as eight Standing Committees might sit each day. From the outset it was certain that not all could be covered effectively – but who was to choose which committees were to be televised? And, more fundamentally, who should undertake the coverage and its administration? The Televising Committee appeared to begin considering these problems in greater depth after they had made the majority of their decisions about televising the Chamber. Indeed, some of the broadcasters were recalled late on in the committee's deliberations to answer questions specifically about their proposals for the coverage of committees. It is not surprising that there were questions which exemplified all the major fears surrounding such coverage.

In a Televising Committee session on 23 January 1989 Anthony Nelson, who originally introduced the motion setting up the experiment, pressed the broadcasters whether the desire of members to see increased coverage of the committees would be fullfilled. Ian Hargreaves, then the BBC's Controller of News and Current Affairs, replied: 'I am sure that is the case; there would be significantly more coverage of Select Committees than is now the case, both because they are frequently sources of news and because of special programming' (HC Select Committee 1989: 141–II, para. 987). But despite this increase in expected coverage there would not be a new programme specifically dealing with the committees, as there was in radio. They were almost all negative about the prospects of live coverage, with only Channel 4's David Lloyd even hinting at a possible slot. The thorny subject of regional coverage was also raised, Bob Southgate of Central TV pointing out that disparate news priorities could lead to different agendas from the networks. Yet the overall tone of the evidence was bullish, leading to comments along the lines of 'We'll be overrun'. Glyn Mathias of ITN tried to allay fears that the Committee Corridor would be overburdened by suggesting that there would probably be only two or three crews on the corridor on the busiest day of the week. This was pounced on by Roger Gale, who considered that crewing at that level would be incompatible with the positive responses to Members' questions concerning committee coverage. An answer from Ian Hargreaves exemplified television's nervousness about the committees as programme material, in comparison with the enthusiasm for coverage by the politicians.

> The impression we sought to give Mr Nelson is that there will be a substantial increase in the amount of Committee coverage on television. There is, at the moment, very, very little indeed. Even if we increase that substantially, which we plan to do, that will not have this Committee Corridor choked with television cameras.
>
> (HC Select Committee 1989: 141–II, para. 1023)

The wooing is progressing. The committees sit simpering shyly in the corner, but the bride's family is not convinced of the groom's prospects!

The report

We need not dwell on many of the questions that were before the Televising Committee; rather we shall note that they left many unanswered. The report differentiated between the Chamber coverage, which it characterized as 'supply-led', and coverage of the committees, which was 'demand-led'. The difference was that the operators tendering to provide coverage for the Chamber knew in advance that the proceedings were to be covered in full and could predict and reasonably expect to recover the cost of provision, whereas coverage of the committees was likely to be highly sporadic, with variable demands and costs. The Televising Committee also concluded that there should not be a defined minimum amount of committee coverage, since this would force the broadcasters to take material that their editorial judgement suggested they did not want. It is interesting to speculate on the degree to which this decision was influenced by the fact that there was no financial provision for the committees in the provisional funding agreement between the broadcasters and the House.

However the decision was arrived at, the report left the ball in the broadcasters' court. Any organizations wishing to film the committees would be able to do so after registering with the Supervisor of Broadcasting (an officer of the House) and satisfying him of their competence. There was to be a pooling arrangement for all potential customers, with those wanting to take live coverage having priority over anyone wanting recorded material. In addition the 'Approved Operators' were to 'devise suitable arrangements to evaluate, on a weekly basis, any bids for coverage for the following week's Committee meetings and to allocate crews accordingly from within pooled resouces' (HC Select Committee 1989: 141–I, para. 74(v)).

The ground rules

Before we consider where all these decisions left the broadcasters, the other prime recommendations should be outlined. There was to be a maximum of three cameras per committee room; while the desirability of the cameras being remotely controlled in the near future, was accepted, it was recognized that the additional costs might prove prohibitive for the experiment. Five designated committee rooms were to be equipped for television with additional lighting, in the form of upgraded chandeliers, and improved cooling and ventilation systems. Any meeting which was open to the press and public was also to be available to the broadcasters. The statement of objectives and the rules of coverage for the

Chamber were to apply *mutatis mutandis* to the committees, but it was recognized that the procedures and environment of the committees necessitated additional guidelines. These allowed reaction shots from witnesses, but not from those not giving formal evidence, such as officials attending upon a minister. Broadcasters wanting to take live coverage could not pass on their additional costs to those wishing to record the committee for subsequent use.

'Suitable arrangements'

The broadcasters formed a 'Committee Users' Group' including representatives of the BBC, ITN, the Independent Television Companies Association, Sky Television and Channel 4 – later joined by British Satellite Broadcasting. The potential difficulties, not to say dangers, of the suggested pooling system were discussed and it was quickly rejected. Instead, the Users' Group decided to advertise for an independent company to act as co-ordinator and provider of coverage on behalf of them all. An advert was placed in the press inviting tenders for the contract. It stated that the successful company would be able to provide up to six crews, delivering a mixed signal with a minimum of two cameras per committee room. This implied a maximum capacity of three committees, on the assumption that two cameras could cover the rooms satisfactorily. The requirement for a mixed signal meant that the companies tendering for the work had to provide some sort of switching device that could be used *in situ* to cut between the two or three cameras. The groups were also required to demonstrate a proven track record in political news or current affairs journalism, together with the organizational skills required to administer the flow of demand for footage and the apportionment of costs.

A total of thirteen organizations or groups believed that they fitted this particular bill and put in bids. The organizational character, technical and editorial complexity and suggested costs varied enormously. As much as anything else this resulted from the lack of definition in the original advertisement, leading some of the bidders to conclude that the Committee Users' Group (CUG) did not know exactly what it wanted. This impression was compounded by the absence of any indication from the CUG as to how many committees the successful applicant might be required to cover. It is fair to say that this lack of any guidance on so basic a factor (one that would affect both the costs and complexity of the contract) was largely due to the fact that the members of the CUG themselves did not agree on how many committees they were likely to require, with estimates varying between one and three Select Committees a week and a very occasional Standing Committee. As will be seen later, all the estimates were too low, but the figures do reflect the views given in the broadcaster's evidence about their perception of the committees' televisual appeal as they entered the experiment.

The groom is chosen

The successful contender for the contract consisted of a consortium of three companies. Two were production based and later formed a joint company, Commons Committee Television – henceforth CCTV. The technical provision was provided by the third company, Walshy's, a small and young company whose idea of hiring recently retired BBC and ITN news camera operators to staff the committee contract proved appealing to the CUG and was very successful, both technically for the broadcasters and diplomatically for the House authorities. They had also found a mobile mixing desk and camera control unit that was smaller than, yet just as effective as, any proposed by their rivals. CCTV comprised Seven Days Production Ltd and the Barraclough-Carey organization. Seven Days Production co-ordinated the coverage, acted as clearing house and provided the executive producer, John Underwood. Barraclough-Carey gave the group a depth of current affairs experience and negotiating expertise that reassured the CUG of the overall durability of the bid.

So the stage was set for the marriage of Parliament's youngest offspring and the broadcasting barons' chosen suitor. What did the experiment hold in store for our young lovers?

A TRIAL MARRIAGE

Accommodation is always at a premium in a Victorian building not designed to accommodate a twentieth-century legislature, and the allocation of rooms to the various committees was a subject of much discussion and diplomacy from the outset. As already stated, there were to be five committee rooms equipped to accommodate television, three for Select and two for Standing committees. It is obvious that the committees which the broadcasters wanted to cover had to be placed in those rooms, yet there were still many people with touchy sensibilities to whom this smacked too much of being told what to do. Although one of the most sensitive, this was not the only matter that neeeded discussing on a regular basis: thus a weekly meeting between the House authorities and the broadcasters was convened and chaired by the Supervisor of Broadcasting, John Grist. The House was represented by the senior clerks of the Standing and Select committees, the clerk of the Televising Committee, the Deputy Sergeant-at-Arms and members of his staff. The broadcasters' representatives varied week by week but always included one each from the BBC and ITN at Westminster, the executive producer of CCTV and representatives of Walshys. This body met every Thursday at 10 a.m., when the broadcasters indicated the committees required and the House authorities allocated the rooms before the traditional midday publication of the list of committee rooms.

This timing meant that the TV companies had to have made their decisions about coverage and resolved any conflicts before that meeting. The process began on Tuesday afternoon, when a producer from CCTV obtained a list of the following week's committees from the Committee Office. This list also included the witnesses to be called and a brief description of the subject of the inquiry. This information was then faxed to the newsrooms of all the CUG's constituent companies. The companies were then responsible for the internal dissemination of the information to any potential users. Late on Wednesday afternoon a series of phone enquiries were made by CCTV to those broadcasters who had expressed any interest in coverage for the following week. This frequently ended up with the two largest customers, the BBC's Committee Co-ordinator and ITN's Westminster operation, engaging in genteel horse-trading over what each wanted to see on the list for the following week.

The commissioning process was complicated by the system of payment that had been devised for the experiment. It was in essence a fixed price for a single committee to be divided not by how many companies wished to take it but by the channels on which they broadcast. Thus, if a committee was of interest to three ITV companies, their share was one-third of 'Channel 3's' charge, but that cost was dependent on whether Channel 4, Sky or the BBC wished to use it. The BBC's position was also confused by this method of accounting, in that if coverage were being bought for a Westminster programme then that was one share for BBC2, but if the news operation were also interested then the cost increased for a BBC1 share. Other factors added to this complicated structure; for example, the cost of a crew for one day was not significantly greater than for one session, morning or afternoon. Thus, if there were committees morning and afternoon they were cheaper, but if two committees were required simultaneously then the cost was higher for the second crew. The end result of all this complexity was that each time an editor expressed interest in a committee it would cost a different amount, indeed the cost would occasionally be in an inverse relationship to its potential interest – the fewer companies wanting a committee the higher the cost to each. This was a particular problem when committees had a specific regional interest. Because of the timetable it also led to a situation in which companies had to commit themselves to buying coverage before they knew its definite cost. This might not have worried news editors in days of yore but greatly affects the decisions of today's cost-controlled news staff.

Go forth and multiply

Despite these structural obstacles the majority of requests for coverage were met, not least because of a considerable degree of agreement between the major users over their editorial priorities, and a significant level of co-operation between the BBC and ITV companies over regional coverage. Indeed, the offspring of this marriage were plentiful: over the thirty-four parliamentary weeks that the experiment was running a total of 112 Select Committees, 21 Standing Committee and 8 Grand Committee sessions were covered – some 50 per cent higher than the most optimistic estimate from the broadcasters before the experiment began. Although not on the scale of a conversion on the road to Damascus, this phenomenon deserves some investigation, especially as the committees were having to compete for their places on news agendas with a significantly increased number of items from the Chamber.

No single reason can be identified to account for all the additional interest, but there are several contributing factors. A significant element must have been the cost, for although the formula was complex it did mean the greater number of companies that took the coverage the cheaper it became for all. This had a self-fulfilling effect: the more people judged it worthwhile to take coverage of the committees, the more economical it became and the easier it was to order more. Yet to say this was the major factor would be untrue as well as cynical, for it was in the content of the evidence sessions themselves that the real reason lies – they were entertaining as well as informative. There was courtroom drama, with cross-examinations by extremely effective barrack-room as well as professional lawyers; there was soap opera, as inquiries such as the Agriculture Committee's investigation into 'mad cow disease' continued over the weeks; and there was a sense that anything could happen, that the rules of combat were not as restrictive as they were on the floor of the Chamber. Of course, none of these attributes on their own would have been enough had the subjects of their investigations not been of interest, but they did create an atmosphere in which a suggestion to cover a committee was not greeted with suspicion.

Coming to you live and direct

When they had originally given evidence, the terrestrial broadcasters had indicated that there was very little chance of any committee being covered live. Indeed, only Channel 4 held out any hope at all, with their News and Current Affairs Commissioning Editor, David Lloyd, describing their plans as 'a gleam in the eye' (HC Select Committee 1989: 141–II, para. 1011). So it was a measure of the sea change that had occurred when the BBC decided to abandon their scheduled programmes on the afternoon of 4 December 1989 in order to broadcast an hour of live Select Committee evidence. The committees thus exposed were the Treasury and Civil Service Committee (examining the then Chancellor John Major on his autumn statement and economic policy) and the Public Accounts Committee interrogating the Permanent Secretary at the Department of Trade and Industry, Sir Peter Gregson, about the sale of the Rover Group to British Aerospace. The programme was judged an immediate success in editorial terms, with many people expressing delight at its exciting content. That delight was compounded when the audience figures of over a million viewers were released – although not exactly of *Dallas* proportions, it was considered a good number for an unscheduled mid-afternoon programme on BBC2. Such was the interest that it even spawned an item in the 'HP Sauce' column in *Private Eye*, alleging that the chairman of the Treasury Committee, Terence Higgins, had manipulated the timing of members' questions to fit in with the TV coverage. (A clever trick, as the live sections of the two committees were decided at the time rather than in advance.) It is only fair to point out that Sky News had already taken several Select Committees live during November, but its impact on the general public was limited by its delivery system. It is also difficult to gauge the potential audience figures, since they were not at that time part of the BARB audience research system. It must be born in mind, however, that it would largely be the impact on the viewers which would eventually decide whether the experiment was judged a success or not. For many backbenchers, the committee coverage was seen as a way of showing their electors where they were when they could not be seen in the Chamber, as well as illustrating the good work that they were achieving in committee – an area that had previously been regarded as being 'behind the scenes'.

Cinderella gets a good press – the groom's family background

How true was it that the Select Committees had been disregarded by the press? To assess this we have to know a little of the history of their coverage prior to the introduction of the cameras. A report in 1980 by Anne Davies for the Outer Circle Policy Unit analysing the first parliamentary year of the new departmental Select Committees suggested that the press had reacted favourably to them from the start. A new Government was in power and one might have expected that the political pages would already have been filled, but it seems that the parliamentary reporters saw in the new bodies a potential source of copy, both during the evidence-taking sessions and on the publication of their reports. Additionally, BBC Radio 4 started *Inside Parliament*, a weekly programme specifically designed to cover the work of the committees. Indeed, such was the press interest during their first year that Edward Du Cann MP was able to claim on Radio 4's *Analysis* programme on 13 August 1980 'in recent weeks the papers have been filled, absolutely filled, with Select Committee reports and comments'. The credibility given to their reports undoubtedly came in part from the cross-party composition, but the number of column inches they generated was surely related to their subjects. Monetarism was installed at the Treasury, and its analysis by the Treasury and Civil Service Committee led to headlines such as 'The Budget: MPs take on Howe and the Mandarins' (*Financial Times*) and 'Sir Ian Bancroft faces the Jury' (*The Times*). In that first year many committees chose what Enoch Powell called 'red hot departmental policy matters connected with current news stories' (Davies 1980: 55) and in doing so attempted to engage the media as allies in the scrutiny of the executive.

Among the contentious issues tackled in that first year were the Soviet invasion of Afghanistan, the 'sus' laws and the Education Committee's unorthodox investigation into the future of the Promenade Concerts. In doing so they created media interest, but if they were to maintain it they had to gain influence over Government policy, and at a seminar held after the 1983 election several parliamentarians were claiming this had been achieved. The chair of the Energy Committee, Sir Ian Lloyd, said that it had persuaded the Government to revise its fiscal regime in North Sea oil-depletion policy (Englefield 1984: 71). It was stated that the Foreign Affairs Committee had influenced the debate on the repatriation of the Canadian Constitution and 'persuaded the Canadian Government to accept some of its thoughts about how the Canadian Prime Minister might accommodate the Canadian Provinces regarding that legislation' (Englefield 1984: 42). The 'sus' laws were repealed and the Proms returned to the Albert Hall, but were all these policy changes really related to their exposure to Select Committee and subsquent media scrutiny? There is little reliable evidence to answer this question, but it is interesting to note that in the published account of the 1983 seminar (Englefield 1984) and in many other works analysing the Select Committees such as *The New Select Committees* (Drewry 1985) and *Parliament in the 1980s* (Norton 1985) there is precious little mention of the press coverage.

Cast your bread upon the water

Despite this underlying question about their influence, the Select Committees continued to gain coverage, albeit frequently specialist in its nature. At the 1983 seminar George Cubie, then a Deputy Principal Clerk in Parliament's Journal Office, stated: 'the Committees have had a huge amount of press coverage. Perhaps you do not always read the small print on the Parliamentary pages of the heavy papers, but the press coverage has been very good' (Englefield 1984: 66). Radio 4 carried on with its weekly committee programme, now renamed, less ambiguously, *In Committee*. However, it was the investigation into the Westland Affair that really began to rekindle a regular media interest. The exchange between Dr John Gilbert and Leon Brittan over the leaking of the Solicitor-General's letter about Westland has rightly become a classic example of parliamentary cross-examination. To what extent the final report on that business was conclusive is debatable, but that it was the fullest public airing of the issues is undeniable. It can be contended that this became the norm, with the evidence-taking sessions becoming the closest that the press, and thus the public, came to hearing what was being discussed along the corridors of power. The inquiry by the Social Services Committee into the NHS reforms were carried out at the same time as the review by a cabinet committee. The first was conducted in public session, while it was not officially admitted that the second even existed. Yet those involved in advising the minister had to bear in mind the information placed in the public domain by the Select Committee.

It was probably because of this effect that the committees began to fall in love with their new swain as he increased the public's knowledge of their work and the information that they uncover.

The rocky road to love

In fact, the road was nowhere near as rocky as it might have been. The House authorities, the broadcasters and the committee officers all recognized the desire of the politicians to see the coverage of the committees do well, and all went out of their way to make the experiment a success. However, some minor problems are worth mentioning, if only to demonstrate the degree to which the 'experiment' was precisely that.

The euphoria over the first BBC live transmission might well have been short-lived if all subsequent programmes had suffered the problems encountered in the second attempt. This took place on Wednesday 13 December 1989 and consisted of coverage from the Trade and Industry and Foreign Affairs committees. The former was investigating the so-called 'Golden Shares' in privatized companies and the latter considering policies concerning Hong Kong. The programme covering them went on air as planned and went across to the Trade and Industry Committee as soon as it began. Unsurprisingly the coverage opened with a shot of the committee chairman, Kenneth Warren, introducing the witness, the then Secretary of State, Nicholas Ridley, and asking him the first question. So far so good. What was not expected was that during Mr Ridley's answer the cameras would remain on Mr Warren. Indeed, they remained on him for the first few minutes, and we have to be grateful that Mr Warren has no unpleasant personal habits when chairing a committee, for if he had they would have been exposed to a very large audience that morning. A technical fault in the committee room had absorbed much of the set-up time. This had been followed by some rapid, but inaccurate, plugging which led to the situation where the output of a single camera rather than the mixing desk was being fed to the TV companies. The fault was swiftly rectified, once a message had been delivered to the engineer in the room, but it was this communications aspect of the system that was exposed as inadequate by the event. When a television company undertakes a live outside broadcast (here defined as anything away from a studio) it normally demands some control over the way in which the outside broadcast is to be run. At the very least it wants communication with the director in charge of it. But in this case the man in control was in the room in which the committee was meeting, so that no conversation was possible, and because of a House ban on radio communications a message had to be passed via a commercial bleeper service to Bernard Hesketh, who was the Walshy's liaison man. He came to the phone, listened to the problem and then had to run to the committee room in question, force his way to the far side of a crowded room and whisper into his colleague's car. This unsatisfactory state of affairs was rectified later in the experiment, but it required an acceptance that a problem existed before a solution could be found.

The jealousy of a former lover

An article in the *UK Press Gazette* on 25 December 1989 gave voice to a growing resentment towards television on the part of the remainder of the press gallery. It claimed that in committees 'the large number of camera operators and technicians left barely any room for newspaper reporters'. There were, in fact, four extra personnel in the room, three camera operators and the director, but the podia on which the cameras had to stand did remove about eight additional seats. However, the article went on to complain that this had led to reporters being excluded from 'two major Select Committee hearings because of lack of space in small House of

Commons committee rooms', 'and those who did gain access were 'crushed up against the wall barely able to take notes'.

That the rooms were full and difficult to work in was undoubtedly the case, but that this was solely, or even primarily, the fault of the arrival of television is open to doubt. As any member of that select band of journalists who regularly undertook coverage from the Committee Corridor before the introduction of the cameras could vouch, both of these problems were already present, and the degree to which they were exacerbated is debatable. That it became a bone of contention can be explained in several ways. First, television coverage itself was engendering more interest in the committees among the more senior members of the press gallery who had not worked the Corridor for some time and were therefore not aware of the accommodation problems. Second, the resentment over many issues surrounding the introduction of cameras into the Commons was voiced through this issue. Third, television coverage was inducing more members of the public and witness's advisers to take up their rights to be present in the small, mixed public and press area. Whatever the reason, it did not develop into a major row and the offer of a feed of the more popular committees delivered to the press gallery viewing room was accepted.

There's none so blind as them can't see

In this case what couldn't be seen was the Thames. All committee rooms overlook the river, and some Members were outraged that the needs of balanced lighting meant that during sunny days the blinds over the windows were pulled down. The great British art of compromise was brought in to play, and when you next look at a committee room in summer you will be able to see newly commissioned Venetian blinds – allowing both sides of the argument to claim victory.

The same happy outcome has yet to be achieved for various problems encountered over the provision of sound from the committee rooms. As is frequently the case in the House, the organization and working practices covering this area of life in the Palace have grown up in a haphazard fashion. The equipment is owned by a company called Westminster Audio, rented to the Property Services Agency (a government body) and operated by a variety of different people. In Select Committees they could be employed by Westminster Audio itself, Guerney's (the

Select Committees' transcription company) or BBC Radio, while in Standing and Grand committees Hansard insisted that its committee sub-editors operate the mixing-box. The sound system was originally designed as an enhancement and transcription aid, not for broadcast; and by broadcasting standards it is also getting old. This led to occasional complaints over the quality of the sound and the operation of the mixing-boxes by non-broadcast-trained staff. This inevitably led to friction and a feeling that the newcomers had territorial ambitions over existing jobs and editorial controls. At the end of the experiment this problem was still to be resolved, but it is one that can be remedied by a mutual understanding of the needs of the various parties involved, combined with a not insignificant investment in new equipment – although out of whose pocket that should come is a moot point.

The Standing Committees

The role of the Standing Committees has been explained earlier but we should spend a short while looking at how they fared in the battles for coverage. When representatives of the Chairmen's Panel appeared in front of the Televising Committee before the experiment began, they accepted that they would not get as much coverage as the Select Committees. One of them, James Lamond, put it like this:

> We realize that the Standing Committees would be facing severe competition from the Select Committees. They may be a bit more glamorous perhaps, if that adjective can be applied. We see this as an opportunity to bring before the public the very important work that goes on in standing committees.
> (HC Select Committee 1989: 141–II, para. 107)

This realistic assessment of the competition facing Standing Committees was correct; by the end of the experiment, 45 Standing and Grand committee sessions had been covered in comparison with 112 Select committee sessions. This was, however, a valiant attempt to explain the legislative process at one of its dullest stages. One potential change in the nature of the Standing Committees was hinted at in the same session. Michael Shersby referred to the viewers and said: 'Some of us hope that there will not be quite so much post being opened as they see us at work' (ibid., para. 1092). At least one Opposition backbencher went into print later in the experiment saying that precisely this had happened and that the quality of debate in the sessions when the cameras were there had improved. More cynical observers claimed that it just elongated the time spent in committee, increased the likelihood of a guillotine and, more important, did not change the Government's mind about anything. Whichever view you take of the argument, it is one of the few areas of the experiment where the outcome was close to the prediction.

As the figures show, it was also correct that there would be less coverage of Standing Committees in comparison with the Select Committees. Valiant efforts were made in some quarters, such as a decision by Mike Broadbent, the BBC's Commons TV Editor, to cover the passage of two bills through the committee stage even if they would not normally have fought their way on to the running orders. ITN's *Parliament Programme* also made similar attempts. Even these endeavours to make sure that the full range of the legislative process was brought before the public were not without their hiccups, the most annoying of which will continue to plague the coverage of Standing Committees until the present timetable for the ordering of committees is changed. The Thursday morning deadline for the production of a list of committees to be televised creates this timing problem. The broadcasters and the whips concerned with a Standing Committee are placed in the position of having to guess the stage a committee's debate will have reached up to five sessions in advance of the cameras' arrival. This is an almost impossible task, yet the cost is too high for the cameras to be set up for a series of sessions, on the offchance that the committee will reach the particular clause or ammendment that is of interest. This is likely to remain as large an obstacle to the coverage of Standing Committees as their sometimes obscure content.

LIVING HAPPILY EVER AFTER?

As the experiment began to draw to a close the inevitable question arose – had it worked? Had the prophets of gloom been correct, or had the arrival of the cameras seen the beginning of a new age of electronic democracy? And our two lovers had to turn to each other and ask: 'Has it been good for you?'

For the broadcasters the simplest answer would seem to be

found in the figures showing the number of sessions recorded – 157 represents a level of interest well in excess of expectations. If further evidence were necessary, then the week of programmes dedicated to the committees that ITN ran on Channel 4 could be cited. These were from the *Parliament Programme* stable and consisted of five two-and-a-half-hour programmes in the week beginning 23 April 1990, subtitled rather cheekily 'In Committee'. The BBC, for its part, produced two special programmes to coincide with the publication of specific Select Committee reports – that from the Home Affairs Committee on the Crown Prosecution Service and that from the Environment Committee on the pollution of beaches. A third programme on the report of the Trade and Industry Committee on the sale of the Rover Group was postponed when the committee decided not to publish its report when expected but to take further evidence – a case in which the schedulers and programme makers had a heavy reminder that they are totally at the mercy of the parliamentary timetable!

But what had the parliamentarians made of the trial marriage? One effusive tribute came in a memorandum of 26 April delivered to the Televising Committee before their review of the experiment was published. It came from Terence Higgins, and began:

> As Chairman of the Liaison Committee I have no doubt that the experiment in televising Select Committees has been a considerable success. Many more meetings of Select Committees have been televised than I thought likely. My impression is that the use made by the broadcasters of televised proceedings has been balanced and interesting. The coverage has been important in bringing home to members of the public that when there are often few Members in the Chamber many are heavily engaged in committee work.
>
> (HC Select Committee 1990: 265–II, 144–5)

Another example of this view emerged during an interview with the chairman of the Agriculture Committee, Jerry Wiggin. He was asked if there had been a discernible difference between the press coverage of two of his committee's inquiries – first into salmonella in eggs and second into BSE, the latter with the cameras in, the former without. He replied: 'I think the BSE inquiry probably got better reported, I think had the cameras been in the salmonella inquiry the public would have understood the issue better. I would be prepared to say the television has encouraged all sections of the media.' From these examples one can gather that the reception along the Committee Corridor had been good, but what of the House as a whole?

The Televising Committee published their review of the experiment on 11 July 1990. In an accompanying press release it was stated that the coverage of committees had been 'successful from a technical and administrative point of view, with the sole exception of the operation of microphones in Standing Committees'. Hardly fulsome in its praise, but not very negative either. At a press conference to launch the report Sir Geoffrey Howe, then the Leader of the House and as such chairman of the Televising Committee, felt that the reaction to the committee coverage had been mixed, but had persuaded the reluctant that the committees were here to stay and that it had enhanced their public reputation and effectiveness. He also expressed the personal view that the committees made 'superb natural television'. The view of the Televising Committee as a whole can be gauged from its recommendations. Some of the main ones were that the present contractors should be kept on during a 'roll-over' year while permanent arrangements could be organized; that the broadcasters should review the pricing structure; that two additional committee rooms should be made available for television; and that the highest priority should be given to the use of remotely controlled cameras for committee coverage (HC Select Committee 1990: 265–I, para. 173).

Despite some reservations, the conclusions were mainly positive, as was the Commons reaction to the whole report. So, after the debate and eventual vote in favour of the permanent introduction of the cameras, what did the future hold for our lovers as they faced a lifetime together?

A rosy future?

In conversations with various members and chairmen of committees, it was obvious that the mechanics of the experiment had worked remarkably well. The major reservation was over the introduction of remote-controlled cameras, although even here there was some degree of variance. Terence Higgins, who had begun the experiment strongly advocating their rapid introduction, felt that the experience of it had changed his mind. In an interview he explained his position thus:

One is aware of the cameras – they are fairly intrusive, even though the cameramen are very good and professional. There is a case therefore, from a convenience point of view, for remote-controlled cameras. But I'm a little worried that we'll find that a single person operating the remote-control cameras will be rather less good than the present cameramen.

This reflects the views of some broadcasters who feel that the quick-fire nature of the Select Committees is not well suited to a remote-control system. However, it is likely that the pressure for such a system will become irresistible, once someone has found the considerable sum of money needed to introduce it.

Accommodation proved less tricky than expected, with the reallocation of committee rooms not as much of a problem as many had predicted. Indeed some of the officials of the House were admitting privately that it was now easier to move committees for reasons other than the cameras, because their members had become used to being moved for television. But the need for new larger rooms was exposed by the increased interest in the committees. Because of this their greater use of the Grand Committee Room (off Westminster Hall) is likely to increase, if they can displace the Private Bill Committees that frequently use it at present but cannot be televised because of their quasi-judicial nature. In the longer term it may be that the suggestions for purpose-built committee rooms to be provided in the planned new parliamentary buildings will prove an appealing option. These could have better ventilation, lighting, acoustics, press and public facilities, as well as a design that would make television both better and less obtrusive.

One other controversial topic has already been referred to the House Accommodation Committee. It is the present rule that cameras may not be admitted to press conferences called to publicize a committee's report if they are held in the normal committee rooms. The reasoning is that the press conferences are not part of the proceedings of the House and as such not covered by the televising rules. This tends to lead to a structural imbalance between the report itself and the earlier sessions. The committee members themselves are split on this aspect of the rules, but it is an area that is likely to come under increasing pressure for change in the not too distant future.

Togetherness

So what use are the broadcasters going to make of the available committee coverage in the years to come? ITN has announced its desire to repeat its experiment of a week of special programmes. Sky News will continue to broadcast 'major' committees live, whenever they believe the editorial content deserves such treatment. When the terrestrial broadcasters were questioned in January 1989 before the experiment, all indicated that they had no plans to launch a new programme dealing specifically with the committees. And so it was the BBC who made the most dramatic change of programming after the experiment, by launching *Scrutiny* immediately after the Queen's Speech in November 1990. In providing a television competitor for Radio 4's *In Committee*, they had fulfilled one desire of the parliamentarians, as well as exploiting a particular vacant broadcasting niche. In doing so one might say the new husband was providing a worthy first anniversary present to his young wife.

Ultimately, did the television coverage of the committee matter? Did both partners enjoy the experience? Terence Higgins put it like this: 'The committees have gained, but I think the House as a whole has gained, because it shows what is going on in areas that might otherwise have been behind the scenes.' No star-crossed lovers these; Cinderella is at the Media Ball and loving every minute of it.

Part III

Assessments: the politicians' perspectives

Chapter 5

Televising the Commons: a backbencher's view

Austin Mitchell

Dragging the Commons into the twentieth century by putting them on TV has been an exercise demonstrating the worst features of constitutional advance in this conservative country. Obviously necessary if the Commons are to do their job in an age when most people rely on television for their news, the advent of MPTV was delayed for far too long by fear, disguised as high principle. It was grudgingly accepted at the end of a long process of attrition, implemented by improvisation rather than rational planning, then loudly acclaimed in an orgy of self-congratulation as if the result was unimprovable perfection. Indeed our present propensity to bask in the glow of undeserved congratulations, and our feelings of courage and wisdom in merely doing the obvious, are so numbing that the next, necessary, stage of advance – a channel dedicated to parliamentary coverage – is being lost from sight. As a result it too could be long delayed and grudgingly accepted. Indeed there are only two differences between this and other major advances. First, television was pioneered by the House of Lords, the geriatric ward of the constitution for once seizing the initiative instead of blocking progress. Second, unlike other significant changes such as the Reform Bills, the Select Committees and the ending of the Lords' veto, television has had little effect on those whose lives it was supposed to change: the individual MPs.

Let's not kid ourselves. We've been lucky. MPTV has worked well. All the studies that have been done are perfectly correct in describing Commons TV as a success, even if their tone is that of the anxious teacher trying to congratulate a dull and recalcitrant child on how clever he's been in becoming toilet trained – at eight. Yet it has taken far too long. It has been done on the cheap. The success has come by accident. So if there are any lessons to be learned they centre on our misconceptions about our own job. Coupled with our own exaggerated fears of television, these misconceptions have wasted twenty years when we could and should have been developing and consolidating Parliament's role in what is now a media democracy. Instead of the slow build back to relevance we now face a crash course in catching up. Which is why we must get on with the next stage quickly.

A survey based on a sample of one member, Me, indicates that, apart from the physical presence of eight cameras and brighter lighting from ugly but supposedly temporary rigs, television has had minimal impact on the lives of MPs. A slightly higher degree of public interest, a flowering of jokes, the occasional feedback from the public about one's speech or, more commonly for backbenchers, gibes about never making any, or not even being seen alive in the Chamber. Occasionally pressure groups or individuals demand a 'mensh' or request the raising of an issue, so that it may be seen on television, presumably after the same efforts to raise it before a bigger audience on regional programmes such as Yorkshire Television's *Calendar* or the BBC's *Look North* have failed. I have even had a few free suits, perhaps because I looked like an Oxfam dresser, which may be why we all look smarter. Some MPs received make-up kits from British manufacturers, though there's little change here: those who wore make-up before continue to do so. I have also had a pair of shoes given, though frontbenchers have been told not to put their feet on the table and, since I'm no longer so exalted but stand on the Commons Kop, my feet are never seen at all.

These are the sum total of the changes. Not much, but bigger than I personally predicted. It was the media which brought the effect on Members to the fore with a stream of questions about whether behaviour would (or could) deteriorate, whether MPs would (or should) go to charm schools, whether the lights would be too glaring for the really dim, as they have been for the two fools who intially made an occasional practice of attending the Commons wearing dark glasses. None of this has anything to do with the plodding reality of the MP's job but has a lot to do with the media's personalization process. Such trivia became important only because until the experiment was made permanent in July 1990 MPs could block access to broadcasters, and up to 1988 they had exercised that veto largely for personal reasons, particularly fear. We don't have much power. When we use what little we have to resist progress, as we do all too often, we make ourselves an issue.

Yet the real intention of bringing television into the Chamber, and the real effect, was to strengthen Parliament itself. It was to put the Commons back at the centre of a national debate which is now a media debate. All else, including the feelings of the workforce, and its effect on them and their undoubted egos, is secondary and unimportant. In 1980, when I successfully asked for leave to bring in a bill for the televising of Parliament and carried the first successful vote for it by a majority of one, the casting vote of the present, then Deputy, Speaker, the instant assumption was that here was a failed media man's attempt to bring the Commons down to his level and get himself back on the box at the same time. In fact the techniques and histrionics of the studio are irrelevant to a Chamber where close-ups are out and falseness is immediately detected. The necessary arts are clever debating, a useful turn of phrase, a leavening of humour and a clear and compelling argument. 'Make one point. More and you confuse them,' the young Harold Macmillan was told. The same advice holds true today, for, though our presentation is more serious, more fact-packed and, thanks to increased staffs, better researched, a Chamber is not a studio. Those who forget the cameras are there (which is very easy to do) and concentrate on the argument are more likely to be successful than someone superbly trained, beautifully made-up, immaculately dressed and coiffured. The bland leading the blind is for party propaganda, not Parliament.

The argument for TV has nothing to do with that but everything to do with the role of the Commons in a modern democracy. We are not a closed debating society, controlling the executive by debate. Perhaps in Bagehot's day the Commons could exercise the only control governments really fear, by threatening to bring down the administration. Since then, party has transferred that power to the electorate. The executive not only does not fear the Commons, though it can be inconvenienced by it; it controls them through its party majority. So the role of the Commons has changed. It can no longer control, though it can test both Members and arguments, occasionally to destruction. Its job is to dramatize and educate. The purpose of debate is to put the case for and against what the Government is doing. It is intended for the electorate, to give them the raw material with which to decide their vote. That role is futile if it doesn't reach the people.

In the mid-nineteenth century, politics reached a middle-class electorate through a broadsheet press geared to their interests and preoccupations. In the twentieth century a bigger electorate was far worse informed because Parliament chose to exclude the medium on which the majority of the people rely for news and information: television, the modern eqivalent of those newspapers. The most surprising thing about the whole debate is how little this basic argument was broached by MPs obsessed with fear of television, a fear compounded by the fact that its late admission to the Commons would be a confession of their own failure in keeping it out and forcing it to develop its own alternative, and better, political coverage.

TV was essential. All the personalization, the efforts of tailors and charm schools, the pressure for elocution teachers and such trivial froth are irrelevant compared to that basic principle. In any case, though MPs may be short on charm, the only training which could be really useful was not provided: not mastering the dramatic arts but such simple problems as stance, gesture and breath control appropriate to public speech. Few have ever mastered these, as is shown by the incidence of pharyngitis and Kinnock throat. Few now remedied the failure, and the advice of other organizations clamouring to get publicity by putting their case before MPs was mainly trite or confined to playing with close-circuit cameras of the kind which a half-decent organization or party (though not Labour) offers as routine. All useless – though there may have been scope for help in presentation of an argument, even if this is essentially a question of backing and brains, neither being abundant in the Commons.

So the only beneficial training offered was by the Commons TV unit itself: familiarization with the Chamber in its new, and not very different, guise after the installation of the cameras. The Prime Minister and the Leader of the Opposition both had closed sessions. They were then talked through the tapes by their advisers, in an effort to improve performance. Individual shadow and ministerial spokesmen were briefed and given playbacks – 'Look up, not down', 'Speak to the world, not the front bench opposite' and 'Keep the bald spots out of sight' – though most soon relapsed into old habits, a testimony to how easy it is to forget the cameras. Backbenchers got more perfunctory group sessions in which they were merely shown how the system worked. Anything else would be to magnify the importance of mechanics best forgotten. The best training was in the art which should have prevailed before: that of good Chamber speaking. What comes over well in the Chamber is, and was, the serious discussion of serious issues, analysis of the argument, testing, justifying and developing it, and clever interjection. All that also comes over as well on a television which is essentially eavesdropping on the Chamber, not taking it over and dominating as it does in its own forum. Television was never intended to benefit (or harm) the individual members. They are largely irrelevant to it. If they have to make changes in behaviour or type these are necessary changes anyway. TV could, and perhaps should, make life a little more difficult for MPs, but only by creating a wider audience to see them do their job. The purpose is to benefit the Commons as an institution. Individuals are affected only as parts of that.

The House of Commons is an organ of government in the sense that it is a legislative machine run by the executive. Yet its essential function is public education: the open window of government where all must be displayed, the stage for the dialectic which puts over the arguments by dramatization. Those roles are basic to mass democracy. They can be performed only on television. Radio broadcasts are welcome and certainly cheap, but no substitute. Their audience is small (except when radio broadcasts are repeated on television). Listeners are also distracted and annoyed by the hubbub of background sound picked up by the omni-directional microphones. So radio must now fade in importance. Having got in first, it never developed its lead by providing the cheap, continuous coverage of the type still transmitted in Australia and New Zealand, where Parliament has been broadcast since before the war. That radio coverage should also have gone into the offices round Parliament to inform MPs of what is going on in the Chamber, keep them in touch and ready and available to go back to the Chamber as items of interest crop up. In the British Parliament, unlike grown-up legislatures, work has to be done in the offices where it is isolating and insulating. MPs have a right to be kept in touch. The failure to provide this facility is yet another indication of the total disregard of the needs of MPs and the reluctance to provide an environment which facilitates their work.

Fortunately, television has come at last – nearly a quarter of a century after the first (narrow) vote, two decades behind other legislatures, one behind the best coverage overseas in Canada and the US House of Representatives, five years behind the departure lounge (now the green-room) of politics, the Lords. The chief beneficiary is the body which resisted it for so long: the Commons. Coverage on news bulletins has increased by 80 per cent, according to the Hansard Society study (Hetherington, Weaver and Ryle 1990). Coverage on regional programmes – something much more important for backbenchers – is also extensive, bringing MPs to their own electors. Parliament is at last reaching the people, however imperfectly. As a result it can begin to move back to the centre of national interest. It belongs to the people. They must have access to it, even if they do not use that right obsessively. Let them form their own judgements of MPs instead of being dependent on the sketch writers. They may even read those accounts and others, to help form their own judgements. Let them assess for themselves whether an argument is weak, or an approach noble or shabby. Numbers of viewers aren't important, compared to the principle of access. Yet in any case the numbers are comparatively high, up to 20 million per day, cumulatively well over half the electorate in any average week, even if the more devoted programming is watched by only between one or two million.

Because the Chamber reaches the people, its importance is enhanced. It provokes reactions. The arguments get home, as they did on Hong Kong, where Labour's argument for restriction looked shabby, if only because it was; on the Health Service, where the Government looked defensive and evasive; or on the Gulf, where the unity of Parliament reached the world through CNN and C-SPAN. Ministers do not fear MPs but they do fear the electorate who will decide their destiny. So they need only to know that the debate is reaching the people to feel a new influence which should make them more attentive to Parliament. Sensible ministers now have to be seen to listen, to respond, to demonstrate concern, not to behave with the casual brutality of a Ridley, a Lawson or a Hogg. The ministerial steamroller of the elective dictatorship can no longer be driven quite as insouciantly, while any sensitive Opposition will put the people on the front line and say less about its party ideology. In an indefinable, but real, way Parliament is the more important, the stronger and that bit nearer the centre of political preoccupations than it could ever be as a closed debating society. It may not be more respected. That depends on the quality of its debate and the calibre of the personnel. Yet the public perception of those is also different from that of the in-group who've done the judging hitherto.

The second beneficiaries are the parties. The House of Commons is their stage and the cases put there are party cases. Parties are basic to democracy. Yet up to now they have laboured under the handicap of being cut off from the public they claim to lead, because the mass party is dying, the party press is dead, killed by the left's incompetence and the fact that the Conservatives don't need it: sycophantic support is provided free by their sympathetic press. The traditional channels of public meetings and campaigns are atrophying, and six party political broadcasts a year are a pathetic alternative compared to the scale of their task. Now, with the televising of Parliament, a new channel has opened up. It is dependent on the editorial decisions of broadcasters, but these are essentially scrupulous, inhibited by the requirement to maintain balance which precludes judgement and the need to remain acceptable to the Common themselves. In practice, broadcasters concentrate on party spokesmen and ministers, those selected by the parties as their most competent exponents. Which is exactly what the parties want – if not the backbenchers.

The benefits to the individual Member come well behind all this. But, if the 'physical side' which preoccupied the media now becomes irrelevant because the experiment has been made permanent by a majority of 99 and the veto of MPs is therefore abdicated, the boost to individual backbenchers has been something more than a 650th of the collective gain. We have direct input to our constituencies, mainly via the regional companies and BBC regions. We benefit from being shown doing our job, though the audience is still prone to consider that performance equates with a presence in the Chamber which is in fact a bore and a distraction from real work. Personally, I now find it easier to work in the office and watch Prime Minister's Question Time on television, not being an enthusiast for this traditional turd-throwing ceremony. Yet for others the Chamber itself is rather more compelling. The number of oral questions submitted has gone up, particularly for Prime Minister's Question Time. Attendance in the Chamber is higher, particularly at peak time, the live coverage from 3 to 4 p.m. Doughnutting still goes on – not now on the back benches but as a way of being seen clustering round senior figures, doing the nodding dog routine (as seen in the back windows of cars) to demonstrate a grasp of the profundity of the points made by frontbenchers and gain a little reflected glory. In theory this process should reverse if frontbenchers collectively or individually reach a nadir, but in practice there is no limit to sycophancy in politics.

Backbenchers such as Dennis Skinner who take little or no part in committee work but are constantly in the Chamber are now more likely to be viewed as major figures. Which is a little unfair on committee dogsbodies but their lot has also seen a huge gain, for the Select Committees have become the most interesting aspect of Commons work. They were in danger of flagging because they operate mainly behind the scenes, but television coverage has offered Members new careers as amateur Perry Masons, and now there is competition to get on them, as well as on the few Standing Committees that are televised, such as that on the Broadcasting Bill. The Broadcasting Bill Committee was massively over-subscribed; this enabled the whips to use membership as another source of patronage, when they usually have to dredge deep to get people to serve on such committees.

More preparation is now necessary for speeches. Potential quotes, sound bites and jokes have to be thought through. Although the coverage of backbenchers has been reasonable and predictions that television would be dominated by the front-benchers have turned out to be true only for national news bulletins, the prospects of any one Member making an impact are low – except in the MPs own area, where the slight but growing incumbency effect of election may be helped along, marginally. In any case, appearing on television is always ego-enhancing. A halo hangs round anyone on the box and MPs now have a little one. Hedged by that divinity, they may find constituents more interested, more likely to ask questions, but also more likely to make judgements. Members who slavishly followed the line of a Government hurting people by high interest rates, unemployment and bankruptcy, or of an Opposition which wouldn't say what its alternative was, were exposed in a way never possible before. Neither side could make claims about their constituencies or about the delight of their constituents at party policy when these could be quickly contradicted. The constituency focus must be strengthened, and hopefully life may also be made a little more difficult for the 'ministrables' who ignore the growing demands of constituencies in order to dedicate themselves to self-promotion. Stupidity can't be as well concealed, though the House remains over-indulgent to it. If it is to be better brought home, the testing process of interjection and reply will have to be televised, and broadcasting will have to remove the shroud it still draws over incompetence, ignorance and simple idiocy, by making *sotto voce* value-judgements on *sotto voces*.

Because television was so long delayed, more concessions were made to conciliate Members than should have been necessary. The rules of coverage are too cautious, even after the 1990 relaxation. Procedures have not been sufficiently changed to make the most of the House's new role in show biz, the need to hold attention, not pander to dignity, and the need to help backbenchers. The structures were arrived at almost by afterthought as a compromise between Tory enthusiasm for privatization and the desire of others to keep some control. They can be improved, for the whole thing was done on the cheap by imposing on the goodwill of already overstretched broadcasting organizations and inviting loss-leader bids for the prestige of working in Parliament's inadequate conditions. More resources need to be provided to an overstrained committee coverage. Usage would be maximized if the coverage were provided without charge to anyone who wanted to use it for any purpose, especially if Parliament used its authority to pressure British Telecom into reducing the exorbitant prices it charges for links on which it has a monopoly. The aim should be to make Parliament as widely available and as much used as possible. It is a service, like the public utilities used to be, but one which, because it is basic to democracy, should be free.

The problems are minor. The experiment was a great success. No greater than was predictable, but more than enough to prove its value to the doubting Thomases who are always so numerous before any major advance and who built a vested interest in praising with faint damns afterwards. So just in case the chorus of self-congratulations becomes so obsessive and so long-sustained that it obscures the need for further advance to repair the damage caused by the way Parliament was reduced in public standing and effectiveness before television finally arrived, two basic points need to be emphasized. We have succeeded almost by accident. The structure is spatchcock, the Mother of Parliaments has scrounged to get it, and if we end up with the most sophisticated parliamentary television in the world we haven't done so by any rational process of considering why we were doing it, and how effort could best be directed to the real job in hand: that of plugging Parliament into the people, rather than merely admitting television. We have been lucky. The coverage has been good, the contractors excellent, but improvement is a perpetual process, particularly in television.

To have taken this obvious step is not a manifestation of our wisdom, merely something inevitable. We have to move on, and quickly too. Television devours, audiences get bored, interest wanes and Parliament has much to do to rebuild its authority. The Commons, constitutionally central, remain peripheral in the new politics – no longer the politics of parties or institutions but media politics, reaching the people through the media, particularly television. Our delay in admitting the people and their medium into the Chamber has forced television to do, earlier and better, something it would have done anyway – to stage its own political debate as another aspect of its mission to inform and entertain. The broadcasters have developed that debate on their terms, using the politicians rather than giving them access on their own terms, and putting politics in a dependent relationship subordinate to the medium: just another branch of entertainment. They have given that debate a wider audience, a greater standing, and a more central role than it would have if properly balanced by the institutional debate through the Commons. All are far greater than the Commons themselves can command, even on television.

Bringing in television is a step in the right direction, not the end of the journey. It prevents any further slippage in Parliament's long decline into irrelevance. For their part, Neil Kinnock and Margaret Thatcher showed little liking for the great tradition of dramatizing politics by personal duels of the Gladstone–Disraeli, Wilson–Heath type, although Kinnock came to find confrontations with John Major more to his liking. Thatcher and Kinnock revealed a marked preference for putting their own case on the media political circus because it had the audience and because neither was a gifted performer in the Chamber. This perhaps reflected a realistic sense of priorities for a mass electorate, but it was bad for democracy. Television in the Chamber may not dramatically change it. Yet it does force the Prime Minister and Leader of the Opposition to be more active on home ground, to put in more appearances, to challenge each other in the only forum in which they can do that, and to do their duty to democratic debate. In the future it will force party leaders into more confrontations, general debates and parliamentary appearances – just because television is there, and the audience with it. This ends the slide into the irrelevance of the closed debating society typified by the leaders' contempt of the central forum.

We must now build on that, not only to enhance our role in media politics, but to establish our own independent role. Putting television in the Commons makes us just another part of what is still media politics, controlled, staged and run by and for the media. We place another source and additional raw material at their disposal, widen the range of their options, and give the audience new interest. Yet we work on their terms, and still do not have a clearly defined role of our own. We remain subordinate and far from central. We can only strengthen our position by establishing our own independent sphere of operation, our own direct input to the people. That can only come from a dedicated parliamentary television channel screening the deliberations of the Commons and its committees, full time and from start to finish, without editorial intervention or control. We need to supply the people with raw, untreated Parliament, for them to use as they will.

Parliament in the living room and on tap was always the essential objective but the first priority was to get coverage on the major channels, particularly the news and regional programmes which most people watch. Yet the dedicated channel entered the argument even at this early stage as a distraction. Initially the Commons majority against partial coverage was swollen by those who didn't trust the broadcasters. Both were joined by some opposed to television altogether who hid behind the idea of a dedicated channel by arguing that there should be no coverage until it was dedicated, safe in the knowledge that this would postpone it to the Ides of Cable. The television organizations offering to finance coverage would not pay for that. Nor would government. So the best became the enemy of the better.

Right up to the July 1990 debate on making the experiment permanent, the argument for a dedicated channel remained the acceptable face of an opposition which remained, though more feebly, root and branch. Then Roger Gale and Dale Campbell-Savours, both opponents of conventional access, proposed a Doomsday amendment requiring another vote on coverage unless a dedicated channel had been provided within a year. Many supported this initially. They withdrew their support only when it became clear that the proposal was in fact a pistol to the head, not to force a desirable supplementary objective, but to put forward an alternative to the permanence the majority wanted settled. So the amendment was rejected by a majority of 39. But not before the Leader of the House, the Opposition spokesman and several other speakers had emphasized the urgent importance of a dedicated channel and committed themselves to it – by due processes, which means the Ides of Parliament.

It will come. The problems are basically financial and they will determine the two crucial issues of when and in what shape. No terrestrial channel is available, but satellite would also put it on to the cable network as that grows. The new Astra satellite will shortly add sixteen more channels to the sixteen already transmitting, with other, more expensive satellite options also on offer. Such a channel would cost between three and five million pounds, depending on the transponder rental. It would cost even more if simple transmission of Parliament was supplemented, as it could and should be, by public affairs in the *longueurs* when the House is not sitting. The best comparison, C-SPAN in the United States, is financed by the cable industry at a cost of around three cents of every cable dollar. It has a small staff, outside-broadcast facilities, studios and two channels. It transmits the US House and Senate as its basic diet supplemented by public affairs, broadly defined, in press conferences, seminars, lectures, national committee meetings, conventions and phone-ins with senior political figures. The whole is a diet of raw politics and an available resource; a pool to dip into. The material is presented without editorial selection, without overt mediation or pushy presenters building their own personality cults. Viewers are free to make their own judgements, sitting in the producer's chair.

A British C-SPAN is the optimum. It would benefit Britain's political nation: the active, the interested, the civic minded, the concerned, the cause pushers, all those with an interest in what is going on and views about it. They are at present a deprived class. They make the system work, yet they have little to nurture their interest. They are split by party, scattered by geography, alienated from the apathetic majority, rather like lepers. A public affairs channel would feed them, give them a focus, unite them, and provide the two-way flow of arguments, ideas and information that is needed if the Commons debate is to be widened out to involve the nation. Why should they not be able to satisfy their perverse interest in politics as those interested in sport, news, film or even pornography do because all are increasingly catered for by dedicated channels on satellite and cable?

Bringing politics to the people on the medium which has replaced party politics by media politics is the answer. It would make politics healthier, provide a national resource, a lever to lift the lumpen and leaven to give life to the lump. Such a channel would always be a minority one. Yet the political nation is a key minority, and many more would drop in and out, particularly as major issues emerged. No democracy can tolerate a situation in which the information about what is being done in their name, as well as the debate and the basic decisions the nation faces, does not flow out in a flood, but only through the controlled hosepipe spurts of the mass channels.

A dedicated channel would be more expensive than the present coverage. Would the House, which really means the Government, be prepared to pay? It should. It probably won't. There was a strong case, in the early stages of the campaign to get television into the Commons, for a publicly funded television unit of the type which manages coverage in Canada and the United States. There were two main arguments for this. One stressed the principle that it is the responsibility of the Commons to provide this as it provides Hansard. The second made the practical point that he who pays the piper calls the tune: the prospect of taking control out of the hands of broadcasters, whom MPs do not trust, was a way of winning wavering and nervous voters. But since MPTV has been accepted without the Commons TV unit it deserves, and since the Government won't be pressed too hard on this issue because the broadcasters have done such a good and safe job (and incidentally don't require the degree of control a Commons TV unit would provide), it is reasonable to argue that the money which these desirable and proper structures would have cost should, instead, be devoted to a dedicated channel.

Finance for the existing coverage is culled from different sources: broadcasting organizations, the Property Services Agency and such loss leaders as independent contractors are prepared to bear. Why, therefore, should the dedicated channel not be a similarly combined operation, to spread a burden of costs which will be greater? Possible contributors are terrestrial television, which could use the signal, the cable and satellite industry, both currently poor but potentially profitable enough to contribute or provide support in kind. There is also a strong case for educational funding because the channel would be widely used for educational purposes. In such a way annual costs of up to £10 million could be financed – provided there is the will to do so.

Britain has been lucky to get a technologically advanced, efficient and effective Commons television, almost by accident. It has been even luckier that the television organizations have been so conscientious and devoted in their coverage, in providing programmes and in developing the facility. Yet before the chorus of congratulations swells to a crescendo which drowns out even the eccentric mutterings of Roger Gale and Dale Campbell-Savours, we should be clear that television is not a medium which can be ushered in by the back door and left to get on with the job, like a plumber connecting up the water supply. The audience tires. People have to be hooked, served and interested. The medium devours and exhausts. Up to now MPTV has been on its best behaviour, lest a door which it has taken so long to open should be slammed. Although that won't now happen and the medium won't suddenly change its nature and reduce the Commons to *Spitting Image* ridicule, we do have a responsibility to ourselves to avert the potential problems and keep interest alive.

A number of changes would enliven audience interest, including a relaxation in the currently over-restrictive guidelines on coverage, free provision of the signal, and procedural changes to shorten speeches, to reduce the legislative burden on the Chamber and to revive the Standing Committees by allowing them to hold hearings on legislation. All this must be coupled with the speedy provision of a dedicated channel to stimulate interest and sustain democracy. Then at last Parliament would become the dynamic source and the focus of a wider debate radiating from the political nation. Only then would Parliament be doing its job of reaching out, educating, informing, providing a two-way channel, and generally stimulating the national debate that an active, involved and informed democracy needs.

There is now no going back to the vacuous pomposities of the closed debating society, where members misinterpret their constituents, spout unchecked prejudice, grovel for promotion and cloak stupidity, ignorance and incompetence in dignity. Having made this major step, we cannot now sit back and congratulate ourselves. We must develop the coverage, work harder to stimulate and build on our new link with our constituents and do our job better. No longer the dignified creatures Bagehot wrote about, we are clearly in showbiz, adult education, the pressure-group game and good old-fashioned public service. We need to be good at all of them. Most of all, we must do better the job for which we were elected. Nothing can enhance our standing, whether on MPTV or as simple MPs, more than that.

Chapter 6

A sceptic's judgement of televising the Commons

Roger Gale

I was described recently by a journalist as 'an unreconstructed opponent of the televising of the House of Commons'. That, for a journalist, is a tolerably accurate description, although it is also true that my views have modified since the debate that gave the entry visa to the Trojan Horse on 9 February 1988. In winding up that debate for the opponents I offered 'two separate but equally valid grounds – technical and editorial' for the rejection of the motion (HC Debs 1988a: col. 277). Let me review the technical arguments first.

Members were offered, in a joint paper of 20 January 1988 prepared by the BBC and ITV, 'remote controlled cameras which could be mounted below the galleries . . . there would probably be seven and they would be slightly smaller than the current generation of news cameras' and 'a modest increase in the existing lighting level in the Chamber . . . particularly below the galleries'. It was immediately apparent that the technology available at that time meant the installation of cameras that would have intruded upon the back benches and a level of lighting that would have been hot and uncomfortable. The first lighting experiment conducted by the BBC engineers produced an almost universally hostile reaction – even from those most ardent proponents of the 'experiment'.

'But it works in the House of Lords, doesn't it?' was the question most frequently posed by those eager to get the cameras into the Commons Chamber but blissfully unaware of the nature and requirements of television broadcasting. The House of Lords Chamber is larger and of a very different design from that of the Commons. There are positions available for tripod cameras that simply do not exist in the lower House, where the east and west galleries overhang the back benches, casting deep shadows.

'Why does it work in other legislatures?' was another question that begged all sorts of answers. Most other legislatures that we examined provided either fixed places or a podium for speakers – making the selection of pre-programmed shots a simple matter. Most other legislatures have also abandoned the freewheeling nature of Commons debate in favour of a more formal, more rigid and less immediate structure.

This leads directly to the editorial argument. 'Debate based upon an exchange of views in other legislatures has disappeared,' we said. 'Members go into their chambers and read set speeches to camera; they do not take part in debate.'

The advocates of televising deployed, at every opportunity, the argument that 'the public has a right to see and hear the elected representatives at work' and that somehow the admission of television cameras to the Chamber would enhance democracy. The claim is both naïve and ill informed. What we were offered in terms of reporting from the House by the BBC and ITV – who at that time had assumed that it would automatically be they that did the job – was *Match of The Day* and edited highlights used to tart up the *Nine O'Clock News* and *News at Ten* with occasional 'live' coverage of the 'sexy bits' – such as Prime Minister's Question Time and the Budget – and selective forays on to the committee floors. The debate was not about democracy but about journalism and televisual entertainment.

'What is proposed is an experiment, nothing more,' read a letter from the movers of the motion. The House was in fact offered not an experiment but a Trojan Horse. It was abundantly plain that once the cameras were in the press would not allow them to be removed. With the passing of the resolution the name of the game, therefore, became damage control.

THE SELECT COMMITTEE: TAKING ADVICE AND MAKING DECISIONS

The Select Committee on Televising of Proceedings of the House embarked on the tortuous process of determining both the technology and the terms on which cameras would be admitted for the experimental period. The committee was faced with at least three separate decisions. What technology did we require? Who should run the television unit? What conditions for camera grammar (permitted shots) and editorial control should be imposed?

The televisually illiterate – most of whom did not attend committee hearings – accused the committee of deliberate procrastination, and there was an attempt by the Neanderthal tendency to get the cameras rushed in on virtually any terms in time for the state opening of Parliament in November 1988. If the committee had taken the soft option, it would have delivered the House to the mercies of the second-rate outside broadcast technology used in the House of Lords. We believed, and I think that we have proved, that by insisting instead upon state-of-the-art cameras, controls and lighting we could generate sufficient interest in the project to effect very considerable improvements in the quality not only of the equipment we had been offered but of what was in use elsewhere. The engineers rose to the challenge provided by one of the most prestigious contracts on offer and as a result many of my technical reservations have been allayed. There are few who would now quarrel with the technical quality of the pictures leaving the Chamber or with the technical expertise with which they are delivered by a director and small team of camera operators who have become most adept at their task.

The Select Committee's decision to interview independent contractors alongside the BBC and ITN provoked, at the time, consternation coupled with the view that this was merely another ruse to delay the experiment. In fact, I think most members of the committee would now concede that each of the applicants for the franchise brought fresh and exciting technical and editorial expertise to the end result and, as an aside, we should publicly express our thanks to those who were not successful, as well as to those who won the contract. The creation of the House of Commons Broadcasting Unit Limited was a skilful political compromise that gave the House the best of independent enterprise backed up by the combined corporate finances of the BBC and ITV.

The whole package of technology and editorial ideas owes much to the visit that the committee made – again in the teeth of resistance from the 'more delay' faction – to the national and state legislatures in Ottawa and Toronto. Both Ottawa national and Ontario state legislatures have adopted a broadcast unit, established as an office of the Assembly, to reproduce and provide continuous *unedited* transmission of proceedings, commencing with Speaker's Prayers and ending with 'Who Goes Home' – what is known locally as 'gavel-to-gavel' coverage. Both legislatures installed state-of-the-art systems at the expense of the public purse. Similarly, both legislatures established guidelines that are understood and followed by technical staff. Staff in both legislatures are full-time employees, working under Directors of Broadcasting, but answerable to the Speaker and such advisory and editorial bodies as each House has chosen to create. It was the recommendation of every witness heard by the Select Committee that the House of Commons should, in the light of the Canadian experience, fund and install its own state-of-the-art system, staffed by permanent professional employees of the House.

'Control must be in the hands of the Members,' said Canadian MP Mike Breagh. 'The House should not tolerate "info-tainment".' Bill Somerville, Director of Broadcast Services and Communications in Toronto, added: 'This is not a "news show". It is not entertainment. It is Parliament. If people are to see Parliament then they must see Parliament as it is.'

The committee's eyes were opened to the possibilities of modern technology when it was exposed to the OASIS information system in the House of Commons in Ottawa. Every Canadian Member of Parliament has access to television news and electronic Hansard facilities in his or her office, can request replay of any portion of any recorded debate and expect to receive it within about twenty minutes, and can have access to data systems too. If the House of Commons in London was to have television – with all its drawbacks – then should it not have been as part of a fully integrated voice-telephony, data, personal-computer and off-screen information service? The advantages of such a system seem obvious.

We were further educated to the dangers of the experiment by the Speaker of the Canadian House, who told us, bluntly, that 'televising the House rewards the outrageous', that 'it has led to orchestrated removal from the Chamber and unparliamentary language. We have experienced unparliamentary activity . . . spurious use of privilege . . . the use of allegations in preambles to questions and the abuse of privilege through slander. In the press gallery the professionalism has gone. The reporters now watch the proceedings on television.' There were also benefits. 'It has helped control behaviour – we have less drunks in the Chamber – and the standard of dress has certainly improved.'

Overseas experience suggests that television does – as I have predicted – change procedure. 'We pay attention to seating', said Fred Biro, communications assistant to the Leader of the Progressive Party, 'to make sure that we have the right ethnic/female mix in shot surrounding the orator.'

> We are concerned with images . . . we talk in ten- or fifteen-second clips. We give media training . . . pay attention to ties . . . make sure that suits are buttoned. . . . Members don't want to be seen reading papers or attending to correspondence. We know that we are in competition with other news and with the Opposition for the headlines . . . that raises the temperature of the debate.

This view was supported by the communications assistant to the Leader of the Opposition, who told me: 'We issue prepared texts in advance of speeches to make sure that the media have access to the prepared clip. The "issue" is all-persuasive . . . the "better issues" get the coverage.'

Marje Nicholls, political correspondent of the Canadian *Sunday News*, told us that 'the idea of an "experiment" is a nonsense. Once it's in it's in . . . it will trivialize the House and weaken oratory. Public attitude? They used to have NO idea – now they have an inaccurate idea!'

For parliamentarians, though, perhaps the most chilling observation came from the Speaker. 'We have MPs under party caucus control. The televisual MPs are at the top of the whips' list . . . they choose "performers" in preference to the thoughtful.'

Returned from Canada, the committee came to grips with the experience and sought to sift and implement the recommendations and the advice. We achieved, I think, a good technical compromise that combined the insecurity of an experiment – the 'Chinese lanterns' in the Chamber are evidence of this – with the desire for innovative technical excellence. However, the determination on the part of the Government, in an unholy alliance with an impatient Opposition, that no 'public money' should be spent on the exercise meant that proposals for an integrated Members' information service went out of the window, and so the House missed yet another opportunity to take a faltering step towards the twentieth, if not the twenty-first, century. The House of Commons Broadcasting Unit was given guidelines for camera grammar that struck a balance between the rigid uniformity of head-and-shoulders only that we had seen in Ottawa and the free-for-all permitted in the Ontario State Legislature in Toronto. (Curious how some of those who wanted the cameras in only wanted them in so far!)

The main, and most serious, casualty of debate in committee was the proposal that the 'experiment' should be dependent upon the provision of a dedicated satellite broadcasting channel so that those members of the public who wanted to view the unedited proceedings of the House should be able to do so. Without this provision, I personally believed, the suggestion that televising would in any way 'enhance democracy' could only be seen as a pretence. To have insisted upon a satellite channel as a prerequisite of the 'experiment' would not, as some suggested, have delayed the start of the transmissions beyond what had become the totem-pole date of the state opening in 1989. It would not, however, have been achieved without the expenditure of some three or four million pounds of 'public money' on an Astra transponder and Telecom uplinks, and that proved to be the real sticking-point. Those who were prepared to will the ends to enhance democracy were quite simply not willing to will the means.

I do not believe that there is, or will be, a huge audience for the televised proceedings of the House either in edited form or 'live' – particularly in the middle of the night – but as the crux of the argument in favour of televising was that 'the people must be allowed to see' it seems a little perverse to deny the one vehicle by which they could do exactly that! On that basis I was the lone dissenting committee voice that voted against the final report. I felt churlish in doing so, knowing the hard work and intellectual exercise that Geoffrey Howe, then Leader of the House, had put into achieving a series of contortions designed to appeal to most of the House for most of the time – but the stand had to be made.

We fared no better on the floor of the House. An amendment that would have provided for a dedicated channel was defeated with the same arguments that were used in the Select Committee, and further amendments designed to liberalize the camera coverage went the same way in a collusion between Government and Opposition. The 'Not the House of Commons Show', a confidence trick designed to lead the public to believe that they were seeing the House of Commons at work, was under way!

TELEVISING THE COMMONS: THE GROWTH OF 'INFOTAINMENT'

'Our recommendation – with only one dissentient, for rather special reasons – is that televising should become a permanent feature of the House.' So said Sir Geoffrey Howe, as Leader of the House and Chairman of the Televising of the House Select Committee, introducing the debate on the Select Committee's report after one year of the 'experiment' (HC Debs 1990: col. 1223). As the one dissentient I had – and still hold – not one but several reasons for believing that for televising to become the 'permanent feature' that the House has accepted is premature.

During the time between the state opening and the publication of its report, the Select Committee, with its advisers, considered and took evidence upon a range of matters. Consideration was also given to satellite coverage of the proceedings and to the provision of a dedicated channel. Sadly, no useful or meaningful conclusions were reached, and it was this rather 'special reason' which, at the end of the day, led me to reject the experiment as rather less than the 'success beyond almost any expectations' trumpeted by the study for the Hansard Society (Hetherington, Weaver and Ryle 1990: 1).

Televising of the House has, to a large extent, mirrored the Canadian experience. A number of changes in Members' behaviour are evident. Certainly, standards of dress have improved on the Opposition benches, with only a few mavericks defying the best efforts of Labour's image managers and resisting new suits and smart shirts from Marks & Spencer. Officially, there was none before ('Honourable Members do not drink too much'), but the effects of 'dining well' are less obvious than in the past. With the House on best behaviour, it was not until 9 January 1990 that a Member ruled out of order in Standing Committee chose the floor of the House and 'live' television coverage to use privilege in order to make allegations that would never have been made outside the Chamber and under threat of a writ for libel. Members do, now, play to the cameras and write into over-prepared speeches the 'vision bites' that are desirable for the national news or, at the very least, for the breakfast and local television shows. The noble art of 'doughnutting' – surrounding a speaking Member, in an otherwise empty Chamber, with attentive acolytes – has been caught from across the Atlantic, with the refinement of 'poisoned doughnutting' used to embarrass, by distraction on the screen, an unpopular contribution.

Fred Biro's assertion that 'We pay attention to seating to make sure that we have the right ethnic/female mix in shot surrounding the orator' has been emulated in attempts to make sure that the Scots, Welsh, female and black Members and those in marginal seats are well orchestrated around the Opposition front bench at Prime Minister's Question Time, while junior ministers have been hauled over the coals along with ministers and secretaries of state, by Government whips, for scruffy appearance and overt disdain. Whether the cameras have yet ended a ministerial career is a moot point, but they are certainly a factor growing in importance to prestige and power.

There was a time when a Member had to 'hold the Chamber' to make an impact. Now it is much more important to 'hold the Camera'. It was inevitable that the change to behaviour and procedure would be a creeping disease, but the disease has certainly taken hold.

The 'experiment' has also altered the Members' standing in the constituency. 'Saw you on telly last week' is an accolade. The fact that you were part of a 'doughnut' designed by frantic whips and sat for thirty dreary minutes in mute boredom at some ungodly hour is immaterial. If you are there, on the screen, in the Chamber, you are doing your job in the square public eye. 'Haven't seen you on telly yet' is the accusatory version of the same syndrome. You were in Select Committee until a late hour, in Standing Committee until four in the morning, attending a constituency engagement, meeting members of an animal rights lobby, away on the delegation. No matter. You weren't 'on telly', so why weren't you doing the job we elected you to do? We are now in the 'info-tainment' business. Watch us perform with increasing desperation as any general election draws near. The cameras are in, the gloves are off. The only victim will be democracy!

But what is known about audience responses to the broadcasts from the House? The evidence seems very mixed. 'Television news reporting of Commons proceedings has increased by 80 to 300 per cent or more since the Cameras came into the House,' says a Hansard Society press release in April 1990, trailing the publication of *Cameras in the Commons*. Well, which is it? 80 per cent? Or 300 per cent? Or more? Where were these statistics plucked from? 'These are network news figures,' continues the release. 'At the same time programmes such as BBC2's "Westminster" and Channel 4's "The Parliament Programme" have been winning audiences of *up to* [my italics] 250,000 in off-peak morning broadcasts.' As a television producer and director I know many who would have committed suicide at the thought of such dismal figures. What is clear is that television coverage of the House, while satisfying media demands for visual images from the Chamber, has not enhanced the principles of democracy in any meaningful way whatsoever.

The televising of the House has been an outstanding technical success. It would be quite wrong to suggest otherwise. There are remaining and well-targeted criticisms, certainly, of the lighting in the Chamber and of an antiquated sound system that was never designed for the purpose that it now serves. Coverage of the committees leaves a great deal to be desired and is intrusive to an intolerable degree. Overall, though, the engineers, the director and camera operators have offered a clean feed that few would have believed to be technically possible when the 'go-ahead' was voted through in 1988. Bob Longman, engineering consultant to the Select Committee, lists the achievement methodically in an article in the *Journal of the Royal Television Society* for May/June 1990. The installation of newly developed Sony BVP cameras, the creation of a panning head 'a quarter of the size of its predecessors', the application of miniature 'spotter cameras' to enable camera operators to find Members while covering others and the creation of a superb remote-control camera system have all been crucial to this success.

From a democratic and editorial point of view, however, I believe that the televising of the House has, to date, not been the unqualified success that the Hansard Society and the mechanical media have trumpeted in a self-satisfied way, but a transparent failure that has realized the worst fears of many. The public have not been offered the opportunity to see the House of Commons at work. A very few members of the public have seen a very little of what goes on in the Chamber and still less of the activities of Select and Standing committees. Worse, those extracts that have been seen have been highly selective, owing everything to quite acceptable standards of journalists' news values but nothing at all to the hour-by-hour painstaking work of the legislature of the United Kingdom.

It need not have been thus. During the 1989 recess, before the state opening, we approached Astra Television for the brief loan of a transponder on the Astra satellite. With Sky Television handling the transmission, the gift of the signal from House of Commons Television and a free uplink from British Telecom, what became known, fleetingly, as 'MPTV' took to the air at the same moment that the cameras were switched on. It remained on air – 'gavel to gavel' until, three weeks later, the satellite transponder was required for commercial purposes. The technology was there, on time, and faultless. Only the funding was missing – funding that would have made permanent a real experiment in the televising of the House.

If it was galling to hear, in the debate on the second report of the Televising of the House Select Committee in July 1990, the same 'wrecking amendment' arguments that had been heard when the first report was debated a year earlier then it was so only because the case had been proved. It has been the unwillingness of the House either to fund a dedicated channel or to allow others to run one as a commercial enterprise that has prevented a growing number of satellite and cable viewers from seeing the unedited House of Commons 'warts and all'.

It was said in the debate in the House that the American public, on C-SPAN (delivery funded by cable companies, signal provided by the American taxpayer), can see more of the House of Commons at work than can the electorate of the United Kingdom (HC Debs 1990). 'What is the relevance to the lives of the public of a series of impressive, well-considered debates if they hear little of those debates,' said a champion of televising, Austin Mitchell, in an earlier debate (HC Debs 1983b: col. 876). Precisely! I do not, as is clear, believe that televising has done the House, or its procedures and traditions, any service. If, though, we are to 'extend democracy' then let us no longer find reasons why, technically or financially, it cannot be done and let us at least do the job properly 'gavel to gavel'. The Select Committee during the 1990–1 parliamentary session addressed exactly these issues.

THE PERMANENT TELEVISING OF THE HOUSE: MISSED OPPORTUNITIES

During the various debates on the televising of the House of Commons much has been made of the ability of the television cameras to 'enhance democracy', to 'broaden the democratic process' and to make the debates of the House and its business in committees 'more accessible to the people'. For its part the Select Committee on Televising has highlighted the desirability of providing a dedicated channel which, outside sitting hours, would carry committee deliberations, House of Lords debates and other relevant material.

In my view the overriding considerations of the Select Committee, in preparing its report of March 1991 on the arrangements for the permanent televising of the House, were short-term expediency and the attempt to minimize costs.

The committee has considered three options for the permanent televising of the House: (1) a broadcasting unit established as a department of the House; (2) an independent unit answerable to a Select Committee; (3) a variation on the experimental system, the House of Commons Broadcasting Unit Limited (HOCBUL), incorporating the House of Lords, to create an integrated Parliamentary Broadcasting Unit (PARBUL) based upon the HOCBUL model.

Option 1 – an in-house unit – is the system adopted by a number of legislatures, including the Canadian House of Commons which was visited by the Select Committee. (The system is part of a top-quality Members' information service employing technology that is, sadly, not available to the Members of the House of Commons.)

Option 2 – an independent unit answerable to a Select Committee – is, perhaps unsurprisingly, the option favoured by the professional production companies. The alleged advantages of such a system are that it would offer cost savings combined with a freedom from Civil Service bureaucracy and regulation not available through option 1.

Option 3 – an integrated unit on the HOCBUL model – offers neither the in-house advantages of option 1 nor the entrepreneurial freedoms of option 2. It appears at first glance, however, to be relatively inexpensive.

The Select Committee report recommended 'That the permanent televising of the House's proceedings should be carried out by an outside contractor selected by public tender.' That recommendation is, literally, correct, but by binding that outside contractor to the HOCBUL/PARBUL model the committee has selected the worst of all worlds – option 3.

The financing of television on a permanent basis

We therefore recommend that the present criteria for apportioning costs should be embodied in the permanent arrangements,' states the Select Committee's conclusion.

> The broadcasters should finance the equipment and the running costs, the Parliamentary Works Office should be responsible for expenditure on capital works within the parliamentary estate, notably alterations to the fabric of the building, and the House of Commons Commission should fund the Select Committee and any staff, including the Supervisor of Broadcasting, associated with the management of the televising operation within the House itself.
>
> (HC Select Committee 1991: 11, para. 29)

These financial arrangements guarantee that we have a sizeable chunk of option 1, the independent contractor from option 2, but, through the shackles of HOCBUL, we have tied ourselves to 'the broadcasters' in a way that prevents the development of the service and, to a large extent, the realization of funding that might pay for a dedicated channel.

What seems to have been forgotten is that HOCBUL was intended to be an expedient, devised to provide an experiment in the technical televising of the Chamber of the House of Commons at minimal cost to the taxpayer. The original proposals that the BBC and ITV should jointly pay for and run the installation of the necessary camera, lighting and control equipment were ingeniously leavened with the introduction of an outside and independent contractor to provide the studio director and camera operators.

The commitment to the HOCBUL model, however, means that the major commercial market for the signal from the House of Commons (re-use by domestic broadcasters of edited clips and highlights) and the revenue that the sale of much material might generate are tied up in the commitment to machinery and manpower invested by the BBC/ITV broadcasters.

I would argue, however, that it might be more advantageous for the House either to own and run its own unit and to recoup its costs through the sale of the signal, or, alternatively, to make the franchise available, under the supervision of the Select Committee, to an independent operator responsible for the installation, production and sale of the signal to all domestic and overseas outlets. The provision of a dedicated channel and the generation and sale of the signal from the Chamber are, and should be, inextricably linked. In treating them in isolation, I believe the Select Committee has made a fundamental and potentially damaging error of judgement compounding the earlier failure to explore other methods of finance more imaginatively.

The provision of a dedicated channel

It is widely accepted that if the original thesis behind the televising of the House – the extension of democracy to the electorate – is to be realized, then the work of the Chamber, at least, must be made available unedited on a 'gavel-to-gavel' (or 'mace-to-mace') channel without interruption and with added provision of some form of subtitling or signing for those with hearing difficulties. It is also generally accepted that this provision should be made, to the electorate of the United Kingdom, as universally as possible and free of charge.

Proposals for a dedicated channel – and amendments to the Select Committee's recommendations – pre-date the televising experiment. Originally, proposals that televising should be tied to a dedicated channel were dismissed as 'delaying tactics by those who were opposed to the televising of the House', and, it was claimed, a dedicated channel was 'not at present technically practicable'. This view was shown to be erroneous when Sky Television, in conjunction with British Telecom and Astra and with the assistance of HOCBUL, carried gavel-to-gavel coverage on a satellite transponder for the first fortnight of the televising experiment.

Given the lack of available terrestrial television channels it is clear that the public are only likely to be able to receive a dedicated transmission from the House of Commons via satellite to cable head-end and cable delivery system and/or via direct broadcast satellite. The committee has considered – but only on the back of the provision of the signal by HOCBUL – proposals for cable delivery (United Artists), delivery via the Marco Polo (formerly BSB) satellite and via Astra satellite and cable combined (Thames Television).

While cable is most certainly likely to develop as one of the major distributors of entertainment, voice telephony and data of the future, its current audience reach – and that for the foreseeable future – represents only a small percentage of the electorate. Certainly, outlying rural regions are unlikely to have the benefit of cable delivery systems for many years.

The suggested use of the Marco Polo satellite would, undoubtedly, provide a convenient use for a piece of very expensive technology that is embarrassingly redundant and very probably already obsolete. But who would watch it? Marco Polo is viable as a means of delivering the signal from the House of Commons to the cable head-ends and it does have the advantage of direct broadcast reception by those very few people who invested in a 'squarial' receiver dish and equipment. There are certainly squarials available for sale – hundreds of them – but will the public buy them to receive only the House of Commons and, perhaps, some sophisticated business services? Patently not.

The only currently available and viable system for the provision of a dedicated channel is an Astra satellite transponder feeding both cable head-ends (and thus the expanding cable audience) and those with direct broadcast satellite dishes (Sky dishes).

Funding a dedicated channel

The Select Committee identified three sources of finance: cable and satellite subscriptions, sponsorship and public subsidy. The last has been largely discounted but needs to be re-examined in the light of current Government policy, and the potential for a commercial – perhaps publicly underwritten – venture encompassing the whole of the televising of the House and the provision of a dedicated channel has been insufficiently explored.

A basic assumption of televising of the House has been that there should be no burden of finance on the public purse. This in itself is a quaint and inconsistent approach. The House has apparently decided, through the voting lobby, that the British public has a right to see the House of Commons at work, but is unwilling to provide adequate resources to achieve this policy objective. Unless we are prepared to accept that editorial control should rest with the BBC and ITV, we are duty bound to make provision for a dedicated channel, as an extension of the decision taken by the House and – if necessary – to fund the service that we have already decided the public wants!

The precedents for the public funding of information services are already clear. Through the provision of BBC World Service, the Central Office of Information (COI), Government information departments, S4C (Welsh Services), the British Forces Broadcasting Service and Hansard, we commit some £450 million a year to the subsidy of news and information. In this context, the funding required to provide dedicated coverage of the Mother of Parliaments is not large. Indeed, at some £5 million a year, a parliamentary television service would be cheaper than the £9.5 million that the Government has provided for a service to a maximum potential Gaelic-speaking audience of about 80,000 people!

The suggestion that it is therefore neither possible nor proper to wholly fund a C-SPAN (see chapter 13) or Canadian-style system is simply not consistent with recent Government decisions!

It is not, however, necessary for the public purse to pay for the televising of the House and for the provision of a signal by a dedicated channel if the House is prepared to offer the whole franchise to an independent operator, under Select Committee scrutiny, with the brief to provide coverage of both Houses of Parliament in the Chambers, coverage of Select and Standing committees as required, the marketing of the signal to domestic and international broadcasters and the provision of the signal free of charge via satellite and cable to the viewers at home. The operator would also be responsible for the provision of material to the archive and for the sale of archive material, on cassette, to approved purchasers.

With the permanent establishment of a HOCBUL/PARBUL system the committee risks the danger of excluding once and for all, the whole-franchise operator. (It is highly questionable whether an operator would be interested in marketing the leftovers from the domestic broadcasters or, indeed, whether these would yield anything like sufficient funds to pay for a satellite/cable distribution of a dedicated channel.) Quite simply, this option has, because of a fixation with the HOCBUL system, not been adequately explored in the light of the technical success of the televising experiment.

I would recommend that the House replace the HOCBUL/PARBUL model with one of the following options: (1) a wholly owned and fully funded televising unit as an office of the House paid for entirely out of public funds; (2) a wholly owned televising unit operated by an independent manager/contractor chosen by public tender, funding to be underwritten by the public purse but recouped through the sale of material to domestic and overseas broadcasters and business services with any profits in later years accruing to the House; or (3) the award of the franchise to a wholly independent contractor working to Select Committee guidelines and responsible for the sale of the signal and ancillary products, the provision of all technical facilities (including the satellite distribution of a dedicated channel) and the retention of all profit.

These options allow for the possibility of establishing a dedicated channel broadcasting complete coverage of events in both Chamber and committees. It is only such comprehensive coverage that will unleash television's potential to enhance, rather than detract from, the democratic process.

Chapter 7

Televising the Commons: the view from the third party

Charles Kennedy and Caroline Culey

In the past when the House of Commons has reformed itself, there have always been those who have predicted that the reform in question would mark the end of civilization as we know it. The debates on votes for women earlier this century offer a classic example of such pessimism prompted by innovation. The arrival of cameras in the Commons has continued this oldest of House traditions. Gloomy prognoses of dire consequences emanated from predictable prophets warning Members that they would be metamorphosed into mere pawns in the game of 'MPTV' in which broadcasters would be the key players.

More moderate voices raised genuine concerns about the potential consequences of televising the Commons. These ranged from fairly trivial matters such as the possible impact of television on Members' haircuts and style of dress, to substantive worries that broadcasting might present an image of the House as a bipartisan Chamber in which third parties can appear to be marginalized. These latter predictions have, to some extent, both proved correct.

The arrival of a mirror in the Whips' Office of the Liberal Democrats is testament to members' growing consciousness of the need to check their appearance before entering the newly televised chamber; it is perhaps ungenerous to suggest it might also reflect a growing personal vanity prompted by the cameras. An innovation of dubious constitutional significance, the mirror has already proved its considerable utility and convenience.

More significantly, the televising of the Commons has influenced the procedures and conventions of the House in ways which are damaging to the Liberal Democrats as the third party, to the minority parties in the House and to backbenchers from all parties.

But Liberal Democrats have always supported the introduction of cameras to the Commons, believing that television broadcasting of proceedings would lead to increased public understanding of Parliament and greater public accountability. As a party firmly committed to the principle of open government, we believe that the public have a right to see their elected representatives at work. Jim Wallace, Liberal Democrat Chief Whip, speaking on a motion at Conference which welcomed the introduction of the cameras in the Commons, criticized the House for taking so long to drag itself into the television age. He pointed out the obvious irony in a situation where the British public was able to watch the proceedings of the Soviet Parliament in news bulletins long before they could view events in Westminster – not a particularly good advert for the great Mother of Parliaments!

In the House debate on the Select Committee Report in July 1990, we argued that the broadcasters should be given a free hand. While a number of Honourable Members from other parties called for censorship mechanisms, we advocated a 'warts and all' approach to coverage of proceedings. It seemed important that the audience viewing from home should see exactly what they would see from a seat in the public gallery of the Chamber. For this reason, we were extremely unhappy about the restrictions on camera angles which were originally imposed on the broadcasters. The insistence on a head-and-shoulders shot or a standard wide-angle view seemed to be unnecessarily restrictive. It was none the less regrettable that Channel 4 scrapped plans for regular live coverage of the Commons as a result of these restrictions.

Ideally, we would like to have seen a dedicated parliamentary channel, but, since technical difficulties would have delayed the start of the experiment, we felt unable to support an amendment to this effect in the division lobbies.

Prior to the experiment, then, the Liberal Democrats made their support for the introduction of the cameras abundantly clear. From the outset, however, our enthusiastic support for the principle of televising was tinged with concern that, as the 'third party', televising the House's proceedings would in practice prove to be to our disadvantage. It is not only the opponents of televising who envisage potentially damaging consequences stemming from the arrival of the cameras. In fairness to the broadcasters, our fears that we would be 'carved out' of Commons coverage were not wholly their fault. The House of Commons itself discriminates against smaller parties. The complex procedures by which it operates presume the adversarial politics of confrontation between two parties. This presumption is reflected in the fact that Government and Opposition MPs continue to sit directly opposite each other on benches set two sword-thrusts apart. Our principal reservation about televising was that it would magnify the bipartisan nature of the House. We were worried that, by dramatizing the gladiatorial combat between the two major parties, the broadcasters would edit out Liberal Democrat views and contributions completely.

Coverage of Prime Minister's Questions was an issue of particular concern. Every Tuesday and Thursday, Neil Kinnock as Leader of the Opposition was allowed to put a question to the Prime Minister which he then followed up with two supplementary questions. But the conventions of the House meant that Paddy Ashdown was lucky to get called once a week and was restricted to a single question. Our problem was how to explain this to the general public. Superficially, it might look as if the Prime Minister was slapping Paddy down on each occasion, leaving him with nothing to say in response. Kinnock, however, would come over as a real fighter, going back to the Prime Minister twice. On the days when Paddy was not called, we would have a different problem. People might assume either that he was not in the Chamber or that he was not trying to question the Prime Minister. Worse still, if he was seen to be rising in his place but not getting called by the Speaker, his credibility as leader of the third party could be seriously undermined. In any event, the reality was that for 50 per cent of the time the Liberal Democrats were not participating in the twice-weekly 'Maggie and Neil show' at all. Given that it was the one aspect of Commons business which was guaranteed live coverage and extensive highlights, we knew that it would prove particularly damaging to our party.

We were also concerned about coverage of Liberal Democrats in the various regional networks. Given the uneven spread of our parliamentary representation, there were some regions where we did not have a single MP. In some parts of the country, the same was true of the Labour Party. In East Anglia, for example, there was only one non-Tory MP in the whole region, Labour's John Garrett in Norwich. The key concern for us was how the regional TV companies would achieve the required element of political balance in reporting without sacrificing the local flavour of their programmes.

A further aspect of televising proceedings which interested us was how broadcasters would report Standing and Select committees. We hoped that the broadcasters would make adequate use of committee footage and not concentrate exclusively on events in the Chamber. A number of Liberal Democrat MPs have been singled out for special praise for their work on committees in the last few years – Paddy Ashdown on the Education Reform Bill and Robert Maclennan on the Broadcasting Bill, for example. We hoped that such sterling work would not be ignored. Committee work, moreover, shows a different aspect of the House's business. In Select Committees, in particular, cross-party alliances are made and unanimous reports are common. Such committees operate in a way which is closer to the consensus model of politics (which our party has always advocated), rather than the confrontational model. We were therefore particularly keen for the public to see this facet of the House's activities.

The Liberal Democrats expressed some of these fears in their initial submission to the Select Committee on Televising the House, but by the time we were invited to make a second submission concerning the experiment in television broadcasting many of our fears had been realized. News bulletins tended to concentrate on exchanges in the Chamber, and although some of the national review programmes have used committee excerpts the cost of covering committees has proved prohibitive for the regional TV companies. More significantly, our own anecdotal evidence and a number of independent academic studies confirmed that the Liberal Democrats have not been getting their fair share of 'MPTV'. The study conducted at Aston University, for example, calculated that 'before the experiment began, 65% of MPs' television appearances were by Conservative members, 24% by Labour and 11% by other parties. After the experiment had begun, 64% of appearances were by Conservatives, 28% by Labour and 8% by other parties' (Cumberbatch, Brown and Skelton 1990: 3). A second study by the Parliamentary Research Group at the University of Leeds, commissioned by the All Party Commons Select Committee on Televising, expressed concern over the issue of political balance on two counts: 'First, Conservatives typically attracted more coverage than Labour speakers. Second, Parliamentary television was markedly bipartisan, paying relatively little attention to Liberal Democrat Members and Members of other parties' (HC Select Committee 1990: 265–I, 16). Finally, the

Hansard Society's report on televising noted that 'The Conservative Government's domination is plain', although it attributed this to the procedures of the House rather than the bias of the broadcasters (Hetherington; Weaver and Ryle 1990: 14).

In part, we would agree with this assessment. Before the experiment in televising the Commons began, the Liberal Democrats had high hopes that it would lead to the reform of parliamentary procedure. We believed that the public would show a marked lack of sympathy for the more arcane and idiosyncratic aspects of parliamentary business. Not everyone, however, shared these aspirations. Prior to the experiment, the Select Committee on Procedure (session 1987–8) produced a report on this issue. Predictably, they concluded that 'it would not be appropriate at this stage to make any changes in procedure solely for the introduction of television.'

In reality, the introduction of the cameras *has* made an impact on the procedures and conventions of the House. In many cases, the subtle changes which have taken place have served to reinforce the bipartisan nature of the House at the expense of the third parties. In our submission to the Select Committee on Televising in the 1989–90 session, we highlighted four specific changes with significant consequences for Liberal Democrats (HC Select Committee 1990: 265–I, 76–9).

First, we noted that frontbench speeches were considerably longer during the 1989–90 parliamentary session after the arrival of television. We examined the length of frontbench speeches in debates on four key bills in the 1989–90 session and compared them with four equivalent bills from the previous parliamentary session. In the eight debates analysed, the average length of frontbench speeches increased from 38.4 minutes in the 1988–9 parliamentary session to 46.5 minutes in the subsequent session. This suggests that, on average, the combined length of frontbench contributions in major debates increased by around 8 minutes, or approximately 21 per cent in the session after proceedings began to be televised. One of the reasons for longer frontbench speeches was undoubtedly a corresponding increase in the number of interventions. Backbenchers were quick to learn that a timely intervention in a minister's speech was much more productive of television headlines than a lengthy speech to an empty Chamber in the early hours of the morning.

In general, the practice of taking more interventions is to be welcomed. It certainly makes for livelier debates (and better TV!).

The fact that combined frontbench speeches are frequently taking an hour and a half, however, does have serious consequences for the Liberal Democrats. It has long been one of our complaints that our spokespersons are called late in debates when the press gallery has cleared. With frontbenchers taking longer, our speakers are being called even later, frequently missing the all important early-evening news bulletins.

A second and related problem has been the Speaker's increased use of the ten-minute time limit on backbench speeches. One of the most obvious results of televising proceedings has been the increased pressure to speak from all sections of the House. In an attempt to call as many MPs as possible in all major debates, the Speaker has made much more frequent use of his power under standing orders to limit backbench speeches to ten minutes during the specified times of 6–8 p.m. or 7–9 p.m. In previous sessions, use of the ten-minute rule has not usually hampered our party spokespersons. Generally, they have been called early enough to avoid the ten-minute limit. Indeed, when the standing order was adopted, we sought, and received, assurances from the Leader of the House and the Chairman of the Procedure Committee that the rule would not be used to curtail our party spokespersons. One direct consequence of longer frontbench speeches, however, has been that our spokespersons are increasingly at risk of being called after the introduction of the ten-minute limit. In the 1989–90 session, the Liberal Democrats' contribution to four major debates was restricted by the operation of this rule. On a further two occasions, Liberal Democrat spokespersons elected to be called at the 'fag-end' of the debate rather than be restricted to making a ten-minute speech.

For us, this is a particularly unfortunate consequence of televising. It seems doubly unfair that our spokespersons are being forced to make shorter speeches at a time when others are enjoying opportunities for making longer ones!

A third change apparent since the advent of television was the tendency for Opposition spokespersons to make longer responses to Government statements. We came increasingly to feel that Labour Party frontbenchers were making what amounted to a counter-statement rather than questioning ministers. Hansard does not record the times for responses to statements, but one possible way of confirming our suspicions was to measure the length of responses recorded in column centimetres. We compared the length of Opposition responses to statements for December 1988 with those for December 1989. Details are given in table 7.1.

Table 7.1 Length of Opposition responses to statements, December 1988 and December 1989

(a) December 1988

Date	Statement	Spokesperson	Length in column cm
5	Employment for the 1990	Meacher	25.5
6	European Council (Rhodes)	Kinnock	15
6	Sottish Enterprise	Dewar	38
7	North East Shipbuilders	Garrett	21
8	RSG (Wales)	Jones	21.5
12	Clapham Rail Disaster	Prescott	24.5
12	Fisheries Council	Gorman	16.5
13	Public Expenditure (Scotland)	Dewar	43.5
19	Egg Industry	Clark	25.5
19	RSG (England)	Soley	21
20	Chieftan Tank Replacement	O'Neill	9.5
22	Lockerbie Disaster	Prescott	19.5
Average length			23.4

(b) December 1989

Date	Statement	Spokesperson	Length in column cm
5	Atomic Weapons Establishment	O'Neill	24
6	Scottish Public Spending	Dewar	35.5
11	War Widows	Boyes	14.5
12	Strasbourg Summit	Kinnock	26.5
12	Vietnamese Boat People	Kaufman	29
14	Traffic (London)	Prescott	40
18	Welsh Local Government Finance	Jones	26.5
19	Barlow Clowes	Brown	24
19	BR Objectives	Prescott	46.5
20	Hong Kong	Kaufman	27
20	Fisheries	Morley	22
Average length			28.7

Analysis confirmed that our perceptions were correct. The average length of contributions had increased from 23.42 cm in December 1988 to 28.68 cm in December 1989, an increase of

22.46 per cent. To the viewer, this may not seem a significant point. For a minority party spokesperson, however, it may mean the difference between making a response during live TV coverage or missing out altogether. The problem is compounded by the fact that the Speaker is taking a tougher line on backbench responses. During weekly Business Questions, for example, he has made it quite clear that he will accept only one question from each MP. The Shadow Leader of the House, on the other hand, is allowed to make a lengthy counter-statement concerning next week's business.

One oft-quoted result of televising has been the supposed rise in the number of bogus points of order at 3.30 p.m. On Tuesdays and Thursdays, with live coverage, the temptation to be seen on the box has obviously proved irresistible for some Honourable Members. Research into this allegation is, however, difficult. A quick comparison between January 1989 and January 1990 suggests that the number of MPs raising points of order has doubled. The problem is how to define which points of order are bogus and which are perfectly legitimate – a very subjective judgement to make. What is certainly true is that points of order are increasingly becoming a daily feature, and that certain maverick MPs are appearing in this slot with tedious regularity.

The fourth worrying development from the Liberal Democrat perspective has been the way in which we have been squeezed out of Parliamentary Question Time since the cameras arrived. As with debates, the cameras have undoubtedly increased the pressure on the Speaker to call the largest possible number of MPs during departmental questions. This is particularly true on Tuesdays and Thursdays, when there is the added incentive of being seen on live TV.

A comparison between March 1989 and March 1990 shows a marked decrease in the number of occasions on which a Liberal Democrat MP has been called on to ask a supplementary question. Details are given in table 7.2. In the thirteen days of departmental questions in March 1989, the total number of Liberal Democrats called to ask supplementary questions was 18. In the seventeen days in March 1990, the corresponding total was 16.

It is rapidly becoming the case that only our spokesperson is being called to ask a supplementary question and that other MPs with a legitimate constituency interest are prevented from raising it unless they happen to be lucky in the ballot. Unfortunately, another consequence of televising has been that we are less likely

Table 7.2   Number of occasions on which Liberal Democrats were
called to ask supplementary questions, March 1989 and March 1990

(a) March 1989

Date	Department	Liberal Democrats called
1	Scotland	Archie Kirkwood, David Steel, Russell Johnston, Jim Wallace
2	Home Office	Robert Maclennan, David Alton
6	Social Security	Ronnie Fearn
6	Attorney-General	Robert Maclennan
7	Defence	Menzies Campbell
8	Foreign and Commonwealth	Alex Carlile, David Steel
9	Northern Ireland	Paddy Ashdown, David Alton
13	Transport	——
13	Public Accounts	Simon Hughes
14	Employment	Jim Wallace
15	Trade and Industry	Charles Kennedy
16	Agriculture	
20	Wales	Richard Livsey
21	Health	Ronnie Fearn
22	Environment	——

(b) March 1990

Date	Department	Liberal Democrats called
1	Northern Ireland	——
5	Social Security	Archie Kirkwood
6	Defence	Menzies Campbell
7	Foreign and Commonwealth	Russell Johnston
8	Agriculture	——
12	Transport	Ronnie Fearn, Simon Hughes
12	Overseas Development and Aid	Russell Johnston
13	Employment	David Alton, Jim Wallace
14	Trade and Industry	Matthew Taylor
15	Treasury	Alan Beith
19	Wales	——
20	Health	——
21	Environment	Menzies Campbell
22	Home Office	Robert Maclennan
26	Energy	——
27	Education	Cyril Smith, Simon Hughes
28	Scotland	Ray Michie
29	Northern Ireland	Paddy Ashdown

Note: Both lists refer to supplementary questions only and exclude MPs who had
balloted questions.

to do well in the ballot. The number of questions tabled for oral answer each day has been steadily increasing over the past few years. In the 1971–2 session, 11,108 questions were tabled for oral answer. In the 1988–9 session, the number had risen to 23,932.

This mainly reflects an increase in the practice of syndication, whereby PPSs and whips farm out prearranged sets of questions to party members. The object of the exercise is to increase the probability of 'desirable' questions coming up during departmental questions. With only a small number of MPs, the extent to which we are able to syndicate questions is obviously quite limited. With more and more Tory and Labour MPs tabling questions each day, the probability of one of our questions coming up in the top 20 is correspondingly reduced.

Televising proceedings has undoubtedly exacerbated the practice of syndication, and the results for the smaller parties have been devastating. The Hansard Society study quotes the example of Northern Ireland Questions. Prior to televising, the average number of questions submitted to the Secretary of State was around 25, with the majority coming from the various minority parties in Northern Ireland. By 29 March 1990, the number of balloted questions to the Secretary of State for Northern Ireland had risen to over 100. Of the top 20, the ones likely to be reached, only numbers 6 and 17 were from Ulster members. The rest originated from 'outsiders' eager to get in on the act. As a result, both BBC and Ulster TV cancelled plans for live coverage of Northern Ireland Questions.

Our own Scottish MPs have experienced similar problems. In early 1990 the Liberal Democrats had nine Scottish Members, only one fewer in Scotland than the Tories. Our input during Scottish Questions did not, however, reflect these figures. It had long been the practice for Scottish Tories holding English seats to participate in Scottish Question Time, making up for the Conservative Government's lack of representation north of the border. Even those of the least sceptical disposition might have predicted that television would encourage this practice. At Scottish Questions on 31 January 1990, broadcast live in Scotland, the Hansard Society study calculated that the relative amount of time given to each party was: Conservatives 68 per cent, Labour 25 per cent, Liberal Democrats 4 per cent and SNP 1 per cent (Hetherington, Weaver, Ryle 1990: 15). At that date, however, in terms of parliamentary representation, the relative strengths of the parties in Scotland were: Conservatives 13.8 per cent, Labour (excluding Dick Douglas) 66.7 per cent, Liberal Democrats 12.5 per cent and SNP 5.5 per cent. Since it was the Conservative Secretary of State who answered questions, the dominance of the Conservatives over Labour was to be expected, but the so-called 'minority parties', ourselves and the SNP, did particularly badly under that system.

Question Time has, however, turned out to be the one area where the introduction of the cameras may have helped lead to a change in procedure which will ultimately be to our advantage. The Procedure Committee have been concerned for some time about the growth of syndication. The advent of television was undoubtedly one of the factors which encouraged them to examine this issue and produce a report. They concluded that syndication was undermining the whole purpose of Question Time and therefore recommended that it be stopped. The House debated the report and agreed it. Since the beginning of the 1990–1991 session, oral questions must be taken to the Table Office by each MP in person, replacing the system which allowed sheaves of questions to be handed in by the whips. Hopefully, this will lead to a substantial reduction in the number of questions tabled by Tory and Labour backbenchers, giving the smaller parties a more equitable chance in the ballot.

More important, the new system will also restore some power to the Tory and Labour backbenchers. It is important to note that many of the changes we have cited are not just third-party gripes against the two main parties. They are also examples of the erosion of backbench rights in the face of growing frontbench domination – an increase in the power of the executive over the legislature. Perhaps the greatest irony of televising Commons proceedings is that, in allowing the cameras in, the House has merely succeeded in underlining the Government's dominance and its own irrelevance.

Liberal Democrats remain firmly committed to the televising of the Commons, although we do not always like what we see. It would be easy to blame the broadcasters, but that would smack of shooting the messenger. For the most part, broadcasters are simply reflecting what they see – a House of Commons where the political imbalance derives from an unfair electoral system.

Part IV

Assessments: academic investigations

Chapter 8

Televising the Commons: a full, balanced and fair account of the work of the House

Brian Tutt

The House of Commons deliberated for almost thirty years before consenting to the admission of television cameras. This reluctance seems to have been prompted by Members' distrust of broadcasters, vigorously expressed by Norman Tebbit, who warned that television 'would allow unelected politicians behind the cameras to use us, the elected politicians in front of the cameras, to make the points or create the issues that they want to make, not those that we want to make' (HC Debs 1988a: col. 228). MPs' fears were twofold. First they were concerned that television pictures showing Members being fractious, inattentive or just absent might reduce public confidence in the House. Second, there was a related concern that broadcasters might focus on the 'newsworthy' aspects of proceedings and thereby create a misleading impression of the House's work.

The Select Committee on Televising of Proceedings of the House tried to allay these fears in a number of ways. First, it stated that the primary objective of televising must be to give 'a full, balanced, fair and accurate account of proceedings, with the aim of informing the viewers about the work of the House' (HC Select Committee 1989: 141–I, para. 37). To this end the cameras would be operated by an independent contractor who would be answerable to the House. Guidelines for broadcasters established unequivocally the range of permissible camera shots, as well as legitimate uses of pictures from the House in programmes. Finally, the Select Committee commissioned the Parliamentary Research Group at Leeds University to monitor uses of parliamentary material in news and political programming broadcast on satellite, national terrestrial and all thirty-one BBC and ITV regional stations.[1]

This chapter analyses and present some of the findings from the

Leeds study, and evaluates the extent to which broadcasters were successful in presenting a full, balanced and fair account of the work of the House during the experimental period in television broadcasting. The diversity of parliamentary business reported in television coverage, the range of parliamentarians appearing in programmes, and broadcasters' success in achieving political balance in reporting from the Commons are each discussed in turn. The chapter concludes with a detailed examination of the four parliamentary review programmes designed as the primary broadcasting outlets for materials from the House. But first it is important to establish the frequency and prominence with which broadcasters reported events in the Commons.

FREQUENCY OF COMMONS REPORTS IN NEWS STORIES

The frequency with which parliamentary items appeared in the news programmes on satellite and national channels suggests that television coverage of Commons proceedings might legitimately be described as 'full'. Reports from the House, moreover, routinely achieved a high news prominence assessed by the frequency with which they formed the lead news story for the day (see table 8.1).

Table 8.1   Frequency and prominence of parliamentary reports in national news

	No. of parl. stories in 15 sampled days	Average per day	No. of days with a parl. story	% of stories mentioned in headlines	No. of days bulletin led on parl. story
BBC1 *Nine O'Clock News*	51	3.4	15	27	8
ITN *News at Ten*	44	2.9	15	48	8
Channel 4 News	38	2.5	15	47	8
BBC2 *Newsnight*	22	1.5	14	56	7
Sky News 11 p.m. (13 days)	29	2.2	13	40	3

News bulletins averaged at least 1.5 parliamentary stories per programme, with the news broadcasts on BBC1 and ITN averaging about 3 items each day. One-third of all Commons stories were headlined, and on almost half of the occasions when a parliamentary item featured in a bulletin it was the leading news story of the day. Nor was Parliament neglected in the breakfast programmes, with 107 stories on BBC *Breakfast Time* and 166 on *TV-am* during the fifteen weeks of the sample period, although these were typically brief items recycled several times during the programme.

Broadcasters' use of actuality (that is, film of the proceedings of the House) was substantial in national news programmes. Between one-quarter and two-thirds of all news items used film from the Commons, with additional footage being used as background to the commentators' spoken introductions to stories. Broadcasters had previously been obliged to use still photographs of MPs in their introductions to items, but now they could use film of Members at work in the Chamber.

Considerable variation was evident in the uses of actuality across different programmes. Actuality clips averaged approximately 45 seconds, ranging from shorter clips (25 seconds) in BBC *Breakfast Time* to longer items (77 seconds) in *Channel 4 News*, reflecting differences in both programme style and story length in the various news bulletins. For BBC1, ITN and Channel 4 news, actuality clips averaged 25–6 per cent of total item length, but only 10 per cent for BBC2's *Newsnight*. Since news items themselves are relatively brief, typically 160–5 seconds on BBC1 and ITN news, it seems that editors were inclined to broadcast the 'sound bite' in preference to complex lines of argument reflecting time constraints. Parliamentary review programmes were able to show longer extracts, giving MPs an opportunity to speak for themselves, and do more justice to the ebb and flow of debate.

There is, of course, no objective yardstick for judging whether news coverage of the Commons might be considered extensive, although the Hansard Society study (Hetherington, Weaver and Ryle 1990: 2) suggests that television attention to Parliament increased with the advent of the cameras. But given the high viewing figures of the flagship news programmes it seems permissible to claim that many more people than previously were able to see, at close quarters, MPs at work in the Chamber of the House.

PARLIAMENTARY BUSINESS AND MEMBERS OF PARLIAMENT

Before the start of the experiment in television broadcasting from the Commons, MPs repeatedly expressed their concern that broadcasters might focus on the confrontational, televisually

attractive aspects of House business. Consequently, the report of
the Select Committee stressed that 'the desirability of ensuring
the picture of the House's activities portrayed through television
is as representative as possible of its different facets' (HC Select
Committee 1989: 141–I, para. 53). Findings from the Leeds study
suggest that this objective was achieved. Three main points emerge
from the analysis of broadcast coverage of Commons events.

First, coverage of Commons Select and Standing committees
on national television was considerable, with the four major
news programmes devoting between 8 and 12 per cent of total
parliamentary broadcast time to the work of committees. Review
programmes, perhaps predictably, gave fuller coverage to the work
of committees, with 31 per cent of all events on Channel 4's *The
Parliament Programme* focusing on committee sessions.

The proceedings of certain Select Committees were transmitted
live. These broadcasts tended to report those occasions when
committees were questioning prominent witnesses about controversial issues with a high news profile. The rigorous questioning
of Foreign Office Minister Francis Maude about the repatriation of
Vietnamese boat people, as well as Lord Young's involvement with
the sale of Rover at a session of the Public Accounts Committee,
were each reported live. Standing Committees also received
broadcast attention, although it is an interesting commentary
on broadcasters' priorities to observe the proceedings of the
committee dealing with the Broadcasting Bill were filmed on
sixteen separate occasions, while television reports of discussions
on the NHS and Community Care Bill were broadcast on just six
occasions. Broadcasters, it seems, like other professionals, can
become obsessed with their own particular parish pump.

Second, Prime Minister's Question Time did not dominate
anywhere, although it was the largest single Commons event
covered by ITN *News at Ten*, appearing in 38 per cent of
items, compared to 23–5 per cent for the other major news
programmes. In the parliamentary review programmes, the attention paid to Prime Minister's Questions varied between 25 per cent
of total broadcast time in BBC2's *Westminster* and 10 per cent
in Channel 4's *The Parliament Programme*. Broadcast attention
to questions of all kinds (including ministerial questions, Prime
Minister's Questions and Business Questions) was very high in the
flagship news bulletins, totalling 58 per cent of items in BBC1's *Nine
O'Clock News* and 46 per cent in ITN's *News at Ten*. Questions

also formed an important focus in the four review programmes, accounting for 17 per cent of broadcast time in *The Parliament Programme* and 61 per cent in *Westminster*.

Third, television coverage of the House of Lords was virtually eclipsed, with reports from the Upper Chamber constituting only 1 per cent of all national Westminster news stories. National parliamentary review programmes redressed the imbalance in part by devoting between 8 and 12 per cent of items to the work of the Lords. Coverage tended to feature either the large set-piece debates, such as the desirability of prosecuting alleged war criminals resident in the United Kingdom, or potential revolts against Government legislation exemplified by the Courts and Legal Services Bill.

The diversity of parliamentary activities and events presented in programming was complemented by the appearance of a wide range of Members from all sections of the House. Analysis of broadcasters' attention to party leaders, members of the cabinet and shadow cabinet, other ministers and their shadow counterparts and backbench Members reveals three features that are particularly noteworthy.

First, parliamentary television was nowhere merely a 'Maggie and Neil show' as some had feared. Even in the national news programmes, where the emphasis on party leaders was most evident, reports of Mrs Thatcher and Mr Kinnock accounted for 34 per cent of politicians featured on Sky News. On the terrestrial channels, appearances by the party leaders ranged from 28 per cent (of all politician appearances) on *News at Ten*, to 18 per cent on BBC *Nine O'Clock News*, while on the national parliamentary review programmes reports of the Prime Minister and Leader of the Opposition represented only a tenth of references to parliamentarians.

Second, members of the cabinet and shadow cabinet were prominent in much of the Commons coverage, averaging between 18 per cent (*News at Ten*) and 39 per cent (*Channel 4 News*) of appearances by politicians on national news programmes and between 18 per cent (*Westminster*) and 30 per cent (*Westminster Week*) on review programmes. In aggregate, the two front benches received substantial attention, especially from news programmes, with *Channel 4 News* devoting 70 per cent of total parliamentary broadcast time to the front benches. In review programmes, coverage of the two front benches was less extensive but still ranged between 52 per cent on *Westminster Week* and 41 per cent on *The Parliament Programme*.

Third, backbench MPs were not neglected in any form of TV programming. In national news programmes backbenchers made up between 24 per cent (*News at Ten*) and 36 per cent (BBC *Breakfast News*) of all parliamentarians featured, while in the review programmes they comprised between 42 per cent (*Westminster Week*) and 49 per cent (Channel 4's *The Parliament Programme*) of all MPs shown. On regional weekly political programmes, backbenchers formed the largest single parliamentary group featured, accounting for 60 per cent of all parliamentarians featured on BBC programmes.

These figures may, of course, suggest different interpretations. It might be argued, for example, that parliamentary television has been faithful to the concept of cabinet government, presenting viewers with a wide range of ministers dealing with current policies and issues in exchanges with their Opposition counterparts, but not neglecting the contributions of the backbenchers. Others might agree with Sir Anthony Grant MP that televising is 'yet another weapon in the hands of what is usually called the "establishment front bench" to put itself over compared with backbenchers' (HC Select Committee 1990: 265–IV, 137). Absolute yardsticks are not available to provide uncontentious judgements, but coverage of backbenchers suggests they were far more than mere 'supporting players'. Some backbenchers, whether elder statesmen or the dependably controversial, attracted substantial attention, while others were featured when their particular areas of expertise were involved. Overall, backbenchers who made telling points were likely to be featured in television reports without regard to any previous celebrity. In addition, of course, backbenchers called to speak during live broadcasts received air time. Television coverage afforded to backbenchers prior to the experiment was minimal and consequently it would be difficult to deny that the televising of the Commons has raised the public profile of MPs both in their constituencies and among the broader public.

POLITICAL BALANCE

The desirability of political balance in programming is uncontentious, but judgement concerning what constitutes balance and whether or not it has been achieved in a particular programme has proved an obvious source of controversy in current affairs broadcasting. The televising of the Commons has proved to be no exception; indeed, it created new problems for broadcasters. Many different definitions of 'balance' exist which tend to coincide with party advantage. At the time of the experiment in television broadcasting, for example, the Government might have suggested that television coverage would be balanced if it favoured the Conservative Party with 58 per cent of all party appearances since they held 58 per cent of seats in the House. The Labour Party, however, might have pointed to its role as the Official Opposition and, consequently, demanded parity with the Government as well as an automatic right of reply. Liberal Democrats might have argued for a third criterion of balance by suggesting that, since they polled almost 25 per cent of the popular vote in 1987, this figure should serve as a minimum benchmark proportion of air time for their party.

It falls to broadcasters to adjudicate between such competing claims as they make decisions about programme content. With parliamentary stories broadcasters have to maintain a balance not only between parties, but between front- and backbench Members; they need to show the various facets of the work of the House, and the range of parliamentary events; and they must do this within a framework of journalistic conventions and news values. They face a difficult task, and can be sure of complaints if they appear to err in favour of a particular group. The Leeds study used a number of measures designed to gauge party balance in televised coverage of the House. The first recorded the number of actuality contributions made by specified parliamentary groups; the second noted the number of contributions by party to each broadcast item; the third recorded the percentage of total appearances by members of each political party. These measures generated two broad conclusions. First, television coverage of the Commons presented the Chamber largely as a two-party forum. Other parliamentary parties gained negligible news exposure, and achieved only marginally better coverage in review programmes. Second, within this broad two-party emphasis, the Conservatives routinely enjoyed a prominence in programming unrivalled by the Labour Party.

These conclusions can be illustrated in more detail by examining each measure of political balance in turn. The first measure recorded the number of actuality appearances made by designated parliamentary groups in each broadcast item; the findings are presented in table 8.2.

Table 8.2   Number of actuality contributions and occasions in national news and review programmes

	Network news	Review programmes	Total
Prime Minister	68 (39)	146 (62)	214 (101)
Leader of Opposition	43 (31)	51 (29)	94 (60)
Cabinet	39 (32)	323 (139)	362 (171)
Shadow cabinet	20 (13)	145 (91)	165 (104)
Junior ministers	24 (21)	158 (92)	182 (113)
Shadow spokespeople	16 (16)	62 (52)	78 (68)
Conservative backbench	41 (34)	419 (192)	460 (226)
Labour backbench	54 (39)	378 (186)	432 (225)
Liberal Democrats	17 (17)	72 (67)	89 (84)
Other parties	4 (4)	42 (35)	46 (39)
Conservative Party aggregate	172 (126)	1,046 (485)	1,218 (611)
Labour Party aggregate	130 (99)	636 (358)	766 (457)

Note: Non-bracketed figures show the number of actuality contributions. Figures in brackets give the number of items in which such contributions were made.

Two important points emerge from the resulting data. First, the predominance of the two main political parties was pronounced. Liberal Democrat appearances in network news were minimal, while other parliamentary parties – Plaid Cymru, the SDLP, the SDP and the UUP – made no actuality contributions to network news reporting during the fifteen-week sample period. In the review programmes, however, all parliamentary parties made at least a single appearance.

Second, the Conservative Party consistently made more appearances than Labour. This applied both in aggregate for all MPs, and also when Members were analysed by office. Only in a single area – namely backbench coverage on national news – did Labour members appear more frequently than Conservatives. What was particularly interesting was that, as the ladder of party hierarchy was ascended, the prominence of Conservative over Labour appearances became greater, especially in parliamentary review programmes. Conservatives regularly appeared more frequently than Labour, with Mrs Thatcher making twice as many appearances as Mr Kinnock but three times more contributions. This tendency towards 'presidentialism', or what Schatz calls the publicity hierarchy, may have had an impact on public perceptions of the two main parties, with the image of Labour being less conditioned by the official party line than that of the Conservatives.

A second, broad measure of balance examined the number of party contributions to broadcast items, whether via actuality, interviews, discussions or other forms of communication (see table 8.3).

Table 8.3   Party contributions to broadcast items

	News	Reviews	Aggregate	Average contribution per occasion
Conservative	528 (186)	1,577 (378)	2,105 (564)	3.73
Labour	357 (161)	918 (324)	1,275 (485)	2.63
Liberal Democrat	45 (36)	191 (103)	236 (139)	1.70
Others	8 (8)	63 (43)	71 (51)	1.39

Note: Non-bracketed figures show the number of contributions. Figures in brackets give the number of items in which such contributions were made.

Table 8.3 confirms the focus on the two main parties and the overall prominence of the Conservative Party in programming. The table shows that Conservative speakers not only appeared more frequently than Labour, but made a greater number of contributions on each appearance. This suggests that Conservative spokespersons were perhaps more likely to appear in programmes to be interviewed, whereas Labour, particularly in news programmes, tended to appear making a filmed statement in reaction to a particular event.

The pre-eminence of the Conservative Party was underscored by the fact that members made more contributions than the members of all other parliamentary parties combined. It is also evident that the minor parties received proportionately more exposure in parliamentary reviews than news programmes, but since the latter enjoy by far the larger audiences, this can be of limited comfort to the parties concerned.

A final measure for assessing political balance in programmes is the percentage, of total appearances by all MPs, made by members of each party in the various news and reviews programmes (see table 8.4). Again, the Conservatives prevailed over other parties, achieving never less than 50 per cent of all appearances.

Table 8.4   Party members as a percentage of all MP appearances in selected programmes

	Conservative (%)	Labour (%)	Lib. Democrat/ Other (%)
BBC *Nine O'clock News*	60	34	5
News at Ten	53	37	11
Channel 4 News	51	42	6
Newsnight	61	30	10
BBC *Breakfast News*	65	31	5
TV-am	61	33	6
Sky News	56	44	–
BBC2 *Westminster*	50	41	11
Channel 4 *Parliament Programme*	50	38	10
BBC2 *Week in Westminster*	53	36	12
Channel 4 *Week in Politics*	51	41	9

The data suggest a persuasive case for the Conservative Party's prominence in television coverage of Parliament, with the minor parties apparently marginalized in reporting. A number of considerations must be borne in mind, however, when interpreting these figures. First, this pro-Conservative imbalance reflects, at least in part, the inevitable prominence which the broadcast media seem to bestow on all Governments, and which a successor Government of any political complexion might similarly expect to receive. Broadcasters want statements and comment about key political issues from Government, especially senior ministers who are seen as news-makers; by contrast, the role of the Opposition is judged to be essentially reactive.

A second caveat is methodological. In recording the number of contributions by members of the various parties no account was taken of the substance or direction of the contributions: whether critical or supportive of the Member's party. Consequently, the Conservative totals include a number of attacks on the Government by Conservative backbenchers, such as Nicholas Winterton about NHS reform, Rhodes Boyson concerning the poll tax, and Edward Heath on a variety of subjects. Equally, every speech or point of order by Tony Benn or Dennis Skinner, however helpful or otherwise to their party leadership, was recorded as a Labour contribution. The figures therefore record the attention given to Conservative and Labour MPs, not advocacy of Conservative or Labour policy.

Third, the nature of parliamentary procedure seems to have a significant impact on broadcasters' opportunities for producing balanced programming. By definition, the governing party holds a majority of seats, but at the time of the study the Government, with an initial majority of 101, had almost 60 per cent of the seats in the Commons. Consequently, a strictly quantitative and proportionate understanding of balance implies that the governing party should obtain the largest single amount of coverage, regardless of editorial news judgements. But parliamentary procedure increases the appearance opportunities of the governing party. Ministerial Question Time, for example, one of the most popular events with broadcasters, gives the Government an institutionalized predominance over the Opposition parties. Shadow cabinet ministers have limited opportunities compared to their Government counterparts, but, since Government supporters ask questions alternately with the Opposition, each question from the Opposition benches is countered by three contributions from the Government and its supporters. This applies particularly to Prime Ministers' Questions, where the Leader of the Opposition can raise only one issue, whereas the Prime Minister can deal with many topics. Consequently, a review programme may examine three or four issues and be able to show the Prime Minister's attitude to each of them, but the Leader of the Opposition will feature only in one.

The smaller parties suffer the most from parliamentary procedure. While the official Opposition at least receives something close to parity outside Question Time, the other parties can rarely hope to achieve more than one speaker called in each debate. This is, in part, a function of their limited numbers in the House, although the Liberal Democrats in particular might feel that they labour under a double disadvantage, under-represented in the House by a 'first past the post' electoral system, and then marginalized in Parliament.

But broadcasters seek to give a full, balanced and fair account of proceedings and must reflect the House as it is, not as it might be under proportional representation. Nevertheless, the minor parties have not received the coverage they might permissibly have anticipated, especially in news programmes.

REVIEW PROGRAMMES: A NEW DEVELOPMENT

Pictures from the House of Commons have been used extensively in news broadcasts, but to some extent they have been a complementary resource, augmenting the reporting of stories that would have been covered anyway. A more significant advance for parliamentary broadcasting has resulted from the commissioning, by both BBC and ITV, of new programmes devoted almost exclusively to the proceedings of Parliament. Some of these programmes have survived beyond the experimental period. They have offered extensive coverage of all aspects of the work of the House, and are analysed in detail below. To illustrate variations in the approach to parliamentary broadcasting adopted by the different programmes, a case study of the broadcast attention given to the Defence Secretary's statement of 1 February 1990 on the Colin Wallace affair is examined.

Westminster was the daily parliamentary review programme, transmitted on BBC2 from 8.15 to 9 a.m. (8.15 to 8.30 a.m. on Mondays). It was first broadcast on 22 November 1989; it offered extensive coverage of the previous day's proceedings and was almost wholly based on actuality. During the fifteen weeks of the sample period, every item broadcast on the programme incorporated actuality, which comprised overall 80 per cent of item length, the highest for any programme sampled.

In production terms the programme format of *Westminster* was unadventurous, using a series of packages of actuality with brief contextualizing introductions by the presenter, and short voice-over links between speakers. Unlike its Channel 4 equivalent, *The Parliament Programme*, it did not use interviews, discussions or film packages. Consequently, the programme used lengthy uninterrupted extracts from speeches, rather than the quotable 'sound bites' which some Members feared might become the focus of broadcasters' attentions. On 9 January 1990, for example, the coverage of the Pensions (Miscellaneous Provisions) Bill included, among others, four actuality contributions totalling 157 seconds from the minister, Richard Ryder; 60 seconds from the Labour spokesperson, Paul Flynn; 103 seconds from the Conservative backbencher Ivor Stanbrook; and 57 seconds from Liberal Democrat Archie Kirkwood.

The ministerial statement about the Colin Wallace affair, made on 1 February 1990, provides a good example of the style of the programme. In all, the Wallace affair received 30 minutes and 37 seconds of coverage, about two-thirds of total air time, as the programme followed the issue through Northern Ireland Questions, Prime Minister's Questions, Tom King's statement and subsequent points of order. In all it offered 233 seconds of commentary, the major element being a 57-second contextualizing introduction. Actuality-based reporting accounted for 1,604 seconds, almost 27 minutes.

The breakdown of actuality contributions was:

Prime Minister: 5 contributions totalling 236 seconds.

Leader of the Opposition: 3 contributions, 137 seconds.

Cabinet: 11 contributions from King, 1 from Brooke, 376 seconds.

Shadow cabinet: 1 contribution each from O'Neill and Cunningham, 137 seconds.

Conservative backbenchers: 1 contribution each from Aitken, Heseltine and Mates, 138 seconds.

Labour backbenchers: 3 contributions from Rees, 1 each from Benn, Campbell-Savours, Orme and Skinner, 301 seconds.

Liberal Democrats: 2 contributions from Beith, 1 from Steel, 132 seconds.

Ulster Unionists: 1 contribution from Molyneaux, 36 seconds.

Democratic Ulster Unionist: 1 contribution from Paisley, 39 seconds.

SDLP: 1 contribution from Mallon, 44 seconds.

Speaker: 3 contributions, 28 seconds.

Westminster offered the fullest coverage of the previous day's parliamentary proceedings of any review programme, and regularly included items from committees and from the House of Lords. Its overall tone was non-judgemental, and it provided a straight-forward report of proceedings in the style of BBC Radio 4's *Today in Parliament*.

The Parliament Programme was Channel 4's daily parliamentary review produced by ITN, and broadcast from Tuesday to Friday between 12.00 and 12.25 p.m. Presented by Sue Cameron with parliamentary correspondent Nicholas Woolley, it had a wider remit and a greater variety of programme formats than its BBC equivalent. Around 65 per cent of stories contained film of parliamentary proceedings and, in addition to a review of the previous day's events by Nicholas Woolley, the programme

typically carried a couple of interviews or a discussion with
Members, peers or other relevant politicians. Discussion topics
typically addressed recent or forthcoming parliamentary events,
or examined broader political issues. On 29 November 1989,
for example, Marcus Fox and Dennis Skinner reviewed the
performances of Mrs Thatcher and Neil Kinnock in the previous
day's Prime Minister's Questions, the first to be televised.

The programme paid particular attention to Select Committee
proceedings, perhaps reflecting, at least in part, its scheduling,
which made it the first programme with the opportunity to cover the
morning meetings of committees. On 17 January 1990 the lead story
concerned Lord Young's appearance before the Trade and Industry
Select Committee that morning. It also gave coverage to the work
of MPs in Standing Committees, especially in consideration of the
Broadcasting Bill and the NHS Reform Bill. On 9 March 1990 the
programme led with a 539-second item on the Broadcasting Bill
Committee, which included interviews with George Walden and
David Mellor, with actuality of Mellor, Robin Corbett, William
Cash, Dafydd Ellis Thomas, John Greenway, Ted Rowlands and
Tony Banks. The programme also gave regular coverage to events
in the Lords.

A distinctive feature of the programme was the presence, each
Friday, of a guest MP who gave a humorous review of the week,
using actuality clips for illustration. Some tried painfully hard to
be funny; others, such as Sir David Steel and Mo Mowlem, used
the slot as a platform for a particular concern, in both their cases
the need for procedural reform.

Occasionally ITN used the programme as a vehicle for more
general news coverage, enabling them to 'scoop' the lunchtime
news by giving live coverage to particular events, which might at
best have only a tenuous connection with parliamentary proceedings. A prime example of this occurred on 13 February 1990, when
the entire programme was devoted to Nelson Mandela's speech
in Soweto, with a figleaf of parliamentary content provided by
the studio contributions of David Howell and Richard Caborn.
In the event this ITN scoop was something of a disappointment,
since Mandela's speech was delayed. Viewers had to be content
with live coverage of Mandela walking around the perimeter of
the Soweto football stadium.

In contrast to BBC's *Westminster*, it seemed to be editorial policy
for *The Parliament Programme* not to give undue broadcast time

to parliamentary events that had been covered extensively in news programmes the previous evening. This policy was reflected in the attention paid to the 1 February statement on Colin Wallace. The programme devoted 9 minutes and 5 seconds to the issue, of which 125 seconds consisted of commentary, with actuality clips forming a further 420 seconds. The breakdown of actuality contributions was:

Prime Minister: 1 contribution, 20 seconds.
Cabinet: 3 contributions from King, 1 from Howe, 98 seconds.
Conservative backbenchers: 1 contribution from Franks, 29 seconds.
Labour backbenchers: 2 contributions from Rees, 1 from Livingstone, 169 seconds.
Liberal Democrats: 1 contribution from Steel, 52 seconds.
Ulster Unionist: 1 contribution from Molyneaux, 52 seconds.

Overall, the programme was both entertaining and informative to watch, used its limited time very effectively, and had in Sue Cameron an extremely able presenter.

The BBC weekly review programme during the experimental period was *Westminster Week*, introduced by Christopher Jones, and broadcast by BBC2 from 12 to 12.35 p.m. on Sundays from 14 January 1990 onwards. The programme disappeared from BBC schedules with the advent of the new parliamentary session in autumn 1990. Like the daily programme, *Westminster*, it was overwhelmingly actuality based, with interviews or film packages being rare. When interviews were conducted, they tended to be fairly unchallenging, even when dealing with controversial matters, as Lord Young discovered to his benefit when interviewed on 21 January concerning the sale of Rover.

The choice of subject matter was sometimes idiosyncratic. On 4 March, four of the first six items concerned the House of Lords, with only one, the debate on student loans, which might be considered of major importance. The programme usually included a didactic, procedurally orientated item, such as the feature on Ten-Minute Rule Bills on 21 January, and at least one Select Committee item. Prime Minister's Questions were invariably given air time.

The programme gave greater coverage to the frontbenchers than is typical of the other review programmes. This seemed to reflect, at least partly, time constraints. When reporting ministerial questions, Jones tended to paraphrase the questions, speaking over the 'goldfishing' (pictures of a member speaking, with no sound) backbencher, while using actuality for the minister's reply. This emphasis on the occupants of the front benches was exacerbated by the 'Other Business' section of the programme. This feature, which was unique to the programme, offered a succession of approximately six brief items, averaging between 20 and 30 seconds in duration, each item comprising a terse introduction followed by a 10–20-second 'sound bite'. Frequently the items show Government ministers launching new initiatives, with little apparent attempt at contextualization or balance. On 18 February, for example, the debate on the Education (Student Loans) Bill was encapsulated into 20 seconds, and on 3 March David Waddington's statement on international co-operation against crime was dealt with in 23 seconds. Little information was conveyed in these items and it seemed regrettable that such evidently important matters could not be reported in more depth. Clearly the 35-minute timespan was inadequate to give a comprehensive review of the week, but to cover events in such an insubstantial fashion might appear self-defeating.

The coverage accorded to the 1 February statement about Colin Wallace confirms the preference for frontbench actuality contributors. *Westminster Week* gave 56 per cent of actuality time to the two front benches, compared to 48 per cent for *Westminster*, 28 per cent for *The Parliament Programme* and 15 per cent for *Week in Politics*. *Westminster Week* devoted 9 minutes and 23 seconds to the issue, with 111 seconds of commentary and 452 seconds of actuality. The breakdown of actuality contributions was:

Prime Minister: 3 contributions, 91 seconds.
Leader of the Opposition: 1 contribution, 47 seconds.
Cabinet: 2 contributions from King, 72 seconds.
Shadow cabinet: 1 contribution from O'Neill, 43 seconds.
Conservative backbenchers: 1 contribution each from Heseltine and Tredinnick, 40 seconds.
Labour backbenchers: 1 contribution from Rees, 30 seconds.
Liberal Democrats: 1 contribution from Steel, 52 seconds.
Ulster Unionist: 1 contribution from Molyneaux, 37 seconds.
Democratic Ulster Unionist: 1 contribution from Paisley, 35 seconds.
Speaker: 1 contribution, 5 seconds.

Overall, the programme seemed unlikely to attract or retain a 'non-political' viewer with limited interest in parliamentary affairs. The tone was rather staid and unexciting, with Christopher Jones's commentary style being somewhat ingratiating. *Westminster Week* was a strikingly conventional production, especially in contrast to the regional programmes which followed immediately afterwards (see Chapter 11).

A Week in Politics was the ITV weekly parliamentary review programme, produced by Brook Productions and shown on Channel 4 every Sunday between 10 and 11 a.m. during the parliamentary session. (It has subsequently been retitled *A Week in Politics – Second Reading* and supplemented by an additional programme on Thursday nights under the title *A Week in Politics – Late Sitting*.) It was introduced by Vincent Hanna and Andrew Rawnsley, who operated as a highly effective and informative 'double act' and ended most items with a two-minute dialogue on aspects of the issue under discussion.

The programme covered selected highlights from the week's parliamentary proceedings, in both Chambers of the House and in committees. These items were supplemented by studio interviews with MPs and Peers, such as the interview on 25 February 1990 with Procedure Committee member Peter Shore in the wake of the debate on the Conservative MP John Browne and his business transactions. In addition, each programme included a substantial film report on an aspect of parliamentary politics; for example, items on the pairing system (14 January 1990), Labour plans for procedural reform (11 February) and the work of the Boundary Commission (25 February).

A distinctive element of the programme was Rawnsley's 'House Points' feature, a humorous, parliamentary-'sketch'-style piece using actuality from the week's events. On 14 January 1990, for example, he explored the issue of verbal abuse in the Chamber, and featured examples of the genre by Michael Foot, Tony Banks, John Cunningham, Anthony Beaumont Dark and Frank Haynes.

The tone of the programme was lively and interesting, with the emphasis very much on the high politics of Westminster – both events in the Chamber and the gossip of the bars. Hanna typically adopted a world-weary attitude towards the behaviour of politicians, usually introducing items via literary allusions or humorous quotations. The programme employed fuller introductions than *Westminster Week*, emphasizing the wider political scene, tactical concerns and general contextualizing material. It also used a wider range of formats (film packages, studio interviews and cross-party discussions in addition to actuality), and had a more probing interview style than *Westminster Week*. The programme's interest in wider issues was also reflected in its occasional reports from the European Parliament.

The Wallace statement provides a good example of the programme's style. The item totalled 17 minutes and 15 seconds, including 224 seconds of commentary and 467 seconds of actuality. In addition there were two studio interviews, with Michael Marshall, the MP representing Colin Wallace, on the details of Wallace's claims (5 contributions totalling 133 seconds), and Tony Benn on the wider constitutional issues raised by the case (5 contributions totalling 211 seconds). The breakdown of actuality was:

Cabinet: 2 contributions from King, totalling 72 seconds.
Conservative backbenchers: 1 contribution each from Aitken and Marshall, 97 seconds.
Labour backbenchers: 2 contributions from Rees, 1 each from Campbell-Savours and Skinner, 186 seconds.
Liberal Democrats: 1 contribution from Steel, 67 seconds.
Democratic Ulster Unionist: 1 contribution from Paisley, 35 seconds.
Speaker: 1 contribution, 10 seconds.

A Week in Politics was undoubtedly the most successful of the national review programmes. It covered a large amount of ground in under an hour, used a variety of formats, was well paced and excellently presented. It was more entertaining than its erstwhile BBC equivalent, while at the same time being both informative and educational. It was more likely to attract the vast majority of the viewing public who are not habitual consumers of political and current affairs programmes, and thus made an important contribution to broadening public access to the proceedings of the House.

CONCLUSIONS

Members appear to have been satisfied that the experiment in televising the House of Commons was successful in presenting a full, balanced and fair account of the work of the House to the viewing public. Their decision to make the cameras a permanent fixture (by a majority of 99) must be interpreted as offering some endorsement of broadcasters' achievements in this respect.

Coverage of the Commons was certainly 'full', when measured by the substantive use of parliamentary items in news broadcasts, and review programmes created to provide more detailed attention to the work of the House. Coverage could, of course, be enhanced further. Audience figures attained by regular live broadcasts suggest that there may be considerable potential for a dedicated channel, similar to C-SPAN in the USA, devoted to Parliament. Austin Mitchell, Roger Gale and Charles Kennedy each advocate such a development.

Full coverage was also reflected in the breadth of parliamentary events reported, and the attention given to backbenchers. The reporting of Select Committee hearings and the lack of undue emphasis on Prime Minister's Questions were indicative of the range of proceedings presented in programmes. Few aspects of the work of the House escaped broadcasters' attention. The experimental period witnessed the reporting of questions, the passage of legislation, discussion of Private Members' Bills, Private Bills, Standing Committees, emergency debate applications, Opposition-initiated debates, adjournment debates, the presentation of petitions and countless points of order. The House of Lords, while suffering relative neglect as a consequence of the rival attractions of the Commons, still made regular appearances in review programmes. Backbenchers enjoyed considerable prominence in all types of programming but were especially evident in regional output. A powerful speech or a probing question would be reported, whoever the protagonist. Indeed, televising saw the emergence into the public gaze of relatively unknown MPs such as the stentorian Frank Haynes.

The question of balance is, as always, more problematic. The amply documented prevalence of Conservative MPs above others was perhaps inevitable given the nature of both parliamentary procedure and journalistic attitudes towards the Government. But the marginalization of the Liberal Democrats and the other numerically small parliamentary parties perhaps offers greater cause for concern. Any mathematical formula for the allocation of broadcast time to the various parties is fraught with difficulties and, of course, more coverage does not necessarily imply more favourable coverage. Derisory coverage, however, is a different matter, for it implies that ignored voices do not count. In a plural society, it can never be wrong to admit more and diverse voices into the debate.

The advocates of televising the Commons have made ambitious predictions concerning its likely effects. Speaking as long ago as 1959, Nye Bevan argued that television would 're-establish intelligent communication between the House of Commons and the electorate as a whole' (HC Debs 1959: col. 867). Such hopes rest on the ability of broadcasters to treat the Commons responsibly, and to report proceedings in a full, balanced and fair manner. The evidence from the experimental period suggests that this requirement was achieved.

NOTE

1 Acknowledgement is made to Jay G. Blumler, Bob Franklin and David Mercer, who made major contributions to the report on which this chapter is based.

Chapter 9

Audience reactions to parliamentary television

Moira Bovill, Robin McGregor and
Mallory Wober

The introduction of television cameras into Westminster has aroused extensive debate. Some, like Austin Mitchell (chapter 5) believe that it represents an important step in the democratization of the parliamentary process, and may lead to the public's greater knowledge of, interest in and esteem for the workings of government. Others, like Roger Gale (chapter 6), have feared that the televising of proceedings may curtail the frankness of debates, give undue prominence to publicity-seeking MPs and destroy the atmosphere in the House of Commons. At worst the House might be reduced to a forum for political opportunism, with sartorial elegance, 'doughnutting' and the media-friendly sound bites assuming more importance than informed parliamentary debate.

Despite these differences, both those who support the televising of Parliament and those who oppose it are agreed that the right to film proceedings places a heavy burden of responsibility on broadcasters. The producers and camera crews who provide the original feed from the House must select appropriate camera angles, which will dictate the visual frame within which proceedings are contextualized. They may also colour in subtle ways the programme makers' choice of material to transmit, and hence the public's interpretation of events. Since continuous television coverage of House of Commons proceedings is not yet available, broadcasters preparing news bulletins and current affairs programmes are required to use their discretion in choosing which items to transmit from the continuous feed. Programme makers may be tempted to overrepresent dramatic or controversial material. Additionally, there are fears that the audience may be misled about the nature of an MP's role. Consequently the televising of the Commons raises fundamental and important questions about the nature of media organizations and the likely effects of their products on the viewing public.

This chapter assesses some aspects of the reactions of members of the viewing public to the experiment in televising the Commons. How enthusiastically did they respond to the idea of televising the Commons? What were their expectations about the likely consequences? Were their views altered by subsequent experience of the broadcasts? Is there any evidence that filmed coverage of the Commons has increased interest in, esteem for, and knowledge about, Parliament (as was hoped by those in favour of the experiment)? In addition to these factual questions, our research has explored how reactions to parliamentary programming perhaps express other political values and beliefs. How interested were people in politics for example, and what were their views on such important issues as the trustworthiness of politicians, and the fairness of the social, economic and parliamentary systems in this country? Some understanding of where people stand on such issues was felt likely to be the key to understanding reactions to the televising of Parliament.

AUDIENCE RESEARCH

Research stemming from a variety of different academic disciplines and based on a number of competing theoretical orientations has converged during the last two decades and placed increasing importance on the audience as an active processor of media information.

Some early psychological studies of mass-communication effects mirrored the stimulus–response psychology of Pavlov, and, later, B. F. Skinner's behaviourism: the media message was portrayed as a hypodermic needle injecting information into a compliant subject. The inadequacy of this model was increasingly appreciated, and in the post-war years it was overtaken by the audience-centred uses and gratifications approach, postulated by Herzog and Berelson and further developed by Katz and Lazarfeld. This research trajectory is well covered by McQuail in *Mass Communication Theory* (McQuail 1987). Audiences were no longer to be seen as passive, uncritical recipients of the media message but as individuals who actively use the media to satisfy their own needs. Initial research in this area revealed a profusion of needs: there was, however, a high degree of similarity between different researchers' lists. On the basis of empirical research, McQuail argues for four basic reasons why people watch television programmes: for information, to reinforce personal values and identity, for integration and social interaction, and for entertainment (McQuail 1987). Later, reception analysis was developed out of the uses and gratifications perspective, by researchers who criticized its functionalist overemphasis on *why* people use the media and its comparative neglect of *how* people receive media texts.

The uses and gratifications approach and reception analysis suggest that fundamental effects of mass communication are to be traced to the ways in which people actively interpret and incorporate information. The general thrust of this argument has received definitive support from cognitive psychology, which has demonstrated experimentally how human beings interpret incoming information in the light of prior understandings, variously described as 'scripts' or 'schemas', which they have developed as a result of their previous life experience (see Schank and Abelson 1977).

In mass-media research undertaken from a macro-sociological and political (as opposed to psychological) perspective, the new revisionist approach also gives evidence of increasing interest in audience-related phenomena. Those operating within the well-established liberal or pluralist model of society, in which power is seen as widely diffused among a complex of competing power-groups, have traditionally interpreted the media as a 'fourth estate', standing outside the rest of the establishment and acting as a forum for debate. On the other hand, according to the influential neo-Marxist approach, the media are ultimately instruments of social control, exploited by the dominant elite. Using this latter explanatory framework, the Glasgow University Media Group (1976, 1980, 1982, 1985) have done impressive work – although their methodology has been questioned and their conclusions have been contested (see Harrison 1985) – in suggesting how biases grounded in the assumptions of dominant groups in society may affect news reporting, and by inference public perceptions. Latterly the new revisionist movement in media and cultural studies has challenged this radical paradigm from within (see Curran 1990). According to revisionists, social reality cannot be interpreted solely in terms of class interests, or traced to the mode of production. Instead, following Foucault (1978, 1980, 1982), they see power as a complex, situationally determined phenomenon. Where meaning in the media message is for the neo-Marxist largely unproblematic, revisionists stress the ambiguity inherent in communication, which is therefore open to alternative readings. Such insights lead to the revisionist stress on the importance of studying the internal dynamics of communicative texts and add new weight to the audience's role in selecting from among competing interpretations.

The need for close textual analysis of media messages and the importance of examining the knowledge structures, or implicit social theories, which audiences use to help them interpret information, has therefore been generally accepted. Newspaper reports and television programmes are seen as social practices worthy of study in their own right. Their meaning is not considered to be captured fully by methods such as content analysis, and their 'message' is increasingly studied by various techniques of discourse analysis (see Van Dijk 1988: Billig 1990: Downing 1990) which show how meanings are constructed and negotiated in an ongoing dialogue between media sources and the audience. Studies have shown, for example, that audiences develop implicit theories about how the news media work which lead them to believe that they can compensate for distortions they expect from the media (see Fredin and Kosicki 1989). Recent qualitative research within the Broadcasting Research Department of the BBC would extend such observations and suggest that in the case of familiar news and current affairs programmes the audience look to different programme formats to establish different kinds of dialogue, which in turn liberate different insight into complex social and political issues. Separately each programme type (news bulletin or the multiplicity of programmes perceived as current affairs) is limited by the possibilities implicit in the bargain it has struck with the audience: taken together they extend and enrich the audience's capacity to relate to news information. The television audience would appear, for example, to react very differently to perceived bias in news reporting in the *Nine O'Clock News*, which is expected to be impartial, and a programme like *World in Action*, which has established the right to adopt a partisan approach to a particular issue. Similarly a programme like *Question Time* capitalizes on the adversarial nature of British politics, which is enthusiastically entered into by those who enjoy the programme, although the very same people may violently object if a *Newsnight* presenter allows a discussion between politicians to 'degenerate' into a party-line wrangle.

In the case of the televising of the Commons, the ability to witness parliamentary debates in the House and to observe deliberations in parliamentary committees allows the television audience direct access to the workings of Parliament. There is evidence from qualitative reports undertaken by the BBC's Broadcasting Research Department that the audience particularly values television's ability to put them in direct face-to-face contact with politicians. As one respondent commented:

> I'm using 53 years of my knowledge of human nature to actually say whether this man is actually telling the truth. Now that's something very useful. I can't get that from a newspaper. When I read the newspaper I am reading somebody else's opinion.
>
> (BBC Broadcasting Research Department 1990)

People may therefore begin to use different judgement criteria when they see a parliamentary debate, compared to hearing it reported on radio or reading about it in a newspaper. This could conceivably change perceptions about individual MPs, and even eventually modify the public's 'social representations' (see Farr and Moscovici 1984) of politicians and the parliamentary process.

Background to the research

The IBA and the BBC as a public service broadcaster jointly accepted the responsibility to monitor reactions to, and effects of, the televising of the Commons. The IBA was mainly involved in researching the reactions of MPs, while the BBC undertook to explore those of the public. The purpose was to provide complementary studies which would be best understood in the context of research on the contents of broadcast material, described in other chapters. The present chapter covers the BBC's survey of public attitudes and reactions.

The research was commissioned to answer specific questions about public support for the television experiment before it began, and to monitor any changes in the public's views once they had experience of the transmissions. In several respects it follows and extends a model of research developed when television was first introduced into the House of Lords (see Wober 1990).

The first wave of the survey was conducted in October 1989 immediately before the televising of the Commons, with a second wave in March 1990, some three months after broadcasting had begun. This time interval was rather brief if changes in well-established public attitudes were to be assessed. This scheduling was prompted, however, by the need to produce findings which might inform Parliament's decision in July about whether televising of proceedings should move to a permanent footing.

Research method and objectives

In both waves 1,500 interviews were set (1,476 being achieved in the first wave and 1,482 in the second). On each occasion, a forty-minute questionnaire was administered to respondents in their homes. The sample was representative of the UK adult population, boosted to 250 respondents in Scotland, Wales and Northern Ireland in order to allow for more sensitive analysis of these important areas. Results are down-weighted in the reported findings. The research had two objectives. First, to record the public's reactions to the experimental televising of the Commons, and to relate these to other politically relevant expectations, attitudes and behaviour. Second, to monitor possible changes in the public's attitudes, knowledge of parliamentary procedures, and familiarity with the names and faces of particular politicians.

MAIN FINDINGS

Television as a source of information

Surveys regularly confirm that most people regard television as their most important source of information about what is happening in the world. Similarly, the majority (56 per cent) in both waves of the present survey stated that television was their 'single most important source of information' about events in Parliament. This should be compared with the figures of 18 per cent in the first wave and 17 per cent in the second who nominated a newspaper as their most important single source, and 8 per cent in both waves who nominated radio. There was, however, no increase in the numbers naming television as their main source after three months of the experiment.

Reactions to the idea of televising the Commons

Support for the televising of the Commons was widespread from the start. A few weeks before the television broadcasts began, 69 per cent of respondents stated that they thought televising proceedings was 'a good idea', while only 14 per cent thought it a bad one. After the experiment had been running for three months, views were virtually unchanged, with a marginal, not 'statistically significant', shift in the direction of support for the experiment.

Respondents in the second wave of the survey were also asked whether or not they thought the televising of the Commons should be continued. An even larger majority (83 per cent) felt that it should: 25 per cent of total respondents felt this 'very strongly', and 33 per cent 'strongly'. The disparity between responses to the two questions in the numbers endorsing the experiment was due to the fact that a third of those in the second wave who had stated that they thought the experiment was on the whole 'a bad idea', and a quarter who were undecided about it, were nevertheless prepared to concede that it should continue.

In the second wave, once the broadcasts from the Commons had begun, respondents were asked how often they had seen film of MPs inside the House, either on the news, or on parliamentary review programmes like *Westminster* or *The Parliament Programme*. Almost all (99 per cent) of those who had seen the coverage 'often' on both the news and review programmes, compared with less than two-thirds (63 per cent) of those who claimed never to have seen any, felt that the experiment should be continued. Since it is likely that the audience for the special programmes was more interested in parliamentary politics from the outset, this greater support for the experiment cannot necessarily be interpreted as the result of viewing. It can, however, be inferred that those who were most familiar with the coverage were not disillusioned by three months' experience of the broadcasts.

Public assessments of programme formats and the presentation of parliamentary materials was also measured. In both waves of the study most support was expressed for either 'a weekly programme of special interest for your region' or 'extracts on the news', with around seven in every ten respondents either 'very' or 'quite' interested in these options. In the case of the special programmes (with the notable exception of the programme of regional interest) the more frequent the coverage, the less popular the programme option: thus there was more interest in a weekly programme of edited highlights than a daily one, while least interest of all was expressed for 'a television channel devoted to continuous broadcasting'. It is significant, given MPs' general desire to move towards a dedicated channel for parliamentary broadcasting, that almost a half in both waves of the survey stated that they were 'not at all interested' in this option.

The level of interest in the transmissions from the House presents a familiar challenge to broadcasters, since four out of every ten respondents in both waves of the present survey, similarly to the report by Social and Community Planning Research (SCPR) in 1987 (from data collected a year earlier), described themselves as having 'not very much' interest in politics or 'none at all' when asked 'How much interest do you generally have in what is going on in politics?' (see table 9.1).

Table 9.1   Expressed interest in politics

	SCPR: 1986 (1,548) (%)	Wave 1: before Oct.–Nov. 1989 (1,476) (%)	Wave 2: March 1990 after 3 months (1,482) (%)
A great deal	7	10	10
Quite a lot	22	24	27
Some	31	24	27
Not very much	27	27	23
None at all	13	14	13

Source: col. 1, Social and Community Planning Research (1987).

A tendency was apparent for those who were in some way disadvantaged to express little or no interest in politics. Thus among those in the lowest social-grade categories, DE, an expressed lack of interest stood at 60 per cent in wave 1 and at 43 per cent in wave 2, compared to 17 and 19 per cent respectively among those in the upper social grades, AB. Similarly, in wave 1, 50 per cent of those who had left school aged 16 or under had little or no interest, compared to only 13 per cent of those who had remained in full-time education until aged 20 or older. In wave 2, 41 per cent of those with the least full-time education expressed these views, compared to 18 per cent of those with the most. Labour identifiers were also more likely than Conservatives, and women more likely than men, to say that they had little or no interest in political affairs.

Lack of interest in politics was also associated with more cynical evaluations of politicians and the political process, as assessed by agreement with such statements as 'Political parties are only interested in people's votes, not their opinions' or 'People like me have no say in what the Government does'.

Respondents were also asked whether they agreed or disagreed with five statements about equality of economic opportunities (e.g. 'Ordinary working people do not get their fair share of the nation's wealth'), and the relationships between workers and management (e.g. 'Big business benefits owners at the expense of workers'). Following the procedure established by Heath and Topf (1987), scores on the five questions were summed, and a scale established. Respondents could then be divided into three groups – 'high' (those scoring in approximately the top 25 per cent, and perceiving more inequality and division between the rich and the poor), 'medium' and 'low' (those scoring in approximately the bottom 25 per cent, and perceiving least inequality and division). Around half of those respondents who scored high, compared with under a quarter of those who scored low, had 'not very much' interest in politics or 'none at all'.

A lack of interest in politics was therefore more likely to be expressed by those who are in some sense doing less well, and by those who did not identify with, or endorse, what they saw as the dominant economic and political values. These findings suggest that this lack of interest may represent for such people a turning away from a system which they feel has little to offer them – general alienation precedes and explains a more particular indifference.

Interest in politics was also the most effective predictor of support for the televising of the Commons in both waves of the survey. The greater people's interest in politics, the more likely they were to think televising the Commons 'a very good idea'. Once account is taken of interest in politics, other factors such as sex, social grade and length of schooling (normally powerful determinants of attitudes and behaviour) do not significantly improve our ability to predict reactions to the television experiment. In wave 1, scores on the scale tapping perceptions of inequality did, however, help to predict reactions. Those who perceived more inequality and division in society were more likely to think televising the Commons 'a good idea'. In wave 2, however, when most people had some experience of the broadcasts, such beliefs were no longer significant predictors of support.

The fact that only 10 per cent of respondents expressed 'a great deal' of interest in politics (while around four times as many had 'not very much' interest or 'none at all') would help to explain why the actual audiences for the special parliamentary programmes have been, for some, disappointing. While average audiences for both the BBC and ITN flagship news programmes, the *Nine O'Clock News* and the *News at Ten* (both of which show excerpts from Parliament), stood at just over 7 million each during the second quarter of 1990, the size of audiences for the specialized parliamentary programmes has been much smaller (see table 9.2).

Table 9.2   Size of audience for specialized parliamentary programmes

	Average audience (April–June 1990) (millions)
BBC 2	
Westminster	
(Monday to Friday, 08.15–09.00)	0.1
Westminster Live	
(Tuesday and Thursday, 15.00–15.50)	0.6
Westminster Week	
(Sunday, 12.00–12.35)	0.2
Regional programmes	
(Sunday, 12.35–13.00)	0.2
Channel 4	
The Parliament Programme	
(Tuesday to Friday, 12.00–12.30)	0.2

Source: AGB BARB data.

It is, of course, clear that scheduling plays a part – only the most dedicated will tune in to BBC2 at 8.15 on a weekday morning. In addition, the morning and afternoon weekday time slots are unlikely to find many working men and women available to watch, even if they wished to do so.

Expectations about consequences

Respondents in both waves of the survey were asked whether they agreed or disagreed with ten statements about the possible consequences of televising the Commons (see table 9.3).

Table 9.3 Expectations about the consequences of televising the Commons

	Wave 1 Oct.–Nov. 1989 (1,476)			Wave 2 March 1990 (1,482)		
	Agree (%)	Undecided (%)	Disagree (%)	Agree (%)	Undecided (%)	Disagree (%)
Some MPs will play up to the cameras	88	6	6	84	8	8
People will begin to understand more about how Parliament works	84	7	8	82	8	9
People will feel more involved in what is going on in Parliament	74	12	15	70	12	17
People will become more interested in what happens in Parliament	71	15	14	68	15	16
People will be better able to judge the true character of individual MPs	70	15	17	66	15	19
People will be bored by the broadcasts most of the time	63	20	17	63	18	19
It will make MPs work harder	63	15	23	52	21	26
The media will have less power to influence people's views	52	21	27	47	22	30
People will think less well of MPs	35	28	36	33	32	35
It will spoil the atmosphere of the House of Commons	20	22	56	13	19	68

More than eight out of every ten respondents in both waves thought that 'people will begin to understand more about how Parliament works', and around seven in every ten expected that people 'will feel more involved in what is going on in Parliament', 'will become more interested' and 'will be better able to judge the true character of individual MPs'.

On the other hand, similar numbers of respondents were convinced that 'some MPs will play up to the cameras', with eight out of every ten in both waves agreeing. Six out of every ten were also inclined to think that 'people will be bored by the broadcasts most of the time'.

Experience of the broadcasts did not significantly change these expectations. Opinions shifted significantly after the start of the experimental broadcasts in the case of only two suggested consequences. Respondents became less inclined to think that the televising of the Commons would make MPs work harder (wave 1, 63 per cent agreeing; wave 2, 52 per cent agreeing). Second, they became more likely to reject the view that 'it will spoil the atmosphere in the House of Commons' (wave 1, 56 per cent disagreeing; wave 2, 68 per cent disagreeing).

In both waves of the survey, questions had been asked to tap respondents' opinions about MPs and their behaviour, and their knowledge of parliamentary matters. Since both samples were representative of the UK adult population, and the questions had been asked both before and after the transmissions from the House went on air, these questions allow us to explore, if in a rather limited fashion, the extent to which some of the most commonly held hopes and fears were corroborated. Have people become more knowledgeable, for example, about the way in which Parliament works? Is there any evidence that people think MPs' behaviour in the House has deteriorated since the introduction of the television cameras? Do more people think they spend too much time trying to attract media attention? Have people become more cynical or more approving of politicians and the parliamentary system?

MPs and television

We have seen that more than eight out of every ten people agreed that as a consequence of the introduction of television coverage 'some MPs will play up to the cameras'. However, all respondents had been asked earlier, *without specific reference to the effects of the new transmissions*, whether in their opinion 'some MPs spend too much time trying to attract attention on television'. This gives us a measure of perceptions of *present* behaviour (as opposed to conjecture about future behaviour) which we can use to test whether in fact more people had noticed MPs 'playing up' for the cameras. Although the majority in both waves of the survey agreed that MPs spent too much time trying to attract attention on television, there was a significant *drop* in the numbers endorsing this statement three months after the experiment began (wave 1, 72 per cent agreeing; wave 2, 62 per cent agreeing).

Moreover, although more than two in every ten thought that loud cheering and heckling occurred 'all the time' in the House of Commons, and a further six out of every ten believed it happened 'quite often', there was no increase in the perceived frequency of such behaviours following the televising of proceedings. Nor was there any change in people's evaluation of such conduct. Almost half (46 per cent) in both waves of the survey thought it a bad thing, while around one-third felt that it was 'sometimes a bad thing, sometimes a good thing'. Only around one in every eight thought it unequivocally a 'good thing'. Negative evaluations of heckling were related to perceived frequency of occurrence, with those who thought it happened 'all the time' being around twice as likely to think it a bad thing.

It should also be noted that the public clearly wished to see proceedings 'warts and all'. In both waves of the survey the least popular guideline for parliamentary coverage was the rule forbidding the televising of disruption or disorder in the House: 73 per cent in wave 1 and 69 per cent in wave 2 thought this 'a bad rule'. In the second wave of the survey respondents were also given the opportunity to record their overall impressions of the restrictions on broadcasting – on balance were the rules too strict, not strict enough, or just about right? Half (51 per cent) found them 'about right as they are', and around a third (32 per cent) considered them 'too strict'; a mere 7 per cent thought them 'not strict enough'.

Knowledge about MPs and Parliament

More than eight out of every ten respondents in both waves of the survey had agreed that televising the House of Commons was likely to increase the public's understanding about how Parliament works. However, after three months of transmissions there was no significant change in respondents' ability to name their own MP, or his or her political party. Around four in every ten respondents in both waves could name their own MP (41 per cent in wave 1; 44 per cent in wave two), and around three-quarters could identify their MP's party (76 per cent in wave 1; 73 per cent in wave 2). Nor was there any improvement in people's ability to recognize the name, face or political affiliation of fifteen prominent MPs chosen from across the major political parties.

Table 9.4 Knowledge of key parliamentary roles

	Wave 1 (1,476) (%)	Wave 2 (1,482) (%)
The main duties of the Speaker:		
Keeping order in the House of Commons	69	73
Spokesman for the Government	17	12
Keeping the Queen informed about parliamentary business	6	6
Don't know	8	9
A backbencher:		
An MP who does not hold a Government or shadow Government post	66	61
Any MP who sits at the back of the House	16	19
A retired MP	8	8
Don't know	10	12
A frontbencher:		
An MP who holds a Government or shadow Government post	60	63
An active MP	21	16
Any MP who sits at the front of the House	10	10
Don't know	9	10
The duties of a party whip:		
Ensuring that MPs know how their leaders wish them to vote	48	52
Keeping order during debates in the House of Commons	30	25
Punishing MPs who get out of line	8	7
Don't know	14	16

Respondents had also been asked to choose (from three alterna-tives) the best description of key parliamentary roles. In the second wave there was no statistically significant increase in the numbers giving correct answers. A minority of the replies in both waves, however, produced evidence of some interesting misconceptions (see table 9.4).

To probe for further possible evidence of increased knowledge, respondents were given fifteen statements about the House of Commons, the electoral system and the constitution, and asked whether they were true or false. Although there was a small but consistent tendency for more people to choose correctly in the second wave, the increase in the numbers choosing the right answer was statistically significant in only one case. In wave 2 more respondents were aware that MPs were allowed to have other paid jobs (wave 1, 65 per cent correct; wave 2, 72 per cent correct). This can, however, be explained by a political controversy over that particular issue at the time of data collection. In passing it is interesting to note that in both waves more than half (52 per cent) knew that a political party can lose a general election, even if it gets more than half of the votes in the country, while only a quarter (24 per cent in wave 1; 25 per cent in wave 2) were aware that there is no Bill of Rights protecting the rights of individuals in the British constitution. In addition, more than four in every ten people in both waves of the survey wrongly supposed that Scotland, Wales and Northern Ireland had fewer MPs per head of population than England.

Interest in politics was once again the most effective single predictor of knowledge about MPs and parliamentary procedures. Sex, social grade, age and level of education were also strongly related, with men, older people, those in the higher social grades and those with the most education being more knowledgeable. In the second wave the amount of parliamentary coverage seen on news and special programmes was also related to knowledge scores, with those who reported seeing most of the coverage proving more knowledgeable. This additional piece of information marginally increased the ability to predict knowledge scores, once the demographic characteristics already discussed had been taken into account.

The knowledge-gap hypothesis states that the higher socio-economic groups in society acquire information from the media faster than do the lower socio-economic groups; this results in a widening gap in knowledge between the two. Later research (see Ettema and Kline 1977) has suggested that between-group differences in the perceived relevance of information, and in motivation to acquire it, are particularly important. Genova and Greenberg (1979) argue that interest in an issue is a better predictor of a developing knowledge gap than socio-economic status. Our data allowed for some examination of these hypotheses. No evidence whatsoever was found of a widening knowledge gap either between socio-economic groups, or indeed between those with differing degrees of interest in politics.

Attitudes towards the Government and the Parliamentary system

So far we have looked for evidence of changes in respondents' opinions concerning the behaviour of MPs, and in their knowledge about MPs and the workings of Parliament. Broader issues, however, remain to be covered. To help us in this endeavour we drew heavily on questions asked as part of SCPR's series of surveys *British Social Attitudes*: these were designed to explore individual orientations within what were seen as key dimensions of British political culture, and examined attitudes towards the political system, the economic order and socio-legal institutions. The use of these questions also enabled us to establish trend data, which require a minimum of three observations.

In 1986 and 1987 respondents in *British Social Attitudes* surveys (Social and Community Planning Research 1987, 1988) were asked four questions designed to gauge attitudes towards MPs and the Government. The answers tended, in the researchers' view, to 'present a picture of widespread public cynicism'. However, they also noted that as early as the 1959 survey of Britain conducted by Almond and Verba, there had been indications of cynicism about politicians in British civic culture (Almond and Verba 1963). For example, 83 per cent of their respondents had agreed that 'all candidates sound good in their speeches but you can never tell what they will do after they are elected'. Several writers have seen this as a healthy tendency in a political culture, provided that trust in the democratic process is not jeopardized. Commenting, for example, on the 1987 findings, Jowell and Topf (1988) concluded: 'The British public seems intuitively to have discovered that the surest protection against disillusionment with public figures and powerful institutions is to avoid developing illusions about them in the first place.'

These same four questions were asked again in the present survey. In both waves answers to three of the questions were very close to those found by the SCPR researchers in 1986 and 1987, and even earlier by Marsh in 1974 (Marsh 1977), suggesting that we are dealing with fairly stable public attitudes. No significant changes were recorded (see table 9.5).

Table 9.5 Attitudes towards MPs and the Government: percentage agreeing with three statements

	Marsh 1974 (%)	SCPR 1986 (1,548) (%)	SCPR 1987 (1,410) (%)	Wave 1 Oct–Nov. 1989 (1,476) (%)	Wave 2 March 1990 (1,482) (%)
Generally speaking those we elect as MPs lose touch with people pretty quickly	67	70	71	65	65
Political parties are only interested in people's votes, not their opinions	67	66	64	68	68
People like me have no say in what the Government does	N/A	71	69	67	66

Sources: col. 1, Marsh (1977); cols 2 and 3, Social and Community Planning Research (1987, 1988).

However, answers to the fourth question, 'How much do you trust a British Government of any party to place the needs of this country above the interests of their own political party?', showed respondents in both waves of the survey to be significantly more cynical than those who had taken part in SCPR's *British Social Attitudes* research two and three years earlier (see table 9.6).

This change in public attitudes, had occurred, of course, before the televising of the Commons and consequently cannot be held to reflect the presence of the cameras. The televising of the Commons however, during the short time for which it had been monitored, seems to have had little if any effect in ameliorating this element of political cynicism.

Respondents were asked: 'Does the Government in this country have too much or too little power?' Our research produced evidence of a shift during the three months of the experiment (see table 9.7). There was a trend for more people to feel that the Government had 'too much power'.

Table 9.6   Extent of trust in a British Government of any party

SCPR	SCPR 1986 (1,321) (%)	SCPR 1987 (1,410) (%)	Wave 1 Oct.–Nov. 1989 (1,476) (%)	Wave 2 March 1990 (1,482) (%)
Just about always	5	5	4	2
Most of the time	34	32	24	21
Only some of the time	46	49	44	47
Almost never	11	11	20	23
Don't know	4	3	8	6

Sources: cols 1 and 2, Social and Community Planning Research (1987, 1988).

Respondents were also asked: 'Do you think the present parliamentary system is satisfactory as it is or not? How strongly do you feel this?' Comparisons with a Gallup poll of 1986 would once again suggest a slight trend towards greater dissatisfaction (see table 9.8).

Table 9.7   Views on the power of the Government

	SCPR 1985 (1,530) (%)	SCPR 1987 (1,281) (%)	Wave 1 Oct.–Nov. 1989 (1,476) (%)	Wave 2 March 1990 (1,482) (%)
Far too much power	17 } 48	17 } 44	11 } 50	15 } 58
Too much power	31	27	39	43
About the right amount of power	41	44	34	30
Too little power	3	5	9	5
Far too little power	*	1	2	1
Don't know	7	6	5	5

Sources: cols 1 and 2, Social and Community Planning Research (1986, 1988).

Rising interest and mortgate rates and problems with the community charge/poll tax can be supposed to have influenced the most recent figures. All respondents who discussed politics with friends had been asked: 'What in particular have you discussed recently?' In wave 1, after Nigel Lawson's resignation (discussed by 32 per cent), the issues mentioned most frequently were the interest/mortgage rates (by 22 per cent) and the community charge/poll tax (by 19 per cent). In wave 2 the community charge/poll tax had virtually ousted all other topics: it was named by 88 per cent, while discussion of interest/mortgage rates was mentioned by only 9 per cent. Clearly, such issues, and matters of wider concern, must be held to account for increased dissatisfaction with both the Government and the parliamentary system.

Table 9.8   Satisfaction with the parliamentary system

	Gallup 1986 (c. 1,000) (%)		Wave 1 Oct.–Nov. 1989 (1,476) (%)		Wave 2 March 1990 (1,482) (%)	
Very strongly satisfied	10		5		4	
Strongly satisfied	13	41	19	39	15	34
Not strongly satisfied	18		15		15	
Not strongly dissatisfied	11		9		9	
Strongly dissatisfied	14	44	24	49	23	56
Very strongly dissatisfied	19		16		24	
Don't know	15		12		10	

Source: col. 1, Gallup (1986).

Other answers confirmed that distrust of politicians was widespread, although there was no evidence of any change between the two waves in the survey. In wave one only 43 per cent and in wave 2 only 42 per cent agreed that 'most MPs are trustworthy', while around 30 per cent disagreed, the rest being undecided.

Respondents were also asked what they thought ordinary MPs, not cabinet ministers, spent most time doing. In both waves of the survey, although answers spread over all the six alternatives provided, the most commonly chosen was 'working on behalf of their political party' (endorsed by 39 per cent in wave 1 and by 33 per cent in wave 2). Asked about what they thought MPs *should* spend most time doing, a greater consensus emerged, with around six in every ten (61 per cent in wave 1 and 63 per cent in wave 2) choosing 'working on behalf of individual constituents'. This discrepancy between what MPs were believed to spend most time doing, and what the public thought they *ought* to be doing, would seem to highlight a potential source of considerable dissatisfaction.

On the other hand, whereas the majority expressed a lack of trust in the Government, and endorsed the view that economic injustice and inequality were the rule (around seven in every ten respondents, for example, agreed that 'there is one law for the rich and one law for the poor'), support for an established moral order and the rule of law was widespread. Over eight out of every ten respondents in both waves, for example, felt that 'schools should teach children to obey authority', and almost six in every ten agreed that 'the law should always be obeyed, even if a particular law is wrong'. Only in the case of sentencing criminals was a significant difference recorded between the two waves of the survey: fewer felt that 'people who break the law should be given stiffer sentences' (wave 1, 70 per cent agreeing; wave 2, 63 per cent agreeing). This finding is almost certainly the result of contemporary public concern about overcrowding in prisons.

Radical attitudes towards the socio-legal order (registered by disagreement with censorship, stiffer sentencing and unqualified adherence to the law) were only weakly related to cynical attitudes towards politics and politicians. On the other hand, those who were more cynical about politics and politicians, as in the SCPR research, were more likely to support a conflict model of worker –management relations, and to feel that wealth was unfairly distributed in society. Heath and Topf (1987) draw this important conclusion:

> The fact that attitudes towards the economic order are power-fully related to political cynicism brings out how important are attitudes towards the economic order, not only in shaping party politics but also in shaping trust in the Government. In other words our political culture connects economic and political values much more than it connects moral and political values.
>
> (Social and Community Planning Research 1987: 64)

CONCLUSIONS

Our findings demonstrated clearly public support for the decision to continue televising the proceedings of the House of Commons which was taken by Parliament in July 1990. The kind of positive expectations engendered by the experiment are particularly interesting considering the widespread distrust of politics and politicians which characterized the political climate at that time. More than eight out of every ten respondents thought that 'people will begin to understand more about how Parliament works'; around seven in every ten expected that 'people will feel more involved in what is going on in Parliament', become 'more interested' and 'be better able to judge the true character of individual MPs'. After more than three months' experience of the broadcasts, with 94 per cent of respondents reporting that they had seen some of the coverage, the numbers expressing these opinions had not significantly diminished.

Although the survey provided no confirmation of increased public interest in, esteem for, or knowledge about, the workings of Parliament, it must be appreciated that the time interval between the two waves of the survey was such that measurable effects were unlikely to be registered. Findings do, however, provide a baseline for future research in this area. Results suggest that the continued monitoring of public attitudes towards Parliament in the light of the new access to its workings is of considerable importance. Will the apparent slide towards greater cynicism continue, or is it merely a temporary phenomenon, reflecting the Government's particular difficulties at the time of the survey? Given more experience of a televised Parliament, will the public actually become better informed and more involved? If they do, what impact will this have on the four out of every ten who express little or no interest in politics? The answers to these questions are likely to have a profound impact on British political life.

Chapter 10

Business as usual: the impact of television coverage on press reporting of the Commons

Alastair Hetherington and Kay Weaver

In keeping with its 'Gotcha' headline on the sinking of the *Belgrano*, the *Sun*'s comment when the cameras first began broadcasting the proceedings of the House was 'Commons TV voted Big Yawn'. The newspaper's evidence, it turned out, was that there had been no 'big drain' on electrical power that afternoon. Further evidence came from the *Sun*'s television critic, who wrote of 'the biggest turn off this side of Clare Short on Page Three'. The real surprise, however, was that in the following week the *Sun* carried seven reports of Commons affairs – much more than its previous average of parliamentary reporting.

Looking at the first four months of Commons television, it is clear that most newspapers gave much the same coverage to parliamentary affairs as they had done a year earlier. The 'heavy' newspapers were thorough in their reporting, as were some of the regional mornings. There was a marginally greater use of MPs' words in the House and a narrowing of topics in the political pages – the latter not because of television but because of international events. The urgent discussion of international affairs, from the Government's view of sanctions in South Africa to our attitudes to German reunification, had pushed farming and other domestic matters to one side. The newspapers were anyway keeping an eye on television even before the experiment began. Every newsroom now has a screen with Sky or Channel 4 or *Westminster Live* as a mute presence, with the sound turned up only when someone thinks it worth listening. For the most part the print journalists were working much as before.

Journalists have two advantages over the broadcasters, but one big disadvantage. Their deadlines are not as punishingly early as those of television people with programmes on air at 5.40 or 6 p.m., though most of their copy will have to be in before 9 p.m. This extra time can be valuable, since it leaves space and creates more opportunities for political correspondents to meet MPs in the lobby or one of the bars, and thereby to go deeper into the implications of an event. Although it is perhaps not evident to the public, the opportunity to talk informally to ministers and backbenchers is important in testing the atmosphere, looking forward and gauging opinion about coming events. MPs will say things more candidly if they are not going to be quoted directly. The reporters, of course, will want an 'on the record' comment whenever possible, but they may need the informal talk to extend their knowledge. And for the newspaper journalist who is not required to dash at once to the studio or editing room that is a real advantage.

The second gain is in the space available in newspapers to explore issues more coherently and in more detail. Broadcasters must invariably deliver a compact report – two minutes (or about 300 words) if she or he is lucky, 40 seconds (or 90 words) if not. Whatever the brief, it requires considerable skill to get the message over in so few words and with smooth style. Newspaper journalists are not always as self-controlled – and of course what they write may be battered by sub-editors or night editors. (Cardus was right when he wrote about the average sub-editor's room as 'an abattoir': broadcasters can speak their own words in their own way.) Nevertheless, print journalists do have the benefit of writing at greater length and have more freedom of style.

Their big disadvantage – most obvious since Commons television arrived – is that print cannot carry the force, immediacy and drama of *seeing* a major Commons event. That is true both of the Chamber and of committees. Journalists can write eloquently about ministers and Opposition in hard debate, or a committee putting witnesses through tough questioning, but they can rarely match the screen.

Table 10.1 aims to provide some guidance concerning the range of parliamentary topics reported in newspapers, as well as an assessment of the amount of space allocated to Commons coverage. The table sets out the number of items, the total space allocated to them (measured here in square centimetres and using the crude base of five words to each square centimetre) and then, within the larger total, the measurement of 'direct' Commons speech. Set against the mid-February five days of broadcasting, it indicates the difference of scale. The 'heavy' newspapers did indeed have much more space; of the newspapers listed, only the *Sun* offered as little wording as the primary broadcasters, and then with a rather different style.

Table 10.1 Extent of parliamentary coverage in selected newspapers, with television comparison

Week of 16–20 January 1990

	Guardian	Times	Daily Mail	Sun	Scotsman
Commons items	35	51	6	2	28
Total sq. cm	3,513	6,123	1,062	207	3,892
Committees	4	3	2	–	7
Direct quotes, sq. cm	387	336	9	–	242
Page 1 items	2	5	1	–	4

Week of 13–17 February 1990

	Guardian	Telegraph	Mirror	Sun	Glasgow Herald
Commons items	27	24	6	6	32
Total sq. cm	3,688	3,595	644	267	3,592
Committees	2	2	–	–	9
Direct quotes, sq. cm	458	376	13	14	298
Page 1 items	2	4	1	–	4

Week of 13–17 March 1990

	Guardian	Times	Express	Sun	Scotsman
Commons items	41	51	7	3	21
Total sq. cm	3,790	6,232	988	318	3,693
Committees	6	2	1	1	5
Direct quotes, sq. cm	409	390	40	7	224
Page 1 items	2	4	2	1	2

TV comparison 12–16 February 1990

	Nine O'Clock News	News at Ten	Westminster	Parliament Programme
Items	6	5	20	16
Equivalent, sq. cm	405	285	4,320	1,020
Committees	–	–	1	1
Direct quotes, sq. cm	135	96	3,630	810
Top two items	2	2	N/A	N/A

Press reporting of Parliament can also be assessed in a different way, by taking newspapers' front pages as a partial competitor with the major television news.

TUESDAY 13 FEBRUARY

Guardian:	Lead story on sanctions, 'Mrs Thatcher alone'. Reactions in South Africa, UK and Europe run together, including Waldegrave (minister) in Commons 'direct' quotes.
Telegraph:	Lead story on Mandela; second item on electricity costs, Commons, but with little 'direct'. On back page, Waldegrave and others on sanctions, with some 'direct' quotes.
Mirror	No parliamentary story on page 1.
Sun	No parliamentary story on page 1.
Glasgow Herald:	Lead story on Soweto, third story a brief summary of Waldegrave and sanctions.

WEDNESDAY 14 FEBRUARY

Guardian:	Second item, sanctions row in Commons (almost all indirect). Detail on page 6.
Telegraph:	Lead, sanctions row – long report but almost no 'direct'.
Mirror:	No sanctions row report anywhere (in northern issues). Page 1 lead, 'Take your bloody money and go', on Mike Gatting's cricket tour.
Sun:	Not on page 1, but taking much of page 2, 'Maggie and Kinnock in telly war' (of which more later).
Glasgow Herald:	Sanctions, various aspects. Headline 'Runcie proves Thatcher ally in sanctions row', including Archbishop, Mandela, Waldegrave, Kinnock, Bernie Grant and others.

THURSDAY 15 FEBRUARY

Guardian:	Three main stories, all UK political, but none Commons. Lead on mortgages.

Telegraph:	Lead on mortgages up, with brief summary of Commons exchanges at end, about half 'direct'. Main report on City pages.
Mirror:	No parliamentary story on page 1.
Sun:	Not on page 1, but big headline on page 2 'Help home buyers or you'll be out, Mrs T.' And, perhaps to offset that, on page 6 a half-page – at least in Scottish editions – referring to Labour's Scottish leader, 'Donald, you're a loser': 'He's failed the voters. Pals want him axed. He's a flop on the telly.'
Glasgow Herald:	Lead on sanctions, Waldegrave and others.

FRIDAY 16 FEBRUARY

Guardian:	No parliamentary story on page 1.
Telegraph:	Fourth item on 'mortgage alarm'. PM's Questions: 'Worry among Conservatives'.
Mirror:	No parliamentary story on page 1.
Sun:	No parliamentary story on page 1.
Glasgow Herald:	No parliamentary story on page 1.

What emerges clearly from this analysis is the complete absence of parliamentary stories on the front pages of the tabloids. Other stories reported in the press during the week included:

Guardian:	'The Day in Politics', usually page 6 (three-quarters) or 6 and 7 (two half-pages). More about sanctions, Tuesday and Wednesday, almost all indirect. Also on Thursday, with Hurd extensively quoted and four other Commons items. Friday, Chancellor and Kinnock on mortgages, about half 'direct'.
Telegraph:	'Parliament and Politics', usually about pages 10 to 15, three-quarter page. Tuesday, Crown Prosecution Service, Inter-City trains and three other Commons items, almost wholly indirect speech. Wednesday, debate on spending plans (half 'indirect') and four other items. Thursday, Hurd on sanctions ('Tory rift') and four other items; substantial 'direct' quoting. Friday, reports on two committees.

Mirror:	Usually page 2 or page 4. Tuesday, Waldegrave *v.* Kaufman, short, but about one-quarter 'direct'. Thursday, 'Mortgages go through the roof', with some 'direct' quotes from Commons. Friday, mortgages again, with PM's Questions.
Sun:	Also usually page 2. Tuesday, brief item on Waldegrave and sanctions. Wednesday, as noted, Maggie–Kinnock 'telly war'. Thursday, mortgages and Donald Dewar.
Glasgow Herald:	Parliament, usually pages 6, 8, or 9. Tuesday, more detail on Waldegrave, including some 'direct'. Also Scottish electricity costs and four other Commons items. Wednesday, debate on spending plans, row on sanctions; and six other items, including light-hearted thoughts on Mrs Thatcher confined to her Dulwich home by 'the Kaufman regime'. Thursday, Post Office rivals, gas prices, Wallace case and four others. Friday, Scottish steel and five others. Not much 'direct' quoting.

A year earlier, in mid-February 1989, *The Times*, *Guardian*, *Independent* and *Telegraph* were all carrying longer Commons cover – all four at above 4,000 sq. cm during the week. Only *The Times* remained at that level in 1990. The apparent reason lay in the heavy demands of East European and South African affairs, which were taking substantially more space than a year earlier. The televising of the Commons does not appear to have been a factor.

The *Daily Mirror*, however, had more than doubled its Commons material compared with a year earlier, with television almost certainly being a relevant factor. The *Sun*, too, had increased its cover, though it still remained small. Its prize contribution, already mentioned, was its big display on page 2 of Wednesday 14 February – the 'telly war' of Mrs Thatcher and Mr Kinnock. Without the cameras in the Commons, that 'big row' could never have made such a juicy story for a popular paper, complete with a picture of the two major political leaders framed in an artifical television screen. The *Sun* reported that the row was 'watched by millions on TV' and that 'the rowdy scenes were the worst since TV was introduced to the Commons last year' – a legitimate statement, since the level of disorder was without precedent during the session, and backed by Mr Speaker's rebuke, 'This sounds awful', as the two sides shouted each other down.

It might have been expected that some of the popular newspapers would capitalize on television broadcasting by starting to probe into the private lives of MPs, as they do with other TV stars. That has not happened, so far as is known. But the popular newspaper interest in Commons affairs is still far below the attention given by the heavy newspapers and the major regional papers.

The experience of television broadcasting from the Commons is still too young for an assessment to be made of the extent to which broadcasters and newspaper journalists are ready to bring into public debate new aspects or new ideas from the Commons and its committees. Are the print journalists and the television correspondents, for example, willing to risk time and space for fresh topics? Earlier research suggests that there is caution and some reluctance to take up something that is not already accepted as 'newsworthy'. It would be surprising if that were not as true of parliamentary affairs as other public concerns. Given the wide range of Commons proceedings, it seems likely that a tendency will prevail among journalists to report those events which readers or audiences will most readily understand and with which they will identify.

This is part of the so-called 'socio-centralism' that influences nearly all editorial decisions – or, to borrow an American academic's term, 'motherhood values'. It derives from the fact that a great majority of citizens want a peaceful life, not turmoil and conflict. They prefer good news to bad, though inevitably a lot of painful news comes through newspapers and broadcast news. Socio-centralism implies a concern with maintaining the continuity and harmony of the established society, at least in western countries; it is therefore against those who want sudden or violent change. But within that broad 'centralism' there is room for reporting argument, debate, minority views and reform – and it is from these that better government and a better society may emerge. The tide, however, tends to run against those who are looking for reform. (For further evidence, see Hetherington 1986 and 1989, especially the account of the reporting of the Birmingham Children's Hospital problems in 1987–8 in the latter.)

The point here is that, unless there has been an amazing change among news editors in the recent past, topics are unlikely to secure attention unless they are not already at least partly familiar to a particular audience. This seems to be true for both newspapers and television – but newspapers have the advantage of more space and more time, and in some papers news editors who are more imaginative.

In summary, it is hard to identify any discernible impact on press reporting of Parliament as a direct consequence of the experience of television broadcasting from the Chamber. On the contrary, it seems to be very much a case of 'business as usual'.

Chapter 11

Commons television in the regions: creative broadcasting in a constrained environment

Bob Franklin

On 21 November 1989 the first live pictures were broadcast from the Commons, some twenty-five years after Members had first debated whether to televise the House's proceedings. Belated or not, the arrival of television cameras was an important event with undoubted implications for politicians, parties, broadcasters, the public audience and, in a broader sense, the democratic process. Subsequently, the experiment in televising the Commons was judged a success, with some suggesting that it has created a new era for political broadcasting. It is undeniable that few events can have created in their wake so many new programmes designed to report parliamentary and political affairs. But if a new era in political broadcasting is beginning, its advent is nowhere more apparent than in the various television regions. Regional reporting of Parliament has not been a pale imitation of national television, but has presented events in Parliament through a range of creative and distinctive programmes.

This was a particularly creditable achievement, since it became clear, during a series of interviews conducted with regional broadcasters as part of a broader programme of research,[1] that Commons reporting in the regions was produced in a uniquely constrained environment reflecting the influence of both media and political factors. A discussion of these constraints is followed by a review of the new, and often innovatory, programme formats adopted to present the week's events in Parliament to regional audiences. The chapter concludes with a detailed analysis of selected aspects of regional parliamentary broadcasting.

REGIONAL PARLIAMENTARY BROADCASTING: A CONSTRAINED ENVIRONMENT

Constraints on broadcasting derived from five sources: first, the general philosophy underlying parliamentary broadcasting; second, the need to achieve balance in the most complex and varied understanding of that term; third, the concern to avoid duplication of network stories; fourth, shortages of resources defined in a broad way; finally, technical difficulties. The precise character of these constraints varied across the regions, reflecting differences in regional size, the number of MPs and various other factors. On occasion, different degrees of constraint were evident between the BBC and ITV services, expressing varying levels of financial resource, differing scheduling arrangements, as well as the distinctively parliamentary emphasis of the BBC programmes. Certain constraints, however, were common to all broadcasters, whether BBC or ITV and without regard to particular regions; for example, the problems arising from the need to achieve geographically balanced reporting around a typically disparate region.

In the BBC pan-regions the new programmes broadcast in January 1990 were not the product of any regionally based initiative but were part of a co-ordinated response by the BBC to the challenge of parliamentary broadcasting. Regional programmes were a single component in an overall package of programming which embraced a weekly network review of Parliament scheduled for Sunday lunchtime, followed immediately by the eight regional opt-outs – BBC Wales, *Wales in Parliament*; BBC South and East, *Around Westminster*; BBC North-West, *North Westminster*; BBC North-East, *North of Westminster*; BBC Midlands, *The Midlands at Westminster*; BBC South and West, *Westminster South and West*; BBC Scotland, *News Gallery*; BBC Northern Ireland, *Spotlight*.

Regional broadcasters were given a broadly based programme philosophy, conceived by the centre, which stressed that programmes should focus on parliamentary affairs rather than more general political issues. As one producer confided:

There's a fair degree of autonomy in the sense that it's up to us how we present the programme . . . it's entirely a local matter. But some fairly definite guidelines have been laid down about

what we should include. . . . We were not given a blank sheet
of paper and told to make weekly political current affairs
programmes for [the region]. We were given a piece of paper
which said what you are primarily here to do is to reflect the
work of [the region's] MPs week by week.

In interviews some broadcasters expressed misgivings about this
philosophy, claiming it had implications for production formats and
for content and could compromise journalistic instincts. So far as
the latter is concerned, one producer complained that 'everything
we do in the programme must be Commons driven. We're not
at liberty to go off and do some other story which may be a
perfectly good political story unless it's got at least some relevance
to parliamentary material.' In one region where an especially
newsworthy story had broken about a local MP, a decision was
taken not to report the issue, but it caused 'a bit of a ballyhoo'.
When asked if the preference among local BBC staff would have
been for a programme with a wider brief which encompassed
the reporting of such stories, the producer replied discreetly and
with tongue planted firmly in cheek, 'I think it's probably fair
to say that.' Some broadcasters undoubtedly believed that their
professional competence to assess a story's value according to the
criterion of new values had been compromised by this broader
remit for the programmes. 'There is a tension in this programme',
a producer confided, 'between one's natural journalistic instincts
and the various constraints that exist . . . I think you have to accept
that to a certain extent these programmes are a trip around the
parliamentary bay rather than strictly journalism.'

A second constraint on regional broadcasters derived from the
need to achieve a balance in programmes between the various
political parties, the different areas of the broadcast region and
between the front- and backbench Members with constituencies in
the broadcast 'patch'.

The achievement of political balance was undoubtedly the most
difficult and contentious of these three tasks, not least because
journalists in different broadcast regions inherited a disparate
political geography. In the TVS area, for example, each of the
sixty-two MPs was Conservative, while in the Scottish and North
of England broadcast regions a converse political asymmetry was
reflected in substantial Labour majorities. In most broadcast
regions Liberal Democrats were numerically 'thin on the ground'.

The BBC North-East region, for example, with over 100 MPs, could claim only Alan Beith for the Liberal Democrats. Regional broadcasters were consequently obliged to reassess one of the fundamental tenets of their professional culture which suggests that the purpose of regional broadcasting is to 'present the region to the region'. Adherence to such a maxim would have prompted gross political imbalances. Some broadcasters sought a solution to this problem by trying to reflect more the national balance.

Political balance is, of course, notoriously difficult to define. No broadcasters believed it could be achieved by simply reflecting the number of seats held by each of the parties, although this formed one element in the assessment. Equally important was the size of the party's popular vote at the last election. In the Border region, for example, the SNP did not win any seats but secured a high vote in two or three constituencies, thereby deserving, at least in the producer's perceptions, a right to space in programming. But balance need not necessarily be conceived in partisan terms and may simply reflect a weighing of opinions for and against a particular issue; in the words of one broadcaster, 'a balance in terms of getting conflicting views that would make lively interviews'. Most broadcasters, after ruminating at some length on the issue in a quasi-scientific and quantitative fashion, agreed that balance was a 'gut feeling' that was 'very difficult' but 'if you're a news editor day in day out and if somebody asked you to write for 20 seconds you tend to get it right. Your balance comes with experience.'

Occasionally, the need for political balance constrained content, with programme makers subscribing to one of two antithetical approaches, reflecting the degree to which they were prepared to subordinate news values to the need for political balance. A BBC producer observed:

> When you're looking at the particular business in Parliament in a particular week you might say, right, those five speeches or whatever are the five most interesting ones. But in fact it might be that all five are from Labour MPs in a particular week and, although nobody is expecting us to keep a balance between the parties in every programme, in practice we must really have equal contributions from the two main parties. So therefore you are bending your journalistic principles to meet the requirements of political balance and that is obviously a problem.

Not all producers, however, were prepared to let public service commitments militate against judgements driven by news values. An ITV producer, for example, claimed that she intended to be fair to the various political parties but insisted that, 'if they're not delivering, then I won't. I won't show an MP if he's not dealing with interesting issues.'

Broadcasters also believed that programmes should reflect the activities, interests and cultural range of the entire region, rather than focusing on the major urban centres where the majority of population resides, where the centres of regional and municipal decision-making are located and where the greater part of local political activity is sited. One producer, perhaps more conscientious than others, was 'keeping a record of appearances by our MPs by county within the region. There's no obligation to do this but it's my view that we should try and get round the region.' The requirements of regional balance, as with political balance, necessitated occasional compromises of journalistic judgement about the merit of certain stories.

The final constraint on broadcasters imposed by the require-ments of balance was the need to reflect a fair representation of front- and backbench Members in the broadcast area. As with political balance, there were few uncontentious criteria for establishing a front/backbench balance. Most broadcasters seemed eager to include as many local backbench MPs as possible in their programmes. In part this reflected a certain pragmatism. 'We all know', confided a producer, 'that MPs are going to choose whether this continues and my personal view is that it is extremely unlikely that now the cameras are in they'll ever depart . . . but one shouldn't become too complacent about these things. It will be MPs who decide'. Pragmatism aside, most broadcasters' preference for the back bench seemed to signal a variant of public service commitments. Broadcasters believed that frontbenchers were likely to dominate in network programming and, consequently, 'on a regional programme we need to make backbenchers feel that . . . this is their opportunity to get on'. This perceived division of labour between network and regional programming, combined with broadcasters' natural tendency to 'show the region to the region', disposed many broadcasters to favour the back benches.

The third substantive constraint on broadcasters was the need

to avoid replication of stories and items featured in other programmes. One BBC producer remarked:

> The major constraint that operates is the fact that one is trying
> to avoid duplication of our programme with two other BBC
> outlets. One of course is the 35 minutes that immediately
> precedes us, *Westminster Week* . . . the other is one's own
> regional daily programme during the week where they will
> cover parliamentary material on a day-to-day basis.

This can involve scheduled stories being excluded at quite a late
stage in programme production. 'Last week', a producer explained,
'we were planning to run [a particular item] and discovered late on
Friday night that *Westminster Week* were going to run that so we
took it out altogether because there is no sense in repetition within
the hour.'

When an especially newsworthy story breaks nationally but has
particular relevance for their area, regional broadcasters are likely
to decide to continue with the item but are obliged to find a 'new
angle' on the story. When Colin Wallace, for example, alleged a
'campaign of misinformation' about certain politicians during the
1970s, Merlyn Rees, a West Yorkshire MP and former Home
Secretary and Northern Ireland Secretary, was prominent in the
House's calls for a public inquiry. The local BBC editor was
eager to carry the story but was aware that Merlyn Rees would
be 'exhaustively covered in the news and in *Westminster Week*'.
However, 'This one is so big that we still want to reflect it. Our
problem is how to make it complementary rather than repetitive.
So what quotes has he used that they haven't that still bear
an outing?' Similar problems arose in relation to the station's
regional news programme. Again, the solution was to restructure
the approach to the story. 'As for *Look North*'s coverage,' the
editor explained, 'we have to ask: is there a way we can develop
this beyond its simple news coverage, i.e. shall we get Merlyn in?
And that's exactly what we're seeking to do.'

ITV companies faced similar problems, but with less severity,
since the scheduling of their regional programmes did not place
them back-to-back with the network programme, *A Week in
Politics*. Some broadcasters were sanguine about such difficulties.
'It's the old problem that applies to lots of regional broadcasting',
a producer explained. 'If there's a big story on your patch and
it gets on the six o'clock news and then you're coming on at

six thirty with your regional magazine programme, how do you cover it differently? It's an age-old problem and this is just a new application of it.' A further potential source of repetition was the Parliament programme broadcast by the other regional station, although, interestingly, this was rarely cited as a problem.

The fourth source of programming constraints derived from scarce budgetary and other resources. Financial restrictions seemed to be a problem felt more acutely among ITV than BBC staffs, with the latter largely expressing satisfaction with allocated budgets. 'I get 250 grand from them,' an editor observed. 'I am not unhappy with the budget, believe me. I think it's the right size and I can work happily within that budget.' A producer in a different region confirmed this view but added that 'obviously one has the worry that in the first year we're spending a lot of money to make a success' but if the television experiment 'becomes permanent then the BBC will have to reassess how much money they're going to put in on a continuing basis'. Not everyone subscribed to this 'honeymoon', view of the BBC's commitment to parliamentary broadcasting.

Satisfaction with budgets was less evident in the ITV companies. In some regions budgets were unrealistically low and programming could only be achieved by 'creative accountancy' techniques in which the real costs of programming could be lost within other budgets. A broadcaster in one region, with responsibilities for a half-hour parliamentary programme, admitted that 'the above-the-line budget for this programme is £1,000 a programme, which is phenomenally cheap, and it's a bit of a strain. I do a lot of deals to get it on the cheap.' The salaries of the producer and programme researcher were funded by another programme, which was finished ahead of schedule while the presenter was 'in between projects for which we get grants, so there's a little bit of money from that'.

Some broadcasters undoubtedly felt that the Select Committee's suggestion that regional broadcasters should use the signal from the House extensively in programming showed ignorance of the realities of regional broadcasting finances. 'The Select Committee is going to put a lot of pressure on regional companies to carry coverage', a producer complained, 'but this is quite ill informed. I did all sorts of costings and the cost of a satellite feed to a company like this would actually cripple us.'

A second aspect of resource constraint reflected the number of MPs in a broadcast region. It is perhaps unusual to consider MPs as a resource of programme makers but they are the key actors in the drama of parliamentary television. The number of Members in a particular broadcast region, their role and office in their parties and their willingness to participate in regional programming are all factors which restrict or enhance broadcasters' possibilities for programme making. Central Television, for example, with a hundred MPs in its broadcast region, clearly has a good deal more 'raw material' for programmes than the smaller regions. A producer in one region had contacted Members on her patch to explain her ambitions for the programme and elicit their support. 'I met all the MPs', she explained, 'and said: "Look, we can't run this programme without you 'cos we've only got a dozen of you, and if even one of you says you're not interested I'm ten per cent short."' But even in regions with greater numbers of MPs, broadcasters were limited by Members' willingness and ability to participate. Some were keener than others; some were judged by broadcasters to be more 'TV capable' than others. There developed what one broadcaster described as 'the repertory company of MPs which, if you allowed it to be the case, would always get on'. Broadcasters must serve as gatekeepers. But these 'good performers' could serve useful functions for broadcasters. One producer mentioned a local MP whom he described as 'someone who is always good value in the sense that we usually end up with something controversial. . . . So there must be a tendency to let the repertory company perform at the expense of others.' Most broadcasters reported favourable feedback about programmes from MPs in their region.

Certain constraints on broadcasters which were common to all regions can be termed technical considerations. These include the quality of camera shots from the House and the guidelines established by the Select Committee to govern broadcasters' use of the signal. The guidelines were not strictly a technical restraint, since they reflected politicians' intentions that the experiment should be conducted on terms which they had established, but the constraints they generated were technical – relating, for example, to the issue of how a particular piece of film might be edited.

Most broadcasters agreed that the quality of shots was high and better than they had anticipated; most also shared the view that the quality improved rapidly during the very early period of the experiment. But some problems remained. One broadcaster complained about pictures from the House and suggested that 'because the cameras are set high, it's more or less like shooting a football match', adding with evident pleasure that 'it's actually less flattering on the front bench than it is on the back benches.' None the less, 'if the subject matter is interesting that gets over the problem of the quality of the shots.' It is interesting to note that broadcasters' concerns about the quality of shots related to perceptions of the audience reaction to them. 'Television programmes are so sophisticated now', one producer explained, 'that viewers expect certain standards and the sight of MPs goldfishing around is going to look very naff and not the sort of thing I'd like to see.' Another difficulty which arose in this context was the occasional tardiness of the cameras in locating Members, especially backbench Members, who had the floor. 'Sometimes an MP on the back benches can be speaking for ten seconds before the camera finds him or her', a producer claimed, 'and it's a real problem if you're trying to edit. We get those awful wide shots, an anonymous voice, and then the cameras find them and they're finished.'

The Select Committee guidelines were also perceived as a constraint in two ways. First, the initial limitation to the head-and-shoulders shot meant that it was very difficult to establish the geography of the House. 'You still get some visual nonsense', a producer complained. 'They've got cameras all the way round . . . it's a bit like shooting cricket from both ends. The camera crosses the line so you don't know instantly which side of the House you're on.' The changes to guidelines in early January 1990 which allowed wider-angle shots must have eased these difficulties. Second, the restrictions on cutaway shots presented problems for broadcasters, especially in the editing of film. One broadcaster remarked:

> Last week we could have used two minutes of [a local MP] but there was a very odd 30 or 45 seconds in the middle of it. We could have used the front, a cutaway and then the back, but what we had to use was the last thirty seconds. A piece of a minute and a half could have been used but because we were in that constraint we couldn't do it.

In summary, these five factors – programme philosophy, the necessity for balance, the need to avoid replication of network programmes, shortages of resources and technical difficulties – imposed a complex amalgam of potential constraints on regional broadcasters. But, despite these difficulties, broadcasters in both BBC and ITV settings displayed great enthusiasm and energy for the enterprise of parliamentary broadcasting. Broadcasters' commitment to generating creative programme formats, as vehicles for parliamentary television in the regions, was evident in many of the programmes which are discussed below.

REGIONAL PARLIAMENTARY BROADCASTING: THE PROGRAMMES IN OUTLINE

The BBC regional programmes

The BBC regions responded to the availability of the signal from the House of Commons by establishing new programmes designed specifically to carry parliamentary actuality. BBC Wales began transmitting *Wales in Westminster* from the beginning of the experimental period, while BBC Midlands, North, North-West, South-East and South-West launched their programmes in January 1990. BBC Scotland's programme *News Gallery* was oriented more towards current affairs, while BBC Northern Ireland decided against a programme in the Sunday lunchtime parliamentary schedule.

In contrast to the majority of ITV regional weekly programmes, the BBC regional output took its agenda directly from the parliamentary events of the week. This editorial focus had a number of implications for the scope and format of the programmes. The broad objective of the programmes was perhaps best expressed in the first edition of *Wales in Westminster*: 'To show in more detail than ever before how your MP is exercising the power bestowed by the voters.' The programme philosophy emanating from the centre prompted obvious similarities across the BBC programmes, but there is evidence that individual producers enjoyed sufficient autonomy to mould programmes into a form particularly appropriate to the political complexion of their regions.

The substantive common feature of the programmes was that each employed a member of the BBC political staff as the parliamentary correspondent for the region, to introduce brief actuality highlights of the week's events as well as to contextualize some longer stories. The shorter items were typically clips of local backbenchers addressing regional issues. On 21 January 1990, for example, *North of Westminster* used three such items: Mansfield MP Alan Meale introduced an adjournment debate

on a constituency case; Hexham MP Alan Amos questioned
Transport Minister Robert Atkins about improvements to the
A1; and, on film, north-eastern MPs Jim Cousins and Neville
Trotter asked Douglas Hogg of the Department of Trade and
Industry about industrial redevelopment on Tyneside. This type
of material, illustrating the day-to-day concerns of local MPs, was
a standard feature of all the programmes.

Autonomy was evident in a number of areas. First, within the
limits imposed by the events in the House, the agenda was directly
regional. This can be illustrated by examining the lead stories
in programmes across the English regions for 21 January and
25 February 1990. On 21 January each of the BBC regional
programmes led with an item about the community charge/poll
tax – undoubtedly the major political story of the week – which
used actuality from the House debate of 17 January. Actuality,
however, played a relatively modest part in the extensive reports,
which included studio and ex-studio interviews, film packages, vox
pops, computer graphics and other formats deployed to illustrate
the regional implications of the charge and the attitudes of local
councils and publics to the new tax. On the same day, however,
Wales in Westminster led with an item on the Environment
Protection Bill. By contrast, the selection of lead stories on
25 February showed a greater variety of editorial judgement.
South-West again led with the community charge/poll tax, but
both South-East and Midlands gave priority to the future of
the Royal Shakespeare Company, BBC North looked at the
future of shipbuilding in Sunderland and North-West considered
a local immigration case. All programmes featured actuality: the
parliamentary events reported included Ministerial Questions, a
Government statement, a private notice question, a Labour-
initiated debate and a backbench adjournment debate.

The overlap of concerns between programmes was minimal
(with the exception of community charge), reflecting the extent
to which a regional-issue agenda was followed. But a regional
agenda was evident not only in terms of the stories reported but
by broadcasters' willingness to downplay events already featured
in national broadcasting, even where there was a substantial
regional interest. Consequently, on 21 January 1990 BBC Midlands
featured as their third story the Select Committee appearance
by Lord Young concerning the sale of the Rover Group to
British Aerospace; it had already been covered extensively in

the immediately preceding *Westminster Week* programme. This ranking of news stories might also express broadcasters' concern to avoid duplication of issues aired in network programmes.

Regional autonomy was similarly evident in the range of programme formats used in addition to the straightforward reporting of Parliament. All regions invited MPs to participate in studio interviews or discussions, usually responding to film reports embracing actuality. BBC South-West, through an editorial decision to reflect the political complexion of the area, had a substantial three-way studio discussion as the centrepiece of each programme. This involved a Conservative MP (sometimes a relevant minister from a local constituency) and representatives from Labour and the Liberal Democrats, often prospective parliamentary candidates or councillors, who provided a measure of political balance not evident in the composition of MPs in the regions. No other region gave the Liberal Democrats such regular, almost institutional coverage, and most confined their studio discussion to representatives of the two main parties. BBC South-East produced some memorable discussions; especially noteworthy was a debate about arts funding between the MPs Brian Sedgemore and Terry Dicks.

Some programmes preferred interviews to discussions but again managed to give the format a distinctive twist. BBC Midlands employed two presenters who alternated with questions to the interviewee, who had to remain particularly alert since *Midlands at Westminster* was broadcast live. BBC North-West provided the most innovative adaptation of the interview format in its regular 'Question Time' feature. Viewers were invited to phone in questions on a topic which had been trailed in the evening news programme, which were then put to a guest MP. In addition, the viewer judged to have the most pertinent question was invited to make their point in person and was given the opportunity to press the MP with supplementary questions. This proved to be an very interesting element of the programme, providing a good example of public access to the medium. On 21 January, Wyre MP Keith Mans was pressed about the community charge/poll tax and on 25 February Tom Sackville of Bolton West was asked about church–state relations.

A number of distinctive programme formats were adopted by particular regions. BBC North-West had a feature called 'Final Reading', where an invited MP gave a two- to three-minute talk to camera on a particular aspect of the parliamentary week. Again the programme provided an element of access, in this case designed to offer opportunities to MPs rather than the audience. BBC South-West reflected the public service ethos in its 'Parliamentary Answers' service. Each week the programme had an explanatory item on different aspects of parliamentary procedure such as the ten-minute rule, which was dealt with on 25 February. Viewers were invited to submit questions about particular parliamentary protocols. This provided another way of increasing the accessibility of Parliament to the public. A number of the regions sought to inject an educational element; BBC North-West and South-East had items on Private Bill procedure, while a number of programmes explained the detailed provisions of individual pieces of legislation.

The scope of coverage provided by the programmes was impressive. They reported a variety of parliamentary events including Select Committees, and approached them from a distinctly regional perspective. Issues given Select Committee coverage included the Rover sale and RAF low-flying, both significant regional issues. In addition, BBC North covered the Energy Select Committee held in the Civic Centre at Mansfield on 14 March 1990 to get firsthand evidence about the problem of mining subsidence. This provided a further regional aspect to the coverage of Parliament.

Regional programmes made a determined effort to give extensive coverage to backbenchers, who formed 60 per cent of all Members' appearances – a fuller contribution than in any other programme type. It is also interesting to note that backbench 'celebrities' identified as possible subjects for particular television attention (Skinner, Benn, Livingstone, Banks, Lawson, Tebbit, Heath and Heseltine) did not make unduly frequent appearances on regional programmes during the experimental period. That this might have been a deliberate editorial decision seems to be illustrated by the coverage of the parliamentary discussion of mining subsidence during a debate on the Coal Bill. The news programme *Midlands Today* showed actuality of Frank Haynes and *Look North* showed a contribution from Dennis Skinner, but neither Haynes nor Skinner received air time in the relevant weekly programmes. Coverage was instead given to the more restrained contributions of MPs such as Richard Alexander, Harry Barnes, Jim Lester and Alan Meale. Generally the tone of the programmes was serious and informative; very few items were humorous in intent.

The ITV regional programmes

Prior to the cameras' access to the House, most ITV regional companies broadcast a weekly current affairs programme. Many of these programmes were well established – some, like Yorkshire Television's *Calendar Commentary*, having been broadcast for almost twenty years. The remit of these programmes typically extended beyond the treatment of parliamentary issues to embrace more general political concerns. Their focus was predominantly regional and where national issues were discussed they tended to be 'localized' to emphasize the regional dimension. The overwhelming majority of ITV companies incorporated parliamentary materials into these existing programmes, with few scheduling slots to accommodate new programmes. The exceptions to this general rule were Granada, *What the MPs Say* and *Granada This Week*; Tyne Tees, *Points of Order*; Anglia, *Cross Questions*; and Border, *Politically Yours*. Consequently in many areas the same production and presentation teams made relatively few changes to existing parliamentary/current affairs programmes as a result of the availability of pictures from the House.

ITV regional programmes offered a distinctive issue agenda compared to their network colleagues at ITN, and when national issues were discussed regional broadcasters continued to stress the local aspects of the story. Discussion of the community charge, for example, focused on tax levels set by local councils and their effects on local communities. All ITV regional programmes, like their BBC counterparts, tended to employ a wide range of programme formats, including use of actuality clips from the House, film packages as well as interviews with local and national politicians, both inside the studio and in various locations. Indeed, regional programming generally employed a wider range of programme formats than the network programmes and, by a considerable use of 'vox pops', created opportunities for local viewers to voice their concerns about parliamentary issues. Programmes, moreover, tended to feature predominantly MPs local to their broadcast areas. But, despite these similarities, variations were evident in the ways that broadcasters in the different regional companies presented parliamentary issues during the experimental period. Some of this diversity is explored below by examining in more detail the parliamentary programmes broadcast in specific regions.

Border was one of the few ITV regional companies to produce

a new programme as a response to the televising of Parliament. *Politically Yours* contained a fairly high number of actuality clips and focused on parliamentary issues but gave them a regional emphasis. For example, the impact of the Food Bill was considered from the perspective of a local housewife who toured Sainsbury's with Minister David McLean (a Border MP). Border adopted a variety of programme formats, such as studio interviews, film packages and actuality-led stories. In the first edition, for example, there was an filmed item about women in Westminster including an interview with Emma Nicholson MP, a studio interview with an academic about televising the House of Commons, and an 'up the line' interview from London with a newspaper correspondent about the issue of safety in the nuclear industry. Other elements of innovation in programming were evident. One of the editions of *Politically Yours*, for example, fell on St Andrew's Day and the company conducted a poll to establish English attitudes to Scottish separatism. Poll findings were discussed in the programme by members of the Scottish National Party. The programme also routinely featured a quiz for viewers, inviting them to identify local MPs and events from archive footage. The majority of stories, as in other broadcast regions, did feature local MPs discussing parliamentary issues with a regional emphasis. Border's programme, like its BBC counterparts, was specifically designed in response to the availability of the parliamentary signal and was one of the most creative and adventurous of the ITV regional parliamentary programmes.

Central Lobby is one of the long-established ITV weekly current affairs programmes. Transmitted in each of the three Central sub-regional areas, it tended to focus, more than other ITV regions, on general political concerns, which it did not always seek to localize. *Central Lobby* on 14 December 1989, for example, broadcast a very long item of almost 20 minutes' duration, exploring the history of political satire. MPs were not featured in the programme, which focused instead on recent developments and trends in political satire and concluded with excerpts from the company's own extremely successful production, *Spitting Image*. When *Central Lobby* did 'localize' national issues, these were often focused on a broader political, rather than simply parliamentary, agenda. Food irradiation and Nazi war criminals, for example, were discussed without any parliamentary emphasis. When actuality was used, it tended to serve as a 'back-up' or supplement to stories. Coverage of the Trade and Industry Committee questioning Lord Young, for example, was used in an item about the Rover controversy – a distinctly local story.

Granada took the idea of creating a slot to look at the weekly activities of MPs a stage further than most regions. *What the MPs Say* was an example of a new programme which featured a local MP recalling the week's business in the House. This review did not always focus exclusively on the region's MPs and tended to be a light-hearted look at the House's proceedings. On occasion, however, it did not pull its political punches. On 21 February 1990, for example, Frank Field showed Select Committee coverage of Health Minister Kenneth Clarke under intense questioning. In the second parliamentary term, *What the MPs Say* developed into a second new programme, *Granada This Week*, which had a closer affinity to other regional offerings. On 21 January 1990, for example, *Granada This Week* broadcast an item about the poll tax/community charge, focusing on charge levels set by local councils; this included interviews with local MPs and councillors as well as actuality from the House.

Scottish Television incorporated little actuality into its current affairs programme, *Scottish Questions* possibly reflecting the lower profile of specifically Scottish issues at Westminster. Its favoured programme format tended to be the film package. One item, for example, examined issues arising from empty council houses in Edinburgh, followed by an interview with the Lord Provost of Edinburgh. The programme was fairly confrontational in some of its interviews. On 18 January 1990, for example, Donald Dewar was interviewed in an extremely forceful and adversarial manner on the subject of Labour's proposals for an independent Scotland.

In summary, regional parliamentary programming has given extensive and serious coverage to the work of regional MPs and their contributions to both national and local concerns. They have employed a wide range of programme formats, with some proving to be entertaining, informative and creative. Reporting has embraced the full range of the Commons' work, and local backbenchers, rather than frontbench or national politicians, have tended to dominate programming. Television broadcasting from the Commons has, in this respect, been markedly different from its radio predecessor, which prompted little programme innovation among broadcasters, who largely confined themselves to the use of parliamentary materials in existing programming. By contrast, the experiment in televising the Commons has provided a creative stimulus to broadcasters, who have responded by generating a range of innovative programmes. Parliamentary broadcasting has served to underscore the vitality of regional broadcasting and its distinctiveness from the networks.

REGIONAL PARLIAMENTARY BROADCASTING: THE PROGRAMMES IN DETAIL

The House of Commons was presented on regional television in the regular early-evening news and current affairs programmes, as well as in the specialist weekly review programmes often specifically designed to carry parliamentary materials. Several aspects of broadcasters' use of the television signal from the Commons are detailed below. The data are derived from an analysis of 2,442 items of parliamentary reporting, broadcast on satellite and national terrestrial television and on the thirteen BBC and eighteen ITV regional and sub-regional stations, sampled for one day each week across the fifteen-week parliamentary period from 21 November 1989 to 18 March 1990.

First, film of parliamentary events was incorporated into regional news programmes fairly regularly, but was presented extensively in the various parliamentary review programmes. Details of parliamentary reporting in the BBC and ITV regional news services are set out in table 11.1. Two points stand out from the considerable variation in coverage across the BBC and ITV regions. BBC regional services broadcast 1.2 Westminster stories each evening, while ITV companies featured one parliamentary item each evening in their regional news, signalling that news attention to Parliament was routine and high, especially when it is remembered that many of these services are distant from London and lack a specialized presence there. But, perhaps unexpectedly, the geographically more peripheral areas tended to offer their viewers more parliamentary news than stations located close to London. Consequently, among the BBC regions, for example, the greatest amount of attention was paid to Parliament by Scotland, Newcastle, Wales, Leeds, Northern Ireland and the North-West. In ITV the heaviest parliamentary coverage was provided by HTV (Wales), Grampian, Anglia, Ulster and Yorkshire.

Table 11.2 details actuality uses by the individual BBC and ITV services in the regions. Again much variation is evident, with

Table 11.1 Frequency and prominence of parliamentary stories in
regional news programmes

	No. of stories	Average per programme	No. of headlined stories	No. of bulletins (of 15) leading with a parliamentary story
BBC				
Scotland	33	2.2	12	2
North/Newcastle	28	1.9	9	6
Wales	27	1.8	6	1
North/Leeds	23	1.5	10	6
N. Ireland	18	1.2	9	2
North-West	18	1.2	5	2
West	16	1.1	5	4
South-East	16	1.1	4	2
South	14	0.9	3	1
South-West	13	0.9	5	4
East	13	0.8	4	1
Midlands	13	0.8	5	4
E. Midlands	10	0.7	5	3
ITV				
HTV (Wales)	26	1.7	1	–
Grampian	19	1.3	3	–
Anglia	19	1.3	3	1
Ulster	18	1.2	8	6
Yorkshire	16	1.1	9	6
TSW	16	1.1	4	3
Thames	15	1.0	8	4
TVS (Maidstone)	13	0.9	2	1
Scottish	13	0.9	2	2
Central (West)	11	0.7	5	1
Tyne Tees	10	0.7	3	1
Granada	9	0.6	4	2
Central (South)	9	0.6	2	2
Central (East)	9	0.6	5	4
HTV (West)	8	0.5	1	2
Border	7	0.5	4	2
TVS (Southampton)	3	0.2	1	–

the largest number of actuality-based reports in BBC regional
news being presented by Scotland, Leeds and North-West; for
ITV regional news, the largest number of actuality-based stories

was found in the output of Tyne Tees, HTV (Wales), TV South (Maidstone) and Anglia. Incorporation of actuality into BBC regional weekly programme items was greatest for Wales and the North; in ITV weekly programming Granada and Border used Commons actuality most often. Table 11.2 also shows a tendency for BBC programmes to feature actuality more regularly. Over the study period as a whole, BBC news bulletins averaged 18.6 items per programme compared with 13 for their ITV counterparts.

Table 11.2   Use of actuality clips from Parliament in regional programmes

	No. of parl. stories	No. with televised actuality	% with televised actuality	No. of days (out of 15) with actuality-based stories
BBC news				
Scotland	33	8	24	6
North/Newcastle	28	3	11	3
Wales	27	6	22	6
North/Leeds	23	8	35	6
N. Ireland	18	5	28	5
North-West	18	8	44	7
West	16	3	19	3
South-East	16	3	19	3
South	14	7	50	6
South-West	13	5	38	4
East	13	4	31	3
Midlands	13	2	15	2
E. Midlands	10	3	30	2
ITV news				
HTV (Wales)	26	6	23	6
Grampian	19	2	10	2
Anglia	19	6	32	5
Ulster	18	2	11	1
Yorkshire	16	3	19	2
TSW	16	4	25	4
Thames	15	2	13	2
TVS (Maidstone)	13	6	46	5
Scottish	13	2	15	1
Central (West)	11	5	45	4
Tyne Tees	10	7	70	7
Granada	9	2	22	2
Central (South)	9	5	56	5
Central (East)	9	2	22	2
HTV (West)	8	2	25	2
Border	7	4	57	3

TVS (Southampton)	3	–	–
BBC weekly parliamentary			
Wales	25	17	68
North-West	16	11	69
North	14	14	100
West and South	12	11	92
Midlands	12	11	92
East	8	8	100
Scotland	4	4	100
ITV weekly parliamentary			
Granada	16	13	81
HTV (West)	16	8	50
TVS	15	6	40
Border	13	9	69
Anglia	12	–	–
Scottish	11	3	27
Grampian	11	3	27
Yorkshire	11	6	54
Central	9	4	44
TSW	7	1	14
Thames	3	–	–

Second, regional programmes offered viewers a distinctive parliamentary issue agenda compared to their network equivalents. Table 11.3 signals that regional news programmes did not merely ape national news agendas but focused on certain issues and offered viewers a far more extensive treatment and analysis of topics such as transport, housing and the environment than did the national news bulletins.

There was, however, and perhaps unsurprisingly, less coverage of international and foreign and defence issues in the regional compared to national programmes: 17 per cent in national parliamentary news items, 11 per cent in national review programmes, 8 per cent in regional weekly reports and only 4 per cent in items for regional news programmes.

Third, regional programmes featured certain parliamentary events and actors more prominently than other forms of programming. Regional television was quite distinctive for devoting more attention to House debates than any other Commons event. In ITV and BBC regional news programmes, 32 per cent and 36 per cent respectively of broadcast time was devoted to debates; the proportion for all regional parliamentary review programmes was 32 per cent. In national news programmes, however, BBC devoted on average only 18 per cent of coverage to debates, with an equivalent figure of only 22 per cent for ITV news; the Sky News figure was 18 per cent.

Table 11.3   Differences between issue agendas in national and regional news

	National news (%)	Regional news (%)
Northern Ireland	1	5
Health/NHS	2	5
Transport	1	8
Energy	1	3
Environment	1	5
Agriculture	3	5
Law and order	4	6
Housing	1	4
Total	14	41

So far as political actors were concerned, regional television displayed a preference for presenting backbenchers rather than frontbenchers. In BBC and ITV weekly review programmes, backbenchers formed 60 per cent and 50 per cent (averaged across all stations) respectively of all Members featured. In regional news, backbenchers constituted 46 per cent of featured MPs on both BBC and ITV services, whereas figures for the *Nine O'Clock News* (29 per cent) and *News at Ten* (24 per cent) were substantially lower.

Fourth, regional programmes were decidedly different in geographical focus from national programmes. Most stories in the national news bulletins were national in focus (ranging from 78 per cent in *TV-am* to 66 per cent in *Newsnight*), while the national parliamentary review programmes' preoccupation with national events was even more pronounced, averaging 84 per cent of items. But the majority of stories in regional programmes had a local emphasis (see table 11.4). Indeed, in line with a previously noted pattern, inspection of the profiles for the individual regions showed that the most regionally oriented news services came from the more peripheral areas of the country – Northern Ireland, Scotland, Wales, Newcastle upon Tyne and the Midlands in the case of the BBC, and Ulster, Scottish, Grampian, Tyne Tees and HTV (West) in the case of ITV.

Table 11.4   Geographical focus of regional programmes

	BBC regional news (%)	ITV regional news (%)	BBC regional weekly (%)	ITV regional weekly (%)
International	–	–	6	4
National	9	11	22	42
National with some regional	24	29	39	30
Regional with some national	14	6	8	7
Regional	53	54	25	16
Total	100	100	100	99

Fifth, many of the MPs appearing in regional programmes and stories were local and represented constituencies within the transmission areas. In BBC Wales news programmes, for example, all the MPs featured were local in 67 per cent of items and the majority were local in a further 7 per cent of items. In ITV news programmes, Central (West) featured all local MPs in 73 per cent of broadcast items and a majority of local MPs in a further 95 per cent. By this criterion, the most locally oriented of the BBC news services were Wales, Scotland and the West; in ITV they were Central (West), TV South (Maidstone), HTV (Wales) and HTV (West).

Sixth, regional programmes often introduced a different type of non-parliamentary personality or spokesperson into parliamentary stories from those featured in national programmes. Such appearances were not negligible, averaging nearly one per story in both national news bulletins and ITV's weekly regional programmes, and occurring in four out of five stories in BBC regional news and in seven out of ten stories in ITV regional news. Details of the number of such appearances for each of seventeen kinds of non-parliamentary figures in the main programme types are presented in table 11.5. These show a much greater involvement in the regional output (compared with national parliamentary coverage) both of local councillors, officials and other politicians, and of ordinary men and women in the street. This last may reflect local broadcasters' observable tendency to use the 'vox pop' format more than national programme makers.

Table 11.5 Non-parliamentary personalities appearing in parliamentary stories

	National news	National review programmes	Regional news	Regional weekly programmes
TUC	2	–	1	1
CBI	1	–	2	–
Trade union official	26	2	22	8
Industry management	28	8	63	26
City	9	1	–	–
MEP	1	1	3	4
EEC official	–	–	3	–
Foreign politician	18	3	2	3
Media	17	7	11	22
Academic	12	4	12	5
Pressure group	27	4	35	25
Local councillor	10	1	37	26
Local government officer	2	–	21	12
Local politician	9	3	17	21
Civil servant	4	16	6	10
Vox pop	11	1	49	28
Other	35	4	55	27
Total	212	55	339	218

A final but important point about parliamentary broadcasting in the regions concerns the discernible differences between ITV and BBC services. A number of distinctions are evident here.

First, as noted earlier, BBC regional news carried more parliamentary stories than ITV during the experiment. BBC regional stations averaged 18.6 stories over the fifteen-week period compared to 13 for ITV. Similarly, BBC regional news carried more actuality-based items for each station (an average of 5) compared to ITV (average 3.5) and more actuality-based items than ITV in parliamentary review programmes, the average figures being 10.7 and 4.7 respectively.

Second, BBC regional parliamentary programmes and news bulletins featured Select or Standing Committees on more than twice as many occasions as ITV. In news programmes the BBC devoted 14 per cent of parliamentary items to committees, whereas the figure for ITV was 6 per cent; equivalent figures for parliamentary programmes were 9 per cent for the BBC and 4 per cent for ITV. These latter figures are relatively small and it would be wise to interpret them with some caution.

Third, Prime Minister's Question Time featured much more prominently in ITV news and parliamentary review programmes than in their BBC counter parts and accounted for 14 per cent of ITV regional news items and 15 per cent of ITV regional parliamentary items; equivalent figures for BBC news and parliamentary programmes were 8 per cent and 4 per cent respectively. There was also a slight tendency for BBC parliamentary programmes (60 per cent) to devote more attention to backbench Members than their ITV equivalents (50 per cent).

Finally, 46 per cent of ITV regional parliamentary stories were national or international in focus compared to 28 per cent for the BBC, allowing the latter greater opportunities to focus on regionally based stories.

The size of the various ITV companies (distinguished broadly into three groups according to resource levels) had an uncertain impact on parliamentary coverage in the regions. The evidence remains inconclusive, although there were some signs that during the experimental period the smallest companies may have found it difficult to give full attention to Westminster developments with implications for their regions. Border, for example, created a new weekly programme which used a considerable amount of Commons film, but broadcast for only seven weeks because of financial limitations. Two of the other smaller companies, Grampian and TSW, were both infrequent utilizers of Commons actuality in news and weekly parliamentary programmes.

In summary, the interesting and imaginative record of parliamentary broadcasting in the regions has been particularly impressive not only for the amount of coverage but also its distinctiveness. Regional broadcasters have responded creatively to their newly achieved access to the House by generating a range of innovative programmes expressing a wide range of programme formats. Coverage often differed from the national programmes, bringing a regional slant to stories, dealing with distinctive issues, featuring many backbench Members and introducing a broad range of other local voices. This fine record should not be taken for granted, since it was accomplished despite the pressures of many, not least financial, constraints. Regional political broadcasting is not merely alive and well; it appears to be flourishing.

NOTE

1 The Select Committee on the Televising of Proceedings of the House of Commons commissioned the Leeds University Parliamentary Research Group to undertake a study of broadcasters' uses of parliamentary materials across the period of the experiment in public broadcasting of House proceedings. The data for the above chapter are derived from that larger study and consequently acknowledgement of assistance is due to the other members of the group, Jay Blumler, David Mercer and Brian Tutt.

Chapter 12

The implications of parliamentary broadcasting for politicians

Guy Cumberbatch, Brian Brown and Julia Skelton

Austin Mitchell has observed that the televising of the British Parliament 'ends the long struggle to get the Commons on the box. Only a year behind the House's own laggardly timetable, five behind that geriatric ward of the Constitution the Lords, ten behind comparable democracies and twenty-three years after television was originally defeated by one vote' (Mitchell 1990:1). But Mitchell's enthusiastic advocacy of Commons television has been closely matched by other MPs' equally strong feelings against admitting the cameras.

Our evaluation of the experiment in television broadcasting assumed as its starting-point the numerous parliamentary debates on this subject which, by articulating the broad range of Members' own hopes and fears about the likely impact of the cameras on Commons procedures and their own behaviour, offer a useful research agenda of hypotheses. This chapter examines those various hopes and fears.

More than sixty MPs with constituencies in the Central television region were interviewed about their assessments of various facets of the experiment.[1] Interviews focused on two particular concerns. First, what had been the impact of the cameras on MPs' behaviour and, more generally, the 'character' of the Chamber? Second, how successful did Members believe broadcasters had been in presenting an accurate picture of the work of the Commons and in what ways, if any, did they consider this might influence public opinion? Supplementary evidence concerning MPs' responses to broadcasting were derived from interviews with twenty-five political journalists based at the House of Commons, a three-wave survey of public opinion in the Midlands area and an analysis of Hansard for two periods (each of two months' duration) both before and after the experiment.

THE ARRIVAL OF CAMERAS IN THE COMMONS

The intrusiveness of the television equipment

Many Members expressed concern, in advance of the television experiment, that the cameras and other broadcasting equipment might prove intrusive in the parliamentary setting. Only 40 per cent of MPs interviewed, however, recalled any inconvenience arising from the presence of the television equipment at the beginning of the experiment. This figure had fallen to a mere 27 per cent by the end of the experiment, although some members expressed some irritation with the excessive light and heat prompted by the broadcasting equipment.

MPs were also questioned about the presence of cameras in the committee rooms where the arrangements for filming have been very different. In committees, cameras are manually operated and mounted on tripods with other production equipment placed on a mobile trolley. Given the small size of most committee rooms, it is perhaps unsurprising that 71 per cent of MPs indicated varying degrees of annoyance with equipment, with 17 per cent suggesting it was 'very intrusive'. But on occasion the presence of cameras proved a strain for broadcasters as well as Members. David Gilroy Bevan MP remembered a particular session of the Committee on Transport:

> It was extremely hot because of the cameras and suddenly the picture slid down the wall as the cameraman passed out in dead faint. I started resuscitating him and the radio commentary got it all. 'The MP for Birmingham Yardley, Mr Gilroy Bevan, now has the cameraman by the throat.'

The House is undoubtedly less than ideal for the broadcasting enterprise, but the highly valued architectural legacy of the parliamentary buildings suggests that any alterations to facilitate broadcasting would undoubtedly prove contentious. It might also raise questions about how far televising the House should be allowed to transform, rather than simply observe, the work of the Chamber. Nevertheless, MPs' responses suggest the need to explore alternative arrangements in committees now that cameras have become a permanent feature.

The impact of television on Members' appearance

The cameras' potential impact on the appearance of MPs was a focus of considerable media speculation prior to the start of the experiment. The subject prompted humorous reports about MPs attending charm schools to improve their appearance and presentation skills. But the majority of MPs seemed reluctant to admit that they had consciously adapted their appearance for the cameras. A quarter (25 per cent) of MPs admitted adapting their appearance, with less than one in ten (9 per cent) acknowledging a change in their style of dress. A similar proportion (9 per cent) conceded they were more conscious of their posture and body language in the Chamber. The effect of cameras on MPs' appearances was neatly captured by one Member who suggested that, while he was generally 'smarter' and always made sure his 'flies were done up', he felt that overall he was 'not generally bothered'.

But while MPs denied any substantive impact for the cameras on their own appearance they seemed willing to believe that their colleagues had proved more susceptible to such influences. Nearly half (48 per cent) of the Members interviewed believed that other Members had changed their appearance as a consequence of televising proceedings. About a quarter (23 per cent) identified women as a group particularly likely to change their appearance often, suggesting that they now 'wear bright colours'. Since fewer than one in ten MPs were women (and only one in five of our respondents), it seems curious that they should have excited such comment.

The perceptions of political journalists confirmed the marginal changes to personal appearance reported by MPs. Only one in three (36 per cent) of the twenty-five journalists noted any change in Members' appearance. Again, one in three (36 per cent) commented on the 'smarter' appearance of Members generally, while one in five (20 per cent) made specific reference to the darker suits and sudden proliferation of colourful ties worn by Conservative men. One in six journalists (16 per cent) thought that some Members were more careful about their posture and where they positioned themselves within the Chamber; one interviewee echoed the Speaker, Mr Bernard Weatherill's evidence to the Select Committee suggesting that certain MPs now favoured the back benches because of the attractive backdrop afforded by the wooden panelling (HC Select Committee 1990: 265–I, para. 142). Another journalist reported the newly achieved awareness on the part of certain ministers and shadow spokespersons, called to speak from the dispatch box, of the need to try to keep their heads held high to offset the unflattering effects of the steep 38-degree angle at which the cameras are positioned. Another observed that those speaking from the dispatch box were more careful about the positioning of their hands and their papers. A small proportion (8 per cent) made particular reference to Margaret Thatcher's posture and body language when addressing the Chamber. In summary, the evidence suggests that modifications to appearance have been essentially minor.

The impact of television on Members' behaviour

In the numerous debates about televising the Commons, some MPs alleged the cameras would prompt an escalation in various forms of what might be termed 'publicity-seeking behaviour'. John Wakeham, for example, expressed 'the fear that televising our proceedings would inevitably mean a drift away from serious argument towards the sensational' (HC Debs 1988a: col. 210). Another Member claimed, 'the idea that people will not show off in front of the cameras is nonsense' (HC Debs 1988a: col. 203).

When MPs were asked, however, whether they detected a drift away from serious argument in the Chamber, almost nine out of ten (85 per cent) were confident that no such decline in debate had occurred. Of the small number (one in ten) who alleged the cameras had caused such a change, only three Members described the drift as 'large'. When Members were asked if they believed any MPs 'misbehaved' in order to attract the attention of the cameras over two-thirds (71 per cent) responded in the negative. Those MPs (21 per cent) who suggested that the cameras may have had this effect indicated that the criticism applied only to a 'few' of their colleagues.

When asked about any possible 'corrective' effect of the cameras and whether any MPs had stopped 'misbehaving' in the Chamber, the majority (53 per cent) again denied that televising proceedings had influenced behaviour in this way. Nevertheless, more interviewees believed that certain MPs had ceased (30 per cent) than those who thought they had begun (21 per cent) 'misbehaving' as a consequence of television broadcasting. Thus, while a number of Members commented that 'those who misbehaved still do', on balance MPs were more likely to perceive the cameras as having a sobering effect on behaviour.

More than two-thirds (68 per cent) of respondents in the public opinion survey anticipated that televising the House would cause MPs 'to improve their behaviour'. Once the experiment was under way, the figure dropped to 48 per cent, which remains quite high.

To explore MPs' perceptions of more specific forms of disruptive behaviour, such as people 'shaking their fists and shouting slogans' (anticipated by Sir John Stokes; HC Debs 1988a: col. 247), MPs were asked about the frequency of heckling. Just one in seven MPs (14 per cent) in our sample were of the opinion that heckling in the Chamber had increased. A large majority (70 per cent) were confident that the cameras had caused no change in the amount of heckling, while one in twelve (8 per cent) suggested it had actually declined. In evidence to the Select Committee the Speaker, Mr Bernard Weatherill, also indicated that he did not believe that the level of general noise had increased significantly during the course of the experiment. The Select Committee confirmed that the naming of individual Members, expulsion from the Chamber under standing order no. 42 and suspension of the House because of grave disorder each reduced during the period of the experiment compared with previous sessions (HC Select Committee 1990: 265–I, para. 144). When political journalists were asked about perceived changes in Members' behaviour in the Chamber, one in six thought heckling had decreased, while no one suggested that it might have increased.

By contrast, the measures of disruption based on analysis of Hansard reveal results which appear to contradict these perceptions. The proportion of speeches which contained interruptions recorded in Hansard as 'background noise' increased from 15 per cent in the before sample to 22 per cent in the 'after'. Furthermore, the percentage of speeches during which the Speaker intervened was slightly greater in the 'after' sample, rising from 17 to 20 per cent.

MPs were subsequently questioned about specific aspects of Commons procedure. Interestingly, nearly two-thirds (62 per cent) of respondents suggested that the number of interventions during speeches had increased, while none estimated a decrease. This view was echoed by more than one in three (40 per cent) of the political journalists who were interviewed. A slightly smaller proportion of MPs – just under one-half (43 per cent) – suggested that more points of order were raised during debates, and one in five (20 per cent) journalists interviewed expressed a similar view.

In this instance, a comparison with Hansard seems to confirm these impressions. Turning first to interventions during speeches, data indicate that the percentage of speeches during which a Member 'gave way' increased very slightly from 52 per cent before to 57 per cent after the televising. But the number of occasions on which Members refused to give way to their colleagues ('No, I will not give way', etc.) rose by nearly one-third, from 16 per cent before to 21 per cent after the experiment began. It seems that, although MPs demonstrated a greater willingness to concede the floor, this did not match the frequency with which their colleagues sought to intervene. It might be that this pattern was compounded by the fact that Members called to speak were marginally less willing to be displaced from the limelight.

In the case of points of order, the Hansard analysis reveals a particularly striking pattern. During the first 'before' sample (November–December 1988) 44 points of order were raised, with a similar number (39) occurring during the second period (February–March 1989). But these figures exactly doubled to 88 during the first 'after' sample (November–December 1989) and increased sharply to 149 in the final period analysed (February–March 1990). It is also worth noting that increasing proportions of these points of order were disallowed by the Speaker or Deputy Speakers – rising from 27 per cent and 46 per cent in the 'before' samples to as high as 70 per cent in the first 'after' sample, before declining again to 55 per cent in the second. Perhaps most interestingly, the number of points of order raised on Tuesdays and Thursdays (when Prime Minister's Question Time takes place) increased progressively across the four sample periods: from 23 to 30 to 58 and 64 per cent respectively. Given the huge scale of these increases it seems curious that they were evident to only four in ten MPs.

RESPONSES TO TELEVISION COVERAGE

Rules of coverage

Undoubtedly the most controversial aspect of the experiment

in television broadcasting concerned the guidelines established to govern broadcasters' use of materials from the House. The Select Committee's recommended rules of coverage were cautious, although they acknowledged that 'they might need to be modified in the light of experience during the course of the trial period' (HC Select Committee 1989: 141–I, para. 37). They stipulated those aspects of the Chamber which could not be filmed, including the press and public galleries and close-ups of Members' or officers' papers. The 'standard format' for depicting Members who had the floor was specified as 'a head and shoulder shot, *not* a close-up'. Nevertheless wide-angle shots were permitted when different MPs were called to speak or to 'establish the geography of the House for the benefit of the viewers' (ibid., paras 39i–39ii). The committee also instructed that under no circumstances should scenes of disorder be broadcast and emphasized that 'deliberate misconduct designed to secure televised publicity ought not to achieve its aim' (ibid., para. 41). During such incidents, directors should focus on the presiding Speaker or Deputy Speaker. The restrictions on the use of Commons film on television were equally strict: its use in light entertainment programmes, party political broadcasts or any other form of publicity or advertising were all prohibited. These rules were modified a little during the trial period, although it was not always clear to MPs how this had been achieved. Tam Dalyell, for example, asked: 'By what alchemy have the rules suddenly become more and more relaxed?' (HC Debs 1990: col. 1227).

When the Select Committee on Televising of Proceedings of the House of Commons announced the guidelines, many broadcasters and other commentators denounced them as editorially limiting. The BBC Deputy Director-General, John Birt, claimed they would deny viewers a 'full, impartial and meaningful impression of events'. ITN chairperson David Nicholas expressed 'grave reservations', and one media correspondent quoted broadcasters' allegations that coverage 'risks being tedious and unilluminating under such restrictions' (Philip Johnston, *Daily Telegraph*, 18 May 1989).

More than a third (36 per cent) of the MPs interviewed several months into the experiment felt that the guidelines were 'set at the right level'. Slightly more (41 per cent) suggested that the guidelines should be relaxed further.

By comparison, all twenty-five journalists we interviewed felt that the original restrictions on coverage had denied viewers an accurate picture of the Commons. Despite the relaxation of some of the guidelines two months into the experiment, twenty-three journalists still believed they should be relaxed further. Suggested modifications included permitting the use of reaction shots, panning, and the broadcasting of scenes of disorder. One in four journalists (24 per cent) commented that broadcasters should be allowed to show what visitors to the Strangers Gallery and members of the Press Gallery can see.

A similar pattern emerged from respondents in the last of our three telephone surveys several months into the experiment. When asked if they could 'see enough of what is going on' in the House of Commons, just over one-third (37 per cent) replied that they could not, and slightly more (40 per cent) indicated that they had access to 'just about enough'. By contrast, only 4 per cent suggested that they could see 'more than enough'. Perhaps not surprisingly, it seems that dissatisfaction with the rules of coverage was greater among 'outsiders' than among MPs themselves.

MPs were also asked to identify anything that was not currently reported which they would like to see included in transmissions. One-third (35 per cent) were satisfied with the portrayal of the Commons within the limitations imposed. Half (50 per cent) felt there was additional material which should be included in broadcasts and while applauding the existing coverage of Standing and Select committees many argued that additional reporting would be desirable.

MPs were also asked if they thought broadcasters' explanations of parliamentary procedures were adequate. Less than half (44 per cent) were satisfied with the various commentaries. A fifth (21 per cent) of MPs believed that procedures had not been fully or accurately explained and that this constituted a problem, with several reiterating concerns that inadequate explanations could damage constituents' esteem for their MP.

'Newsworthiness' and distortion

The concept of 'newsworthiness' seems to defy any unequivocal definition. Certainly, journalists are obliged to meet tight deadlines, but they tend to develop a finely honed intuition about what constitutes 'good copy', although, perhaps paradoxically, they may not always be able to articulate readily the criteria they use in identifying 'good stories'.

Although it is impossible to define with precision how MPs understood the term, a large majority (80 per cent) agreed that the television companies selected only that material which was considered to be 'newsworthy'; significantly, nearly half of these (47 per cent) saw this as a 'problem'. To explore MPs' responses to broadcasters' treatment of material from the Commons, we asked about some potential adverse effects which had been suggested before the experiment began. Less than half (42 per cent) of the MPs agreed that the television coverage had given a 'distorted' picture of parliamentary procedures. Almost as many (38 per cent), however disagreed with this idea. Nearly two-thirds (62 per cent) of Members disagreed with the suggestion that the coverage had either 'trivialized' or 'damaged the reputation' of the House. But one in eight MPs (12 per cent) did believe that televising proceedings had trivialized their work, and a similar number (14 per cent) felt that it had also damaged their image.

In interviews with political journalists we reminded them that some MPs believed that television was 'only interested in covering the sensational, the bizarre, the self-publicists', and asked them whether they thought that this was fair criticism. Eighty per cent of the journalists defended broadcasters, while the remainder felt there was some substance to these charges. One print journalist said, in broadcasters' defence, 'They have an obligation to be fair, balanced and impartial and they generally stick to it.' Some print journalists had been pleasantly surprised by the television coverage – 'It has not been as superficial as I expected,' said one. Moreover, selecting the 'highlights' was thought to be, as one respondent said, 'the nature of their business'.

When respondents in the public opinion surveys were asked if they thought that 'television is only interested in covering the sensational issues', approximately half of the sample (54 per cent) agreed with this judgement.

Despite the fact that nearly half the MPs felt television had given a distorted picture of the Commons, a significant majority (70 per cent) of MPs interviewed believed that television news coverage had 'improved' since broadcasters achieved access to material from the House.

Perceptions of selection and bias

When Members were asked whether they believed that any channel had selected material from the House in a way which might favour any particular parties or individuals, more than a third of MPs (38 per cent) indicated that they had not seen enough programmes to judge, while the same number (38 per cent) disagreed. Just over one in six (16 per cent) of the Members interviewed believed that the coverage had been either unfavourable or favourable to particular parties. Three Conservative Members believed the Labour Party was favoured in programmes, five members of minority parties believed the two main parties had dominated the coverage, while two Labour members argued that their party had been treated unfavourably.

These results can be compared with the findings from the third public opinion survey, which indicated that more than six in ten (61 per cent) respondents believed that the television news provided a balanced view of political issues. More than a quarter (28 per cent) thought that it was not politically balanced, but only 4 per cent suggested that it was 'always biased'. When respondents were prompted about which channels they perceived to be biased, 20 per cent identified BBC1, 11 per cent ITV, 8 per cent BBC2 and 4 per cent Channel 4. A slightly larger proportion of interviewees saw BBC1 as being 'biased toward the right' rather than 'biased toward the left' (13 per cent compared with 7 per cent). Those who judged ITV to be biased divided equally, with 5 per cent suggesting prejudice in each political direction.

A quarter of respondents (25 per cent) in the public opinion survey felt that a particular party or parties had 'lost or gained' as a result of their television coverage from the House of Commons. Interestingly, nearly one in five people (18 per cent) in the total sample felt that the Conservative Party had 'lost', while just 4 per cent thought they had 'gained'. Conversely, slightly fewer than one in seven (15 per cent) suggested that the Labour Party had 'gained', while only 5 per cent claimed they had 'lost'. These figures need to be understood in the wider climate of political opinion at the time. Thus the proportion of our respondents intending to vote for the Conservatives declined from 33 per cent in October–November 1989 to 22 per cent in February–March 1990. Across the same period, support for the Labour Party had increased from 39 to 42 per cent. These figures reflect closely the findings of other public opinion polls as well as the result of the by-election of March 1990 in Mid-Staffordshire (a constituency located in the sampling area).

Overall there were few complaints from MPs that television coverage favoured one side or the other. Preliminary results from our study of television news and current affairs, however, suggested that proportionately more coverage was devoted to the Conservative Party and its supporters than the Labour Party, both before and after televising. Before the experiment began, 65 per cent of television appearances by MPs were made by Conservatives, 24 per cent by Labour and 11 per cent by members of other political parties. After the experiment had begun, 64 per cent of all appearances were by Conservatives, 28 per cent by Labour and 8 per cent by members of other parties (see chapter 8). The views of MPs and the public, where only a minority charged broadcasters with bias, seemed at first glance to be at odds with these results. There are a number of explanations for this apparent 'mismatch'.

First, the audience, both laypeople and politicians, may not build up an impression of bias or balance simply from the numbers of partisan commentators featured. Second, the varied objectives of the broadcasters, which may often conflict, must be taken into account. The objective of political impartiality, for example, may have conflicted with the desire to reflect reality when the majority of MPs were Conservative. The desire to interrogate legislators in the public interest may conflict with the value of being fair to interviewees. By definition the Government of the day will inevitably dominate the business of the legislature. A simple headcount of people representing the parties of Government and Opposition, moreover, conceals the subtleties of presentation. During the sample period, for example, Anthony Meyer challenged the premiership of Margaret Thatcher – which can hardly have been flattering to the Government.

JUDGEMENTS OF THE EXPERIMENT

Despite some criticism of the television experiment, eight out of ten (80 per cent) MPs in the sample agreed it had been a 'success', while only one in eight gave a definite negative response to this question. Half of those who did not support the televising (5 per cent of the total sample) said that they could not be persuaded to change their minds, since their objections were based on principle. Other dissenters accepted the principle of televising the Commons but would only endorse a channel dedicated to continuous coverage.

Eight out of ten MPs (80 per cent) indicated that they would 'definitely' or 'probably' vote for the cameras to be installed permanently at the end of the experiment. Just under half (45 per cent) of these MPs believed the public have a 'democratic right' to see their Parliament in action, while a further one in eight MPs (12 per cent) believed that the cameras should be there 'on principle'. Frank Dobson, for example, claimed during the February 1988 debate in the Commons:

> In an elected democracy, based on accountability to those who elect us, the principle is clear and has been conceded. Newspapers can report us. Radio broadcasts are made of our proceedings, live or recorded, so there can be no objection in principle to showing us on television.
>
> (HC Debs 1988a: col. 210)

Divisions following the recent parliamentary debates about televising the Commons revealed a growing proportion of support for the televising of proceedings but a lower number of Members voting. For example, the 1988 debate resulted in 318 in favour and 264 against, the 1989 debate resulted in 293 in favour and 69 against and the 1990 debate 131 in favour and 32 against. This last vote, with so few MPs attending, was judged by many observers to reflect Members' view that the experiment had been so successful that the outcome was a foregone conclusion.

When political journalists were asked why they thought televising the Commons was a good idea, almost four out of five (76 per cent) claimed that the public have a democratic right to know and to see how their legislature functions. Two-thirds of respondents in all three public opinion surveys agreed that the televising the Commons was a 'good thing', and 95 per cent agreed that 'the public have a *right* to know what goes on'.

A quarter (24 per cent) of the MPs interviewed had voted in favour of making the cameras permanent, because they believed that televising the Commons gives people a better understanding of politics. One in ten MPs (9 per cent) said that public esteem for the televising had influenced their opinion. By contrast only one in eight journalists (12 per cent) believed that televising proceedings had made the public better informed about politics, although a further two in five (40 per cent) suggested it would have such an effect in the long term. One in five journalists (20 per cent) said it had prompted more public interest in politics, and a further two in five (44 per cent) suggested that it might do so in future.

In the public opinion sample, 61 per cent claimed an interest in 'news about politics', while fewer than one in ten (9 per cent) agreed with the statement 'nobody is interested in watching the House of Commons on television'. But interest in watching Westminster appears to have declined over time. In the last of the three surveys, only one in ten (10 per cent) said they were 'very interested' in watching the coverage from the Commons, whereas 24 per cent had expressed this view before the experiment began. When asked if they made a 'special effort' to watch the Commons, 85 per cent replied in the negative. Respondents in the final survey were asked whether televising the House had increased or decreased their interest in politics; three out of ten (30 per cent) said it had made them more interested – a considerable decline from the results before the experiment began when over a half (51 per cent) of the sample anticipated that it would increase their interest.

Televising the Commons raises much broader issues concerning the accountability of MPs to their public. Some MPs felt that televising proceedings had enhanced public esteem for, and under-standing of, politics, but journalists were less likely to be convinced of this. This perception of the audience seems to reflect a view of the public as a body of people to be informed, educated and inculcated with a greater understanding and respect for MPs' work. This process of 'information giving' is no doubt desirable in a democracy, but it is not a two-way flow. When asked whether MPs were more accountable to their voters as a result of the televised proceedings, one in eight journalists (12 per cent) agreed, while one in four (24 per cent) felt they would become so in the long term. A larger proportion (36 per cent) thought the cameras would not affect MPs' accountability at all, and almost as many (28 per cent) did not know. One in eight (12 per cent) believed the cameras would have no effect on public perceptions of MPs and Parliament.

So far as 'the public' itself is concerned, the proportion of people who agreed that 'because of televising MPs are more accountable to their voters' decreased across the three surveys: 76 per cent anticipated this would occur (in the survey immediately before the experiment began), but several months into the experiment only 59 per cent agreed that this had occurred. Before the experiment

61 per cent of the public interviewed agreed that the televising of the Commons would make their own MP pay 'much more' or 'slightly more' attention to their voters; this figure declined to 44 per cent several months into the experiment. There was a strong prima facie case that televising the House would make MPs more accountable to their voters and pay more attention to them, but the public were less likely to believe this might happen after the House was televised.

Respondents in the public opinion surveys were also asked about parliamentary procedures. A little over half the respondents in the three surveys believed decisions were made in advance rather than as a result of debate. Little change took place after proceedings were televised. Beliefs about heckling, however, changed in an interesting way. The radio coverage of the Commons since 1978 might have been expected to make people aware that debates in the House can become heated and volatile, but the proportion of respondents agreeing that heckling occurs 'every day' in the Commons rose from 64 per cent before the experiment began, to 71 per cent in its early stages, to 78 per cent in the final survey. Changes in attitudes toward heckling were also evident. The majority of interviewees in all three surveys considered heckling to be a 'bad thing' but the percentage of respondents believing it was a 'very bad thing' declined from 50 per cent to 32 per cent from the first survey to the third. This shift is perhaps surprising given the norms of politeness which encourage 'listening' rather than 'interrupting' when people are speaking. Televising, however, seems to have encouraged appreciation of the role of heckling in parliamentary life, as a tool for undermining an opponent's confidence.

In conclusion, it is customary for accounts of the experiment in televising the Commons to claim that it has been a success. Such claims must be examined carefully and be clear concerning the criteria against which success is to be measured. The approval of the public and MPs is one important criterion which seems to have been met. MPs seem generally to be pleased with the televising of the House and their fears about broadcasters' 'distortions', or MPs seeking publicity through outlandish antics, which many expressed in the 1988 and 1989 debates, are not widely perceived to have been realized. Debates about televising the House, moreover, showed a drift in their focus between 1988 and 1990. Initially, the emphasis was on whether the House should be televised at all, whereas later debates became focused on how this should be achieved, whether via the existing television channels or whether through the provision of a dedicated cable or satellite channel offering continuous coverage. It seems that even among the more reluctant MPs there has been a growing acceptance of the House being on television, and a developing interest in how this innovation should proceed.

The success of the experiment may also be judged in terms of the relationship fostered between the public and Parliament. This includes questions about democratic values such as: Are the public better informed? Are MPs more accountable? Is the process of government more sensitive to the public interest? Answers here are less certain, but it seems unlikely that these values have been hindered by the admission of the cameras. However, the extent to which they have been promoted is unclear, and it will only be with hindsight that the effects on the democratic processes can be assessed.

NOTE

1 In addition to the MPs from the Central Television constituencies, two members of the Select Committee on Televising were interviewed and a further thirteen MPs from constituencies adjacent to the Central region. A total of sixty-six MPs were interviewed; fifteen interviews were conducted 'face to face', with the remainder being conducted by telephone.

   The sample was structured to represent advocates and opponents of the experiment in televising the Commons, as well as members of the various political parties. Of MPs interviewed 61 per cent were in favour of the experiment compared to only 55 per cent who voted in support of televising in the House debate of 9 February 1988. Two factors explain this 'over-representation'. First, only a small number of Labour MPs in the sampling region (7 from 37) voted against the experiment, but the need to structure the sample for party balance required the inclusion of a certain number of Labour MPs without regard to their position concerning the televising of the House. Second, only two seats in the region were not held by the Conservative or Labour parties. To guarantee representation of minority-party views, a total of seven interviews were conducted with members of the Liberal Democrats, the Scottish National Party and the Official Unionist Party; all seven favoured the admission of the cameras.

Part V

Assessments: the experience from abroad

Chapter 13

The American experience: C-SPAN and the US Congress

Brian Lamb

Television coverage came as slowly to the United States Congress as it did to the British House of Commons. Thirty years of fits and starts with the medium began on 3 January 1947, when a television camera crew was allowed to broadcast the opening session. 'Aside from telephoto lens dropping from camera to floor of House Friday,' the communications-industry magazine *Broadcasting* reported, 'first telecast of Congress went off as scheduled. No interruption, two cameras used. Lens damaged. No one hurt' (*Broadcasting* 1947: 86). One year later, Claude Pepper, a Florida senator, introduced a bill calling for television coverage of the US Senate and the House of Representatives (*Broadcasting* 1948: 80). Like a similar bill the senator introduced four years before, which would have allowed radio broadcasts, the television bill never made it to the floor for debate, and for the next three decades television coverage of the House and Senate chambers would be limited to the President's annual State of the Union message to a joint session of Congress.

In congressional committees, however, where the topics and the action are often more focused than on the House and Senate floors, television was making inroads. The first known appearance by a television camera in a congressional hearing room was on 30 March 1948, when the Senate Armed Services Committee was considering universal military training (Maloney 1990: 11). The list of committees televised in the early days reflects – and helped shape – the history of the United States in the post-war years: the House Un-American Activities Committee hearings on Communist infiltration of the Government, in 1948; the Special Senate Committee to Investigate Organized Crime in Interstate

Commerce, commonly known as the Kefauver hearings (after their chairman, C. Estes Kefauver, who went on to run for President the next year), in 1951; and hearings chaired by Senator Joseph McCarthy examining Communist infiltration of the US military, in 1954. These hearings and many others in between exhibited for the television audience both good and not-so-good examples of Congress at work. They also served to heighten the debate about broadcast coverage rather than resolve it in television's favour.

Each house of the US Congress is structured in such a way that well-placed opposition can stymie any proposal regardless of how many members support it. In the House, adamant opposition by Speakers Sam Rayburn and John McCormack kept television not only off the House floor but out of committee rooms as well through the 1960s; on the Senate side, filibuster threats by staunch, long-time television opponents like Louisiana Democrat Russell Long discouraged supporters from even making an effort. To its detractors, televised coverage would lead to 'grandstanding' at the expense of real work; they argued that media-smart politicians would exploit their exposure; the public would at best be bored or at worst think that congressmen frittered away their time; and the news media would hone in on the bloopers and blunders – the good 'sound bite' video – rather than substantive issues. 'The Senate is not able to get its work done now,' Senator Long said in 1983. 'It would be even worse if the Senate were on television' (Watson 1983: 1). (These sorts of objections will sound very familiar to those who followed the House of Commons' twenty-year debate over televised sessions.) Even Thomas O'Neill, the House speaker whose support would eventually make television possible, expressed his scepticism of televised sessions by noting: 'We were disgusted with how the major networks covered the Republican and Democratic conventions. If a delegate was picking his nose, that's what you'd see. . . . No wonder so many of us were skittish' (O'Neill 1987: 289).

THE GROWTH OF CABLE TELEVISION

When Congressman O'Neill made that observation, in 1976, a medium that could eventually provide an alternative to the major broadcast networks was already twenty-eight years old. In 1948, in Mahanoy City, Pennsylvania, an entrepreneurial appliance-store owner named John Walson built what is generally believed to be

the first cable television system (Whiteside 1984: 45). Broadcast
signal reception in the mountain town was poor, and in order
to sell television sets Mr Walson erected an antenna on a
nearby mountain and ran a wire from it down to his appliance
store. Sales improved, and for a fee ($100 for installation and
one year's maintainance, $2 a month thereafter) purchasers
of television sets could be hooked into the antenna system.
By mid-year Mr Walson had 727 subscribers, and within the
next couple of years similar services had sprung up in other
communities.

By the 1950s, some owners of what were then called community
antenna systems had begun to experiment with providing their own
programming, and some commercial ventures were being made
into pay-TV, that is subscriber-only access to such programming
as sporting events, cultural activities and movies. Few of these
experiments managed to attract and keep enough customers to
make them profitable, and large-scale ventures with a chance
of success were barraged by a phalanx of broadcasters, theatre
owners and Government regulators. By the 1970s, however,
regulatory sentiment in the United States had begun to turn in
cable's favour, and the industry received a technological boost
in 1975 when the Home Box Office pay-TV service pioneered
the use of communications satellites for nationwide programme
distribution. Pay-TV, thanks to this innovation and the loosened
regulatory strictures, was now free to offer a competitive package of
movies and sports events to cable customers. With an infrastructure
in place, enterprising television programmers soon began to exploit
the opportunities in the new cable market-place (Whiteside 1984:
46).

In 1977 a group of cable operators were considering the idea of
a programming network devoted solely to public affairs. To some
in the industry who favoured the concept, such a network would
help define the infant, still-regulated industry to the politicians and
the regulatory agencies. 'We were getting our teeth kicked down
our throats in Washington because politicians didn't understand
our issues or know who were were,' recalled Ken Gunter, who
ran divisions at a cable company called UA-Columbia (Lamb
1988: 311). The argument wasn't compelling enough initially to
convince the group to finance a new network, but the idea
of such a channel helped break the congressional logjam. In
October of that year, influenced by the fact that cable had the

capacity to provide an unedited, complete telecast of its sessions, as opposed to commercial broadcasters' edited clips, the House of Representatives approved a television resolution by a vote of 342 to 44. It was the culmination of nearly five years of hearings and studies; passage had been immediately preceded by a ninety-day closed-circuit test approved by Speaker O'Neill, who had assumed his office that year.

During debate on the resolution, California Congressman Lionel Van Deerlin, who had a background in broadcasting, summed up the appeal of the new television technology for the House.

> Gavel-to-gavel coverage of the House and Senate proceedings, although they may create no new star competition among the performers, will be available at times and to an extent that no commercial station, certainly no network, could or would provide. It is not within their economic capability. But they might easily be included within the new channel capability of a cable operator.
>
> (Van Deerlin 1977: 35433)

Congressman Van Deerlin also cited the decreasing costs associated with cable–satellite networks ('At today's satellite lease rates,' he estimated, 'the full proceedings of an entire Congress could be transmitted for about $1.5 million a year') and the growing audience that cable was reaching with its alternative programming. He concluded: 'We are, indeed, taking a step toward restoring the government of this land to its own people.'

With the possibility of House telecasts providing a flagship for other public affairs programming, and spurred along by advocates like Mr Gunter of UA-Columbia and his boss Robert Rosencrans, the group of cable operators became convinced of the viability of a cable channel devoted to public affairs and agreed to pool $425,000 for the creation of the Cable–Satellite Public Affairs Network, or C-SPAN.

CONGRESS'S EXPERIENCE WITH TELEVISION

During 1978 and early 1979, C-SPAN put together its operations, a process that included procuring satellite transponder space, constructing a transmitting site and marketing the upcoming service to cable systems. Meanwhile, the House of Representatives worked out the details of its television set-up. The resolution vested authority for devising and implementing the system with the House Speaker, and instructed the Rules Committee to report by February 1978 on alternatives for providing the actual broadcasts. The choices resembled those presented eleven years later to the British House of Commons: a pool arrangement by the commercial broadcast networks; an in-house system totally controlled by the House of Representatives; a set-up operated by the Public Broadcasting System (a non-commercial broadcast network underwritten by Government grants, corporate under-writing and contributions from individuals); or a system run by a commission on broadcasting established by the House. The House eventually decided to follow the Canadian model – the Canadian Parliament first appeared live on Ottawa cable television in 1977, two years ahead of the American Congress – and established an in-house system over which it could retain editorial and technical control. Instructions to the technicians regarding what could and could not be televised were – and still are – strict: cameras must focus on the member or members speaking; prohibited are reaction shots, wide shots of the entire Chamber (this sanction was later modified to allow wide shots during roll-call votes and during 'special order' speeches delivered after the conclusion of legislative business) and shots of the public or press galleries. The coverage is available to all members of the electronic media that are accredited to the House Radio and Television Correspondents' Galleries.

On 19 March 1979, the day the signal became available to the media, the House of Representatives was first shown live on television. The three US commercial networks used clips on their nightly news programmes, and the Public Broadcasting System telecast the first day in its entirety. All planned to return when events warranted, but none had any plans for a long-term commitment to live coverage. News reports treated the début as an amusing anomaly. The *Wall Street Journal* closed its story by quoting an aide to a congressional committee: 'Look at them, all dressed up in their three-piece suits. It looks like a giant ad for Brooks Brothers. If it goes anywhere, it's the end of civilization as we have known it' (Perry 1979: 16). C-SPAN also telecast the first day live – to a potential audience of about 3.5 million households via 170 cable systems. The network had made a commitment to its affiliates to cover the House session on that day and all subsequent days. Initially, the prevailing attitude on Capitol Hill and in the media as to how many people would watch the fledgling service was sceptical, and perhaps best summed up by a PBS executive: 'I can't imagine how many people would sit down in front of their TV sets and tune in cable to watch it. It really is excruciatingly dull' (Perry 1979: 16).

Despite early sceptics, cable-system carriage of C-SPAN grew rapidly as existing systems added the service and new systems were built. And after one year of telecasts, in a survey conducted by political scientist Michael Robinson, members of the House expressed satisfaction with the arrangement, although the proportion of those who said they were 'delighted' with the system was higher among new members of Congress than more senior members (Robinson 1981: 68). A survey of members conducted in December 1979 by the Congressional Research Service looked at the impact of televising sessions upon the behaviour of members. It found that nearly a quarter of the membership was spending less time on the floor since the introduction of televised debate, presumably because they could now watch from their offices; the same number reported that they and their staffs were gaining more familiarity with parliamentary procedures because of TV coverage. The most dramatic change in activity found in the study was a sharp increase in one-minute speeches, which are short remarks delivered at the beginning of each day. In September 1978, for example, there were 88 one-minute speeches delivered during the eighteen days in session; in September 1979 there were still eighteen days of meetings but the number of one-minute speeches had climbed to 153 (Davidson 1981: 4–11). (Eighty-eight per cent claimed that they had delivered no floor speeches since television was introduced that they would not have delivered otherwise, yet three-quarters of the members felt that their colleagues were speaking more frequently.) The report concluded that after one year with the system 'televised sessions seem to be firmly established in the House', primarily because they offered such a practical advantage to members wanting to follow House business without going down to the Chamber. It continued: 'The originally predicted or feared effects – "grandstanding" and the like – have attracted much comment from members, but the overall impact on the House does not seem significant.' The report closed with the caveat that the reach of House television was still narrow, and that as cable television expands and the proceedings are made available to more and more homes, it is entirely possible that public interest and feedback will be far more intense than they have been thus far. This could affect the conduct of House business in ways that we cannot possibly foresee.

(Davidson 1981: 19)

Over the course of the next decade there was only one episode in which television coverage affected the conduct of House business in a major way. In 1984 a group of Republican congressmen, calling themselves the Conservative Opportunity Society (COS), became frustrated that they could not, as members of the minority party in the House, bring issues in their legislative agenda to the floor for debate. They launched a concerted effort to take their case to Congress and the American people. The linchpin of their campaign was the use of the close-of-business 'special orders' period. Although remarks made during the period are not part of official business – that concludes before special orders begin – they are still televised; hence, viewers at home were listening even if fellow House members were not. (The number of households that could watch C-SPAN had reached 17 million by spring 1984, but the network has never subscribed to a ratings service to measure how many people are watching at a given time. Georgia Congressman Newt Gingrich, a COS leader, estimated then that at any given time 200,000 people were watching House telecasts on C-SPAN.) House Democrats began to feel unsettled by the partisan content of the speeches; in particular, they complained to Speaker O'Neill that in at least one instance the Republicans, taking advantage of the rule requiring that the cameras focus only on the person speaking, had deliberately given the impression that the House Chamber was full and that, indeed, Democrats were present but not inclined to reply.

In May 1984, a month after he said in an interview that House television 'is here to stay now. . . . There'd be a hue and cry if you were to turn it off' (O'Neill 1984), Speaker O'Neill responded to the entreaties of his party members by instructing the House television technicians to take wide shots of the Chamber during special orders. A firestorm of partisan invective ensued, fuelled no doubt by the fact that the Speaker had the rules change executed not only without notice, but right in the middle of a special orders speech by a Republican congressman. The Speaker even took to the floor to defend his move, and his remarks were so strong that the parliamentarian ordered a portion of them stricken from the record. When the smoke cleared, the policy of panning the Chamber during special orders remained intact, and, even though the presence of television cameras had precipitated a nationally publicized partisan war, the episode did not threaten their continued use.

In a sense, the virtues of House television were confirmed once and for all two years later when the US Senate, where just one determined opponent could have prevented it, allowed television coverage of its proceedings. A six-year debate in the Senate, which mirrored many of the earlier concerns of the House, was brought to a close when the television measure won the support of the then Senate minority leader Robert Byrd. Senator Byrd, who had previously opposed televised Senate sessions, managed to convince his colleagues that lack of television exposure was causing Congress's Upper Chamber to lose ground in the public perception (Fritz 1985: 10). The première of Senate television in June 1986 was accommodated by C-SPAN II, a companion network to C-SPAN that was initially launched to 5 million households.

C-SPAN PROGRAMMING

Eleven years after its first signal went out over the satellite, C-SPAN is still referred to by most people in one way or another as the channel that televises Congress, even though just ten months after its début it had added other programmes to its schedule. The first non-congressional programme, and the first programme that C-SPAN produced itself, was a seminar of the Close Up Foundation, an educational organization that brings high school students to Washington for a firsthand look at the federal government. Luncheon speeches and question-and-answer sessions with reporters, sponsored by Washington's National Press Club, joined the schedule in 1980; long-form footage of presidential election campaign events was aired in the fall of that year, and the coverage was supplemented with what were probably television's first daily nationwide viewer phone-in programmes. Coverage of congressional hearings was inaugurated in January 1981 with Senate confirmations of President Ronald Reagan's new cabinet. More programming 'firsts' followed – and found room on the schedule when C-SPAN began telecasting twenty-four hours a day in September 1982: coverage of the annual meetings of

America's governors and mayors, interview programmes, daily phone-in programmes with journalists, national political party conventions, and special events like protest marches and rallies in the US capital.

Some programmes naturally draw more national attention than others. The network seems to find whole new audiences when it airs presidential election events. (Campaign staffs have said that they find such coverage especially useful to their jobs.) Complete, uninterrupted coverage of hearings – televised in prime viewing hours – into the Iran–Contra affair was another such event. In November 1989, C-SPAN's telecasts of the House of Commons became one of those programmes that stands out for regular viewers and attracts new ones. To a nation that was once taken aback when TV correspondent Dan Rather made a flip remark to President Richard Nixon, the sight of a country's pre-eminent politician undergoing a ritual of booing, laughter and invective – for a regularly scheduled 15 minutes twice a week – is at first a shock and then a learning experience that invites comparison with our own system. ('All we have are predictable presidential news conferences', said a high school teacher. 'I like the fact that the head of government has to come in and take his lumps.')

The House of Commons is not the only British programming available to the C-SPAN audience. The state opening of Parliament has become an annual feature. And, thus far, the network has travelled to London twice for week-long telecasts about British government and society. Finally, the BBC World Service is a twenty-four-hour-a-day feature of a new C-SPAN offering called C-SPAN Audio 2. Along with C-SPAN Audio 1, which transmits a variety of international short-wave services along with live congressional hearings that cannot be fitted into the television networks' schedules, the audio services are available to cable systems for carriage on their cable–FM radio hook-ups or to accompany their alpha-numeric channels.

THE C-SPAN AUDIENCE

Who is watching – or listening – to the four C-SPAN offerings? Most broadcast and cable networks, seeking advertising support, need the answer to that question, updated continually in terms of ratings points and audience share. The cable industry, however, created C-SPAN as a public service without regard to the numbers. Indeed, as Congressman Van Deerlin pointed out in the 1977 television debate, cable's channel capacity allowed such a service to be created without the numbers-driven decision-making that hems in commercial broadcasters. Yet even the most altruistic business executive would want some indication that his philanthropic enterprise was getting some use, and surveys show that it is, and that the number of households tuning in is growing. A study from November 1988 estimated from polling that 32 million adults in 21 million households tuned in to C-SPAN on a regular basis (Clancey 1988: 1); the figure for households was nearly three times that found in a 1984 survey (Robinson and Clancey 1985: 1), and the increase suggested that politically minded viewers 'found' C-SPAN during the 1988 presidential race. Future studies will determine whether the number has continued to grow.

If people are watching, has their viewing had an effect on the political process? Since C-SPAN was created there has been no massive increase in voter turnout (it has continued to decline), and no propensity among those who do vote to 'throw the rascals out' or to re-elect them at higher rates (98 per cent of congressmen who seek re-election still win it). The impact of C-SPAN has not been a grand rewriting of the American political tradition; rather, it is a collection of short stories. Here are a few.

Richard Armey was a tenured economics professor at North Texas State University when he began to watch sessions of the House on C-SPAN. 'I began to feel a more intimate relationship to the process,' he says. 'I began to feel that these folks weren't bigger than life and that, in fact, most of them weren't bigger than me.' One day it came to him: 'I finally just said, the job's not being done right. I need to go do it myself.' In 1983 Professor Armey began his challenge to the incumbent as an underdog, but won in November 1984 by a narrow margin and has been re-elected every two years since. 'C-SPAN changed my life,' he admits (Lamb 1988: 5–7).

Newt Gingrich is another congressman who credits C-SPAN with a change in his career course. A leader of the House Republicans' COS group, Congressman Gingrich in 1989 was elected by his party colleagues to the post of Republican whip – the second-highest position in the minority leadership. He says that the high profile he attained in his use of television to purvey his party's message helped him win the job. Yet he feels that televised sessions of the House provide more than just a conduit for members to reach a wide audience; they create a massive, electronic, participatory town hall: 'C-SPAN has created the opportunity for an audience to participate in a serious and systematic way in the House of Representatives,' he says. 'It allows, for those who care, the opportunity to see, live and unedited, the process of self-government in an extraordinarily complex society' (Lamb 1988: 117–20).

Jane White, a housewife in Scottsdale, Arizona, watched C-SPAN while she sewed, and she soon came to realize that 'all those years of watching C-SPAN was like being in a classroom.' Her studies came in handy when she and other residents of her neighbourhood reached a point of frustration over an on-again, off-again state highway project through their community. She watched C-SPAN telecasts of campaign management seminars and honed her oratorical skills by observing members of Congress; her chief lesson was that brevity is the soul of persuasion. 'When I'm making a speech to the City Council, I don't want to drone on and on,' she says. 'I found out the best way was to make it snappy' (Lamb 1988: 350–2).

In 1986 Michael Herschede, a Vietnam War veteran, had a job working the late-night shift high on a West Virginia mountain, where he monitored satellite feeds for a local TV station. One evening he watched a C-SPAN overnight replay of a congressional hearing on the possibility of live prisoners of war still being held in South-East Asia. He began to read voraciously on the topic and to watch and tape other hearings. When he learned that a fellow veteran had begun a march across America to publicize the plight of prisoners of war and missing in action, Mr Herschede joined him in Cincinnati, Ohio, and headed west with him along US Route 50 across the continent to Los Angeles, California. They gave interviews to 173 newspapers, thirty-five radio stations and twenty TV stations. 'C-SPAN changed my life,' he asserts. 'I can safely say that along US 50 there are many people whose lives have been changed because of C-SPAN' (Herschede 1989).

Father John Putka, who taught at a Midwest Catholic high school, used C-SPAN's telecasts of House floor sessions in his political theory class. One group of students was so taken with the special orders concept (and influenced by Father Putka's ability to convey enthusiasm for politics and law-making) that they introduced the legislative procedure into their student government classes. 'Several of my students have become "C-SPAN junkies",' he wrote in a letter to C-SPAN:

> Many of them have become fascinated by the use of special orders to call attention to specific issues. Congressman Newt Gingrich, Vin Weber, Bob Walker, and others are well-known to the students, and in discussions they refer to what 'Newt' or 'Bob' or 'Vin' had to say on the House floor with so casual a reference that you would think that they were referring to mutual friends or someone in school.
>
> (Lamb 1988: 285–8)

Richard Cohen is a congressional correspondent for the *National Journal*, a weekly magazine that boasts a small but high-powered Washington readership. Like many reporters who have earned their bylines trudging the long corridors of the Capitol, Mr Cohen has discovered the convenience of armchair observation. He told his readers in a column, 'Through the magic of coaxial cable, I may never again enter the galleries to watch the House or Senate. In the comfort of my suburban living room, I can watch government in action at any hour of the day.' He believes he is not alone in enjoying the benefits of easy access to Congress. 'People now have a better understanding of what's going on. They may not like it, but the point is that they're closer to it, and that's good' (Lamb 1988: 66–8).

Tony Maidenberg, former mayor of Marion, Indiana, and now a state senator, devoutly believes in the virtue of political participation. 'If we want to preserve it, we sure as heck better participate in it,' he admonishes, and he encourages students to visit city council meetings, attend the state legislature, and 'tune in to C-SPAN, because whatever people are concerned about is eventually going to show up somewhere on C-SPAN'. The lessons to be learned are not only political – they can be personal as well: 'I guess C-SPAN has shown that the bottom line, whether you are talking about the Marion City Council or the Senate Judiciary Committee, is by and large men and women trying to do a good job' (Lamb 1988: 244–7).

Whether congressmen like Richard Armey and Newt Gingrich, housewives and blue-collar workers turned political activists like Jane White and Michael Herschede, teachers like John Putka, reporters like Richard Cohen and local politicians like Tony Maidenberg are novel exceptions or the tip of an iceberg is for political scientists to determine. Nevertheless, they are members of a network of homes that on 18 June 1990 passed the 50 million mark, making C-SPAN the United States' seventh-largest basic cable programming network.

Chapter 14

Televising the Bundestag

Heribert Schatz

If the attitude of the British Parliament towards televising its proceedings can be considered 'reluctant' (Franklin 1989: 1), the attitude of the German Bundestag can perhaps best be described as 'welcoming'; indeed, the term 'open house' would not exaggerate current arrangements for television broadcasting. Bundestag plenary sessions are televised live or as edited highlights in news programmes, and many of the more important sessions of committees, as well as meetings of parliamentary parties, are also reported. Television crews can film in the lobby, in the offices of the House and its Members, or in the environs of the parliamentary buildings. During 1990 this openness extended to the Volkskammer, the Parliament of the former German Democratic Republic. Its sessions were covered by West German as well as GDR television until October 1990. In this way, television coverage played a significant role in the process of German reunification.

THE HISTORICAL DEVELOPMENT OF TELEVISING THE BUNDESTAG

The first television broadcast from the Bundestag was on 6 October 1953, some thirty-six years before television coverage of the House of Commons. The Bundestag's decision to admit the new medium of television, to complement existing press and radio coverage of its proceedings, seemed curious at first glance, given there were fewer than 100,000 television sets in the Federal Republic at that time.

This policy of openness towards television reflected the fragile and fledgling democracy existing in West Germany after the collapse of the Nazi regime in 1945. The Allied powers, as well as the growing democratic forces in the three western occupation zones, had agreed that the need to re-educate the German people in the fundamental requirements of a democratic way of life was an urgent task. But democratic institutions had to be reconstructed from scratch. Political parties had to be re-established, and, above all, politicians had to try to regain both the confidence and the esteem of the people. The media faced similar difficulties, since radio and newspapers had been compromised in public perceptions by Hitler's *Gleichschaltung* (normally translated as 'co-ordination'; i.e. Nazi totalitarian control). Consequently Parliament and the media shared a common basic interest. Both needed to create a new legitimacy by proving their democratic commitments and their effectiveness within the new institutional framework of political democracy. In the words of the then Speaker of the Bundestag (Bundestagspräsident), it was necessary to develop a 'healthy national feeling and a democratic consciousness'. Parliament, as the central aspect of the new democratic state, must not suffer the same lack of democratic mass support which led eventually to the collapse of the Weimar Republic; the Bundestag must be made popular from the outset (Wendt 1979).

This belief in the need to 'popularize' the Bundestag was shared by most Members of the House, despite some opposition from the parliamentary parties and the all-party Parliamentary Advisory Committee (Ältestenrat – a committee of senior parliamentarians drawn from all parties). Consequently, thirty important plenary sessions were transmitted live between 1953 and 1955, including the four-day debate on the European Defence Community in February 1955. From the beginning, the coverage was fairly extensive, with nearly forty hours' live reporting supplemented by commentary and interviews from the Bundestag. In the following years live coverage of important occasions became commonplace. In July 1956, for example, there was more than twelve hours' reporting of the debate on compulsory military service, in May 1957 there was nine hours' coverage of the debate on atomic legislation, and in 1957 more than eight hours' live debate on Chancellor Adenauer's governmental declaration.

This first phase of televising the Bundestag, characterized by extensive coverage, ended abruptly in March 1957 when the Speaker, Gerstenmeier, in consultation with the Ältestenrat, stopped live coverage of the plenary sessions for the remainder of the legislative period. There were a number of reasons underlying the decision. There had been disagreements between the various political parties concerning the order and timing of parliamentary speeches during what were known to be 'peak viewing' times. Further problems arose from the indiscretion of some camera close-ups which generated complaints from Members that they had been filmed while reading a newspaper, yawning or eating. Even the contents of one female Member of Parliament's handbag were shown in close-up on the screen. The party leaders, moreover, with the support of the Speaker, complained about panning shots which revealed rows of empty seats; they suggested 'the dignity of the House' was being threatened by such camera shots.

After this decision few live broadcasts were permitted, with coverage being restricted to edited recordings (exceptional matters such as the governmental declaration by the Federal Chancellor in the newly elected third Bundestag in November 1957 were broadcast live, as noted above). These restrictions, which remained in force until the end of 1964, reflected the supremacy of the Parliament's institutional interest, strongly articulated by Gerstenmeier, over the particular interests of political parties and some of the Members of Parliament. The restrictions were eventually lifted on 11 January 1965, when free access to the plenary sessions was once again granted to television broadcasters. The Board of Chief Whips, however, retains a veto power but has never deployed it (Deutscher Bundestag 1983: 1034).

The first nationwide television programme was broadcast by ARD (the Arbeitsgemeinschaft der öffentlich-rechtlichen Rundfunkanstalten Deutschlands). In 1963 the second German television channel, ZDF (Zweites Deutsches Fernsehen), broadcast its first live coverage from the Bundestag. The new station wished to extend political broadcasting and began consultations with the Speaker and the Board of Chief Whips. As a consequence the plenary hall was equipped with additional lighting and fixed places for three cameras. ARD and ZDF both established their own television studios in Bonn and agreed to co-operate in the enterprise of televising the Bundestag. If one station was covering the sessions live from the Bundestag, the other would restrict itself to edited inserts for the evening newscasts; the costs of the technical equipment necessary to broadcast from the House were shared.

The first major event reported after the readmission of television cameras was the debate on Chancellor Erhard's governmental declaration on 7 December 1965. But within a year there were further difficulties concerning live coverage from the plenum.

The Speaker of the Bundestag received more than 500 letters from viewers complaining about the allegedly bad behaviour of Members of Parliament during live coverage of the debate on the governmental declaration of Kiesinger, who had been elected as Erhard's successor to be Chancellor of the coalition of CDU/CSU and SPD on 1 December 1966. Gerstenmeier considered again the possibility of restricting television broadcasting from the Chamber but interestingly on this occasion was unable to assert himself over the various parliamentary groups. The failure was strategic. The new governmental coalition was uncertain of its popularity and could not afford to set aside any opportunity for publicity. With hindsight, these events can be considered a moment of considerable historical importance, even a turning-point, at which the communication interests of political parties began to predominate over the collective interest of the Bundestag as a legislature.

Subsequently, since 1979 in colour, television has covered live on average 20 per cent of each of the 200 to 250 plenary sessions per legislature (Barth 1985). Special occasions have tended to attract even more extensive coverage. ARD and ZDF, for example, broadcast forty-five hours' live coverage from the hearings relating to the emergency laws at the end of 1967. The most intensive television coverage prompted by any single event was the constructive vote of no confidence against Chancellor Brandt and the passing of the *Ostverträge* during April and May 1972. Across a three-week period there was 'saturation coverage', with live reporting from the Bundestag and the lobby, broadcasts from the rooms of the various parliamentary parties, the corridors, the lifts and the restaurants of the Bundestag. As well as ARD and ZDF's permanently installed cameras, eight additional ARD camera teams with mobile ENG cameras were working in the House. Other media were represented extensively. In addition to the 350 members of the Federal News Conference (Bundespressekonferenz) and the 250 foreign correspondents accredited to Bonn, some 300 guest journalists from home and overseas arrived to report the story. Approximately 100 photographers and camera crews from twenty-four television stations and three newsreels crowded into the press tribune, the lobby and the adjoining rooms.

This massive media attention was broadly welcomed by Members of Parliament as well as the general public. But it prompted serious discussions in the press coupled with allegations that television's role in reporting Parliament had become exaggerated and might result in an impoverishment of political debate where the lowest common denominator of response might prevail (Gaus 1972). The debate, however, seems to have had little influence on parties' attitudes towards televising Bundestag proceedings. All important plenary sessions are covered by television, either live (mostly broadcast during the morning from 9 a.m. to 1 p.m.) or as inserts in the public television news. Table 14.1 shows the coverage during the last two legislatures.

Table 14.1   Coverage of the Bundestag's plenary sessions on public television[1] (tenth and eleventh legislatures)

Year	Length of coverage (hours and minutes)			Topics receiving most lengthy coverage	Length of topic coverage
	ARD	ZDF	Total		(hours and minutes)
1983	49.58	41.54	91.52	'Double decision' of NATO	10.20
1984	48.05	35.28	83.33	1st reading of Budget 1985	8.00
1985	58.00	26.10	84.10	Governmental declaration and debate	5.25
1986	46.45	39.32	86.17	1st reading of Budget 1987	7.34
1987	38.33	44.14	82.47	2nd reading of Budget 1988	6.16
1988	35.47	44.30	80.17	Election of the Speaker; 2nd reading of the Health Reform Law	6.36
1989	40.48	50.29	91.17	Governmental declaration and debate	5.55
1990[2]	22.50	26.08	48.58	Governmental declaration and debate on German unification	15.46

Source: Pressezentrum des Deutschen Bundestages (unpublished survey).

Notes: [1] On a seven-year average ARD has broadcast about 53 per cent, ZDF about 47 per cent of the total coverage.
[2] Last session: 23 August 1990. ARD figures include 11 hours 36 minutes of coverage by the 3rd programme of ARD stations.

The commercial programmes of RTL Plus and SAT1 which can now be received in many parts of Germany carry reports of the sessions of the Bundestag in their news programmes but without any live coverage. The two nationwide public TV channels, however, report the plenary sessions of the Bundesrat, the second chamber of the German Parliament, and of the Landtage, the Parliaments of the Länder. Such coverage is quite rare and tends to reflect only very important occasions; the most recent coverage of a Bundesrat session, for example, concerned a debate on electoral law and the process of German unification.

RULES OF COVERAGE

The general rules governing television's admission to the Bundestag in 1953 gave no detailed consideration to questions concerning how the organization of television coverage might be achieved. Issues such as the degree of editorial control to be exercised by the broadcasters were left undecided. Following a brief debate in the Parliamentary Advisory Committee, the various parties consented to accept the rules that had been recently agreed to govern radio broadcasting. This new agreement had in turn been prompted by complaints from the Members of the House, particularly members of the CDU/CSU during the first legislature (1949–53). They criticized broadcasters' editing of recordings of plenary sessions on a number of grounds, alleging arbitrary editing of their speeches and a lack of balance in reporting the contributions of different parties in the House.

In response to the growing criticisms, the Superintendent of the Norddeutsche Rundfunk decided to cancel the transmission of a weekly review of the parliamentary proceedings (*Die Woche im Parlement*). This caused new protests by the parties and some journalists. In subsequent discussion the programme directors and editors of the broadcasting companies and the Parliamentary Advisory Committee agreed a solution which had implications for the forthcoming television coverage: it was decided to leave decisions concerning what should be reported to the broadcasters. In return, broadcasters committed themselves to be fair, objective and balanced in their coverage of the proceedings. The consensus was short-lived, as the terms 'fair', 'objective' and 'balance' soon came to be interpreted differently. The new medium of television was eager to demonstrate its technical capacities to the public using close-up shots to reveal the Chamber to a degree of intimacy which offended Members of the House. Complaints about television cameras' lack of discretion were commonplace.

Since these initial difficulties, broadcasters and the Bundestag seem to have agreed a *modus operandi*: 'fairness' of television coverage now requires observance of the 'rules of journalistic decency' which have resulted from the mutual co-operation of politicians and broadcasters over a number of years. In practice these rules require that Members of Parliament (as well as members of the Federal Government and of the Bundesrat) may not be filmed in 'private' acts such as eating, drinking, reading newspapers, yawning or cosmetic activities like combing their hair, powdering their noses or using a lipstick. There is a light signal on the wall of the plenary hall to warn members when television coverage is about to start. The camera is allowed to show only what is relevant to proceedings. Consequently cameras may, for example, show Members of the House who are yawning or empty benches only if they help to demonstrate that a particular speech is boring. Similarly the hands of the Federal Chancellor tearing slips of paper into pieces may signal high tension in a fierce cross-party dispute, while a close-up of a Member's newspaper may be used to contrast its headlines with the content of an ongoing speech. Reaction shots are also permitted, although until recently possibilities for a full range of reaction shots were limited by the absence of cameras behind the Speaker's podium. It is a substantially more liberal regime of broadcasting guidelines than currently prevails in the British House of Commons. Even 'live' interviews are not what they seem. They are usually conducted only after a 'dress rehearsal' in which the questions for the interview are talked through. Journalists defend this practice by claiming that the live interview must work well at the first attempt (Reumann 1980).

A consensus between broadcasters and politicians concerning the rules of fairness was achieved tolerably easily, but attempts to define 'objective' and 'balanced' coverage proved more contentious. Agreement on this latter question finally emerged from a process of mutual adaptation by the political parties and public television which had already begun towards the end of the 1950s. A brief digression is necessary to explain this process. After the collapse of the Hitler regime, the Allied powers discussed the reshaping of the broadcasting system in the western zone. Eventually they agreed on a British proposal which offered the BBC as a possible model for public service broadcasting that might guarantee the desired distance between state and media. Broadcasting was, moreover, to be organized in a federal system, with six broadcasting companies being founded initially, some of them even prior to the establishment of the new *Grundgesetz* (Basic Law or 1949 constitution). They joined to form the Arbeitsgemein-schaft der öffentlich-rechtlichen Rundfunkanstalten Deutschlands (ARD), which, following the split of the North-West German Broadcasting Company (NWDR) into two autonomous institutions (NDR and WDR) and the establishment of the Sender Freies Berlin and the Saarländishe Rundfunk, consisted of nine members. In 1960 the Deutsche Welle and the Deutschlandfunk were added as federal broadcasting stations and in 1961 the second German television station (ZDF) was founded by treaty between the Länder. Broadcasting laws and elaborate guidelines defined the democratic tasks of the broadcasting stations. Pluralistic super-visory boards (Fernsehrat (ZDF) resp. Rundfunkräte) monitored broadcasters' observance of guidelines and guaranteed autonomy of programme makers from commercial, political and ideological influences. But the boards soon ran into difficulties. The growth of television during the 1950s was matched only by politicians' enthusiasm to try to control this new medium, which they believed possessed substantial potential for persuasion of audiences. Politi-cal parties tried to legitimate their efforts to influence television by reference to the Basic Law of 1949, especially article 21. They argued that media should be used not only for conveying neutral political information but for a range of public relations activities by political parties. Some politicians wanted to bring television wholly under their control. In 1961 Adenauer tried to establish 'German Television Limited' but the Federal Constitutional Court declared the company unconstitutional because broadcasting was judged to be within the jurisdiction of the Länder (the 'regions' or 'states') but not the federal state. The organizational structure proposed, moreover, could not guarantee the necessary autonomy from the Government.

After this defeat, the CDU/CSU, quickly followed by the other parties, began to pursue an ill-disguised policy of reducing the independence of the public broadcasting network. This was not, of course, an official policy or a programmatic commitment so much as what might be termed 'politicization by stealth'. The party politization of the supervisory boards of television and the political penetration of the companies were the starting points for this policy. It soon became commonplace for Directors-General of television stations to be appointed by the political parties in proportion to their parliamentary strength. The fixing of radio and television licence fees, combined with limitations on advertising time, were used by political parties as levers that could be used to apply pressure on broadcasting companies. Detailed observational studies of television programmes conducted by research teams commissioned by the parties provided ammunition for attacks on 'critical' editors and journalists. Broadcasters who 'deviated' from the norms of 'expected political behaviour' frequently found themselves the subject of intense political pressure which typically resulted in the 'dissidents' either giving up their opposition or leaving their job.

These political pressures on broadcasters continued into the 1980s. The CDU/CSU crowned its media policy when it was finally successful in opening the public broadcasting system to commercial influences. The recent development of this duopolistic broadcasting system was facilitated by the Federal Constitutional Court in 1981 when it acknowledged for the first time that the commercial stations and programmes were compatible with the Basic Law. A subsequent ruling in November 1986 opened the way for the establishment of an explicitly 'dual' broadcasting system. The overt purpose of such a scheme was to increase the range and plurality of programmes. The real, if covert, purpose of the CDU/CSU was to place new pressures on public television in the hope that they would suppress any inclinations to be critical of style or content of policy, as well as the qualities of the parties' senior politicians.

The substantive and important consequence of this protracted process of 'domestication' of broadcasters is that public television in Germany has lost its aggressiveness or any sense of being a fourth estate. Investigative political journalism and critical coverage of domestic policy is restricted to the press (*Der Spiegel* or *Stern*); it has no place in television. The *Bonn Cartoon* of WDR is harmless compared to Central Television's *Spitting Image*. Critics of television use the pejorative terms 'court reports' (*Hofberichterstattung*) or 'proclamation journalism' (*Verlautbarungsjournalismus*) to describe the rather 'prudent' style of journalism which characterizes public television.

Television coverage of the Bundestag is merely part of general coverage of politics and consequently is subject to similar expectations by the political parties. For their part, television editors and journalists in Bonn seem to have internalized these expectations.

Complaints by the political parties are no longer necessary to produce 'objective' and 'balanced' television coverage of Bundestag proceedings. Balance is looked for across a range of programmes, rather than in each particular item of coverage, which enables television editors, despite these restrictions, to make coverage of parliamentary proceedings interesting, informative and entertaining. It is broadcasters' professional 'know-how', so vital to reach a public which is not very interested in politics, that guarantees television will not completely lose its autonomy. Politicians, moreover, are reliant on broadcasters to achieve some of their objectives and consequently the relationship between the two groups cannot simply be characterized by any asymmetrical dependence; it is fundamentally symbiotic.

THE TECHNICAL ASPECTS OF TELEVISING THE BUNDESTAG

Television pictures from the Chamber are originated both by public television broadcasters and by a rather modestly equipped 'house channel'. The former produces the greater part of the output seen by the public. The house channel and public television each use the pictures generated for their own distinctive purposes. The house channel was established in 1970 and is run by the press and information centre of the House, which provides coverage of the plenary debates using two rigid cameras; one faces the Speaker's place, the other the Government bench. The signal is transmitted to the offices of the Members and the parties in the House. At the same time the signal goes to the Federal Press and Information Office, which transmits it by a local cable network to the main federal ministries, the parties' headquarters and most of the press editors' offices in Bonn. The signal cannot be used beyond this local service because of its poor technical quality. It is largely an in-house (literally) service whose main function is to inform Members of the Bundestag and officials in the ministries about the progress of a particular debate so that they know when it is their turn to speak or when it is necessary to attend for a vote. If Members want a recording of a speech, perhaps to show in their constituency, they usually have a video recorder in their office and can record it directly. Newspaper editors' offices are provided with the house channel as a free service from the public purse to support their work. The officers of the Bundestag use recording of debates to supplement the written records. If public television wishes to cover the proceedings live, its signal is also fed into the local network of the Federal Press and Information Office, giving viewers an opportunity to choose between the two channels.

This division of function between the Bundestag house channel and public television has never seriously been called into question. In 1986, however, a proposal to revise the arrangements so that only the Bundestag provided the signal was discussed. Schulte, the Chairman of the Committee for Parliamentary Procedures of the Bundestag, and SPD Member of Parliament, claimed the subjects selected for coverage by the television broadcasters reflected their own priorities rather than the interests of the Bundestag. Television allegedly was only interested in appearances by eminent politicians, the 'political heavyweights'.

Schulte's initiative found support among backbenchers but eventually failed, because of the likely cost of the operation (they spoke about DM 10 million per year) and the lack of support for the proposal among parliamentary leaders, who were of course the major recipients of the media coverage. Representatives of public television objected, on the grounds that the pictures would be of an inferior technical quality and would be too 'official' in character, avoiding panning shots along the empty benches or demonstrations on the public areas.

At present it is not clear whether the house channel will expand its service to the new plenary hall currently being constructed. The decision is now complicated by the uncertainty about whether Bonn will continue to be the location for the Bundestag following German unification. The ground plan for the new plenary hall has provision for a minimal and maximal alternative. If the minimal plan is adopted the two rigid cameras will continue to cover the Speaker's place and the Government bench; the maximal alternative provides for at least seven cameras with telephoto lenses. Five of these cameras will be mounted on the horseshoe-like gallery above the circular plenum on both sides of the central 'federal eagle' at the front of the hall, making it possible to televise all speakers in their places. The cameras used will be automatic and guided to the person speaking by a process of electro-acoustic feedback. The cameras will be an improvement on those currently in use but are unlikely to achieve the standards of the public television cameras.

In the future, public television broadcasters will have at their disposal four instead of three cameras in the gallery and also a special room for editing. The entire investment cost for cables, camera and equipping the direction room are estimated at DM 6 million. So far as broadcasters in the commercial television sector are concerned, they seem to have no plans for more extensive coverage of parliamentary proceedings. RTL Plus and SAT1 will take their pictures from the press gallery as previously. No technical improvements are planned for coverage of proceedings of the Bundesrat.

TELEVISING THE BUNDESTAG: THE DEBATE

The discussion concerning the admission of television cameras to the Bundestag in the 1950s bears a remarkable similarity to the recent debate in the British setting. The major difference seems to be that in Germany there has been, from the outset, a consensus among political parties about the need to implant the Bundestag in the consciousness of the German people by making its functions and procedures readily accessible to the public via television. The history of parliamentarianism in Germany made a persuasive case for the fairly extensive reporting of parliamentary procedures in all media; it continues to do so. Many advantages have been claimed for live televising of Bundestag proceedings: the immediacy and impact of television images compared to other media; television's authenticity and its ability to deliver 'an unvarnished portrait of Parliament'; its ability to illustrate the divergent political positions of Members; the desirable effect of making the political process comprehensible; its educational function, especially important for people with little interest in political affairs; its propaganda impact, essential to overcome traditional German 'anti-party prejudices'; and, before reunification, its power to promote the German parliamentary variant of liberal democracy by contrasting it with the so-called people's democracies east of the Iron Curtain (an argument especially forceful because of the possibility of receiving West German television in the former German Democratic Republic). But these cross-party arguments, supported by television journalists as well as Members of the Bundestag, failed to convince everyone. There was and remains opposition to the cameras, although this ultimately has never been compelling. Five arguments are usually offered against admission of cameras.

First, there was a concern that televising debates might damage the 'dignity of the House'. The best-known advocate of this view was the Speaker of the House, Gerstenmeier, who was concerned to establish the institutional identity of the Bundestag in the late 1950s and early 1960s. He believed that the 'high house' might be transformed by television from an autonomous political subject into a manipulated object of broadcasters, whose programmes might focus on arbitrary and humorous events at the expense of the more serious work of the Members.

Concerns about a populist presentation of Parliament were accompanied by the belief that television's concentration on the plenary sessions would revive prejudices from Weimar days about Parliament as a mere 'talking-shop' (*Schwatzbude*). Much of the real work of the Bundestag, moreover, is achieved in committees, where television is not always permitted access so as to allow committee members the discretion necessary for frank discussions. But television pictures of empty benches in the Chamber could produce a misleading image of the activities of the House.

Concern for personal rights and the protection of data formed the basis of a second complex of objections. A number of indiscreet close-ups of the contents of the handbag of a female Member of the House, of a note scribbled by a Minister during a debate, of Adenauer eating a sly piece of chocolate, and of Members yawning, scratching their heads or reading a newspaper, prompted these worries (Gerhardt 1954). Concerns about data protection were expressed by the Speaker and the Parliamentary Advisory Committee, who were afraid that unduly curious cameras might zoom in on the confidential documents lying on the table for the Members during the plenary sessions. This was one of the reasons for the temporary abandoning of television in the Bundestag from 1957, as well as the subsequent prohibition on photographs agreed shortly afterwards (*Saarbrücker Zeitung* 1963).

Third, Members have repeatedly voiced their concerns about the advent of a 'television democracy', with changes in Members' behaviour prompted by the new medium. Members' changes to their clothing or even their gestures were accepted as harmless consequences of television's preference for 'goodlookers'. But these minor matters soon gave way to concerns that television might encourage ministers and Members to concentrate their attentions not on their political opponents in the House but on delivering a 'theatrical show' designed to arouse artificial controversy for the amusement of the viewing public and to promote their own electoral prospects. In brief, the political proceedings of the institution might become wholly subordinated to the requirements of television. It was this concern about television democracy which provided the second reason for the temporary termination of televising the Bundestag (*Bulletin der Bundesregierung* 1955). Fifteen years later it came up again in the wake of the very opulent televising of the debates of the *Ostverträge* (Gaus 1972).

Today this point is no longer a focus of discussion because it is almost universally assumed that television democracy has arrived. Politicians' speeches embracing carefully selected issues are now delivered to targeted audiences with the aid of television. The Bundestag, however, did not adopt one of television's proposals to make the proceedings more 'suitable' for live coverage by concentrating the 'interesting' points of the agenda in the morning so that television could cover the session live without disturbing the viewing habits of their audiences in the afternoon. Other suggestions were similarly provocative. Broadcasters suggested, for example, that Members should be obliged to attend these sessions to avoid the panning shots along the empty benches which proved so irritating to the public (Hopen 1987). Lueg, now director of the WDR editor's office in Bonn, actually requested a faster pace to the exchanges in debate, similar in style to a programme called *Aktuel Stunde*, 'The Actual Hour' which with its 'ping-pong effect' would be much more acceptable to television audiences (Lueg 1980: 154).

A fourth objection recently voiced concerns the rise of the so-called 'publicity hierarchy'. The phenomenon has both political and media origins. First, the political leaders in each of the parties try to reserve television prime time for their own appearances. This, they allege, is justified on the grounds that they are more able than lesser luminaries to convince the viewing public of a particular policy issue. For their part, media are fascinated by the 'cult of the personality' and tend to present only the better-known and more attractive people. So the 'political heavyweights' tend to dominate the screen while the majority of Members have little chance to appear. When the Bundestag was first televised, political leaders' attempts to monopolize the cameras resulted in bizarre if not grotesque proceedings. Some backbenchers would filibuster from the start of a particular televised session in order to pass the microphone, rather like a baton in a relay race, to one of their party's senior figures at a later stage in the debate. On occasions, ministers used their constitutional right to speak immediately to the House, at precisely the moment when the cameras began to whirr. When television failed to play its part in this process there was conflict. In July 1975, for example, the television cameras, as a result of technical failure, stopped broadcasting at the very moment that Straub, the leader of the CSU, wanted to start his televised speech (*Süddeutsche Zeitung* 1975).

The Parliamentary Advisory Committee tried to undermine this phenomenon by reducing speaking time. But the publicity hierarchy continues largely unaffected. As a result, the televising of Parliament has focused on key individuals and has been criticized for encouraging audiences to watch primarily key personalities (the Chancellor doesn't look too good today) rather than concentrating on the issues under discussion.

Analysts suggest that the group of Members who enjoy the bulk of media attention constitutes no more than 10 per cent of the House membership. These media preferences are clearly disadvantageous for publicity-conscious backbenchers, who from time to time stage increasingly wacky stunts to attract television's attention. One Member, for example, paddled across the Rhine in a canoe, while another took a hen to his office, claiming he needed a fresh egg every morning (Dubber 1979).

A fifth set of objections to the televising of the Bundestag focuses on the possible implications for the television audience. Most observers anticipated favourable consequences stemming from the decision to broadcast proceedings, with television creating a public which was better informed about current policy issues. But some journalists and politicians were anxious about the effects on the audience. On occasions when television coverage of proceedings has been particularly extensive, as happened in spring 1972, it has been argued that too much live reporting could annoy the public because their favourite diet of programmes had been replaced by political subject matter. It was suggested, moreover, that television would encourage a passive attitude towards politics among the public, perhaps resulting in a decline in direct political participation. Televising politics, it was argued, might replace the active citizen with the spectator cast in the role of a 'dead head at the political theatre' (Flottau 1972).

Some of the objections raised here – for example, concerning the growth of television democracy and the emergence of the publicity hierarchy – relate to phenomena which have emerged in many contemporary polities during the 1970s and 1980s. They seem, however, to reflect a much broader pattern of change in both political and media systems than can be explained by the introduction of television into legislatures. The latter is more likely a symptom than a cause of such 'malaise' in the body politic.

TELEVISING DEBATES: THE AUDIENCE REACTION

Public television tries to report the political parties in a balanced way, but a 'governmental bias' is clearly evident in the coverage of the Bundestag. Studies show that the Government tends to be the major beneficiary of coverage, no matter which party is in power (Schatz *et al.* 1989). This reflects the fact that the Government is the initiator of events more frequently than the Opposition. The Government also possesses the authoritative definers of events – ministers, senior politicians, heads of departments and so on. A content analysis of approximately 200 hours of television newscasting on public and commercial stations across a three-week period in autumn 1985 and spring 1986, revealed frequencies of appearance for individual ministers, parties and institutions as displayed in table 14.2.

The table shows that appearances by the Federal Government were twice as frequent as aggregate figures for Members of the Bundestag and the various political parties. It must be remembered, of course, that some appearances by the Chancellor and his ministers took place in the Bundestag. It is very striking, however, that while the Opposition party was televised relatively often the Leader of the Opposition, Vogel, enjoyed only a tenth of the number of appearances given to the Chancellor (23 compared to 206 cases). Even Genscher as Foreign Minister and a prominent member of the FDP establishment enjoyed a relatively high publicity profile. If the percentages of the appearances by the Government and its supporters in the House (excluding the category 'Bundestag in general') are aggregated, the resulting ratio in favour of the Government is 9.2 to 1.6. Faul (1989: 37) has very similar results.) Analysis of the news on commercial stations revealed an expected predominance of entertainment, with only scant attention devoted to political news; again the editors focused

Table 14.2 The Federal Government and the Bundestag in television newscasting

	Frequency of appearances (%)	No. of appearances
Chancellor Kohl	1.9	206
Foreign Minister Genscher	1.1	118
Other members of cabinet	4.9	519
Government altogether	7.9	843
Bundestag in general	0.8	86
Government coalition (CDU/CSU–FDP)	1.3	143
Vogel, Leader of SPD in the Bundestag	0.2	23
Remaining Opposition (SPD, Greens)	1.4	144
Bundestag altogether	3.7	396
All persons and institutions (including 25.8 per cent GDR and foreign affairs)	100.0	10,653

Source: Schatz *et al.* (1989).

very squarely on the Federal Government. The Bundestag received little coverage.

Public interest in television broadcasting from the Bundestag was initially quite considerable. Special occasions, such as debates on the *Ostverträge* and the (unsuccessful) vote of no confidence against Chancellor Brandt, enjoyed high audience rating figures; an estimated 43 per cent of potential audience viewed the latter event. The report of the 'Brandt debate' in the evening news on ARD was seen by over 60 per cent of total audience. But such figures are rare. The extension of parliamentary programming, which began in the 1970s, seemed to coincide with a levelling of public interest. The trend in viewing is still downwards. Figures for the year 1986 (with approximately 24 million television sets in the Federal Republic of Germany) show peak viewing figures of 5 per cent for coverage of the Bundestag with average figures nearer to the 1 per cent mark. Coverage from the Bundesrat achieved even smaller figures, the highest in recent years being 0.08 per cent (Rose 1986). These reductions in television audience figures seem to reflect a dramatic decline of interest by the public in political affairs more generally. More recent survey data showed that households which could receive the new commercial programmes, either directly by satellite or by cable, displayed dramatic changes in viewing habits. Consequently the main evening news of the public stations ZDF and ARD (*Heute* at 7 p.m. and *Tagesschau* at 8 p.m.) lost about 20 per cent of their former audiences, while audiences for the late-night news on both channels were down almost 40 per cent. Politics and current affairs programmes generally reported reductions in audience size of between 30 and 50 per cent. These audience reductions for public television were not compensated by a growth in figures for the commercial stations, since equivalent programmes were not broadcast. The mass public has, it seems, turned its attention to the new entertainment programmes and away from political matters (Darschin and Frank 1989).

TELEVISING THE BUNDESTAG: LESSONS FOR BRITAIN

A comparison of televising the Bundestag with television broadcasting from the British House of Commons must begin by noting a German peculiarity. The democratic institutions established in West Germany in 1949 needed to create a legitimacy which the British House of Commons achieved over a long and unbroken period of parliamentarianism. One of the major purposes underlying extensive television coverage of the Bundestag proceedings in the 1950s and 1960s was to help establish a similar tradition. Televising the Bundestag has been used self-consciously to introduce national political issues to the viewing public and to promote participation in the democratic political process.

Despite these initially different starting-points, there have been many subsequent parallel developments in German and British parliamentary politics. Undoubtedly the most important is the development and intrusion of party politics into all facets of political life and institutions. This has had a number of consequences. Policies, more than ever before, are formulated and presented in Parliament and other settings in a way that is intended to be eye-catching and to make them readily marketable to the electors. Attempts by the political parties to limit the independence of the public broadcasting system, which seems to be a feature of many western democracies, are also an inevitable consequence of an increasingly adversarial party politics. Television, presumed to be the most effective medium of communication with electors, seems a natural focus for competitive party activity. Parliamentary debate is also changing in character. Parties increasingly consider parliamentary debates not as a vehicle to convince Opposition parties within the House of the merits of particular policies, so much as an opportunity to demonstrate to the public that they are serious politicians, aware of the key problems confronting society and possessing leaders capable of resolving them. Indeed, the publicity hierarchy which offers disproportionate appearance opportunities to the politically prominent is not so much a product of the media as an expression of the rationality of party politics with its tendency towards constant campaigning and professionalization of public relations. Televising the Bundestag makes these processes more visible but it does not create them.

The report of the Select Committee on Televising of Proceedings of the House, presented in May 1989, seemed to suggest that Members believed something that had proved not to be the case in Germany – namely that coverage of parliamentary debates would achieve high viewing figures from an interested public. In Germany, experience suggests that it is best to give editorial control completely to broadcasters because only the professional skills of editors and camera operators can guarantee a tolerably acceptable level of public interest in parliamentary proceedings. Unedited coverage coupled with strict guidelines on camera shots is quite simply boring television.

Experience from the Bundestag, which seems to be confirmed by the American Congress, also suggests that live coverage of parliamentary proceedings does not by itself change the habits of individual Members in the long run. It is true that initially Members may pay more attention than previously to the quality both of their outfits and of their rhetoric, but they would do so for press journalists without the presence of television cameras. No parliamentary 'greenhorn', moreover, has ever built a career on being telegenic. Television may exaggerate Members' qualities but it does not create them.

The German experience also suggests that television does not damage the 'dignity of the House' in the way that some Members of the Commons seemed to fear. In Germany the rules governing coverage, which leave the privacy of the Members intact and guarantee that potentially negative aspects of coverage like empty benches occur only in relevant contexts, have developed as a consequence of a more general 'domestication' of political television. In Britain the process has not yet developed this far, but the rules of coverage established by the Select Committee guarantee that broadcasters respect the traditions of the House.

In conclusion, on the basis of the German experience the House of Commons should encourage television coverage of its proceedings but do so without an extensive system of editorial control. We live in a television age and it is television which brings most people into contact with politics. People are accustomed to choosing the programmes they wish to see according to their own needs and interests. If television coverage of the Commons is too bland and unattractive, all the preceding debates and efforts of broadcasters and politicians will be worthless. Viewers will simply select a different programme by pushing the buttons on their remote control.

Chapter 15

Europe on the move: the travelling Parliament roadshow

Tony O'Donnell

INTRODUCTION

The increasing television reporting of the European Parliament reflects the institution's own rising profile. It was directly elected for the first time only in 1979 but, since November 1982, has televised its own proceedings. Recordings as well as live pictures were available free of charge to any broadcasters who were interested. Subsequently, television coverage of the Parliament's sessions in Strasbourg has grown inexorably. But while the introduction of the cameras at Westminster in 1989 did not present an unknown or unfamiliar institution to the television audience, since both Lords and Commons have been established for centuries, in 1982 when the European Parliament was first televised it had only been in existence for twenty years. In the European setting the televising of parliamentary proceedings has enhanced in very positive ways public perceptions of both the European Community and its Parliament.

The decision to create an in-house television unit and turn the cameras on in Strasbourg was resolved straightforwardly, and without the protracted and bashful *Angst* that preceded the eventual – and at first merely provisional – admission of cameras to the House of Commons. The decision came against a background of growing unresponsiveness by broadcasters who had prepared, in conjunction with the European Broadcasting Union, a comprehensive framework for extensive international coverage of the first direct European elections in 1979.

Siune, McQuail and Blumler observed that being the very first Euro-poll brought distinct advantages: 'Its standing as a first-time event gave it a certain novelty value, and its authoritative, cross-party sponsorship . . . a legitimate claim to attention.' But there were disadvantages: 'the lack of established rituals, and precedents for coverage . . . general unfamiliarity as an event . . . and a potential lack of interest for the general public' (Siune *et al.* 1984: 257).

Subsequently, television broadcasters seemed to ignore the work of the first directly elected MEPs. Figures for the average number of journalists present at the 1981 plenary sessions, two years into the lifetime of the legislature, were 20 per cent down. Similarly, aggregate hours of television coverage transmitted, although a crude measure, revealed that output had more than halved over the period. In addition to this apparent media indifference, there were the daunting problems for systematic television coverage posed by an institution spread between Strasbourg, Brussels and Luxembourg. The logistics of securing a transmitted TV image from the European Parliament were invariably more challenging for news desks and assignment editors than a score of pictorially more interesting, or just plain simpler, stories which were nearer to hand. More often than not, the selection of these was also easier to justify in terms of the editorial budget.

One way to improve media coverage would be to establish a team of technical 'sherpas' to provide interested journalists and broadcasters with the technical means of recording, preparing and transmitting reports on the latest parliamentary events. But before that team of pioneers formally opened shop in 1982, to a uniquely international clientele, numerous technical, political and even cultural questions required careful consideration.

ESTABLISHING THE TELEVISION UNIT: TECHNICAL AND OTHER PROBLEMS

The basic decision to go ahead was a relatively simple matter compared to the substantial difficulties and complexities involved in its implementation. Perhaps the most problematic aspect of the operation was the itinerant nature of the Parliament's business, reflecting – then as now – member Governments' inability to agree on the question of the parliamentary seat. Business was conducted in three different cities (and seven, now nine, languages). Plenary sessions were (and still are) held monthly in Strasbourg, with a summer recess during August and a compensatory second October session. Until quite recently, moreover, sessions alternated between Strasbourg and Luxembourg, the home base of nearly all the Parliament's administrative secretariat of 3,000 staff. To complicate matters further, meetings of the eighteen specialist committees were held in Brussels for two weeks in every month. Assuming that no definitive pronouncement could be expected on the matter of the seat, technical options for the unit had to be kept as flexible as possible. The solution which seemed to meet most of the requirements was a custom-built outside-broadcast van, which could be driven to wherever Parliament was meeting and used as the core of the television operation.

The specifications for the vehicle which were eventually put out to tender sought, naturally enough, the very best of European technology; these were met by a combination of Mercedes auto-motion and Bosch television engineering. The vehicle possessed two mixer consoles that permitted recording to continue while simultaneously feeding already taped and edited material to line for transmission. The vehicle had the capacity to synchronize and balance four video cameras, once they were unloaded and rigged.

Other technical problems required resolution. The choice of videotape format had been based on the results of a questionnaire circulated to all Community TV stations. Replies showed that favours were divided fairly evenly between the B-format system of EC manufacture and the US-originated C-format. Three B-format machines were incorporated in the outside-broadcast vehicle, and it was decided to base all recording, editing and archives on that system. The final signal could be sent in either PAL or SECAM.

A C-format machine was also bought in order to accommodate customers who wanted to take recordings away in that format, and at the express request of the European Broadcasting Union the format range was further extended by the purchase of a BVU editing unit. The format game has been unending. At the time of writing, a majority favours the beta format, and the TV unit moved to anticipate demands for video in the new format. The master archive continues to be in 1-inch B.

The decision to retain all video recordings of debates means that at the close of every Strasbourg session cassettes are shipped to home base in Luxembourg where they form an ever growing library. Recordings were linked to a computer installed in the outside-broadcast van, enabling a production assistant to time-code every contribution to a debate, and make possible the retrieval of a sequence for copying or editing. Together with basic production notes, the cumulative print-outs formed the basis of a system of logging for recordings. Consequently anyone curious to learn Mrs Barbara Castle's thoughts on farm prices in 1983 may, should they so wish, find the appropriate video recordings.

Equipped to follow Members in their peregrinations, the television unit next addressed the singular operational problem of internal and external communications. Members of the European Parliament do not, of course, speak with one voice, but in their national language. The television unit went into production the year after Greece joined the Community, adding a seventh working language to Danish, Dutch, English, French, German and Italian. Spanish and Portuguese membership in 1986 added two more. Consequently, the technical team could expect to be collaborating with both broadcasters and politicians in production activity where any combination of these nine languages might be spoken. Faced with the prospect of a Tower of Babel with edit suites attached, it was decided for internal working purposes to follow the practice of the European Broadcasting Union and to use French and English as core languages. Fluent liaison with the EBU would be crucial for the successful electronic distribution of Parliament pictures via Eurovision. And, in any case, informal communication between staff in all of the European Community institutions tended to take place in one or other of these two languages.

The recruitment of the team itself meant expanding the already existing audio-visual unit of the Parliament – an arm of the Directorate-General for Information and Public Relations. Advertisements for a series of nineteen posts – director/producers, camera operators, video engineers and technicians – appeared in leading media publications throughout the Community. Good French and English and a taste for travel were preconditions among the many qualifications demanded of applicants.

THE UNIT AT WORK: BASIC PRINCIPLES

One of the initial goals of the operational team, envisaged at the planning stage, was the systematic recording of all parliamentary debates. But an eleventh-hour decision by the Parliament's bureau, as the management committee is universally known, to withhold authorization for recruiting the full complement of staff obliged a considerable rethink. The unit instead adopted a policy of reacting to requests from television stations for specific assistance and, within the limits of the reduced team's remaining capacity, recording as much as possible of the plenary proceedings for archive purposes. Early on, it became practice to record major debates, debates on urgent topics, visits of heads of state and government, and all important periods of vote.

The two basic rules of thumb governing free access to Parliament's facilities were that the client should be a broadcaster and that allocation of technical assistance be made according to the fundamental principle of 'first come, first served'. These are ground rules that have survived intact, despite the radical changes in European broadcast production and the steady, almost remorseless, increase in the pressure on a unit which has remained unaltered in size.

The original guidelines identified several groups as potential 'customers' for parliamentary television services: freelance broadcasters; broadcasting organizations; Members of the Parliament; political groups; pressure and lobby groups; researchers, and so on. Priority, however, was to be given to the broadcasters. But non-broadcast customers would have to pay. Parliament's guidelines were unequivocal concerning the latter. Facilities were to be offered free to broadcasters, but 'there should generally be charges for . . . other access.'

Although falling short of comprehensive gavel-to-gavel coverage, the first full year of operations in 1983 produced encouraging results, with the number of television reports of Parliament's work in session increasing by 100 per cent. While one may accept the veracity of the sceptics' cautionary tales about 'lies, damn lies and statistics', a strong claim can be (and is) made for explaining this veritable upsurge in parliamentary reporting by reference to the newly available technical assistance offered by the European Parliament itself.

There can be no doubt that, at that time, some editors and correspondents harboured significant doubts about the nature of the exercise. Some were simply sharing the sentiments of the celebrated Walter Cronkite, who informed a convention of American news directors in the 1970s that he was tired of being told what was news by 'sociologists, psychologists, educators, parents, bureaucrats and politicians' (Speakes 1988). Others were wary of the possible compromise involved in using Parliament's own facilities to report news stories about the Parliament – a reluctance stemming from the stout tradition of editorial independence present in most (but by no means all) of the European Community television stations. Anxieties concerning the sanctity of editorial freedom remain the chief misgiving of programme makers, with the records for 1983 and the first half of 1984 showing a marked increase in parliamentary coverage, but a continuing tendency for broadcasters to make their own technical arrangements.

In the second full year of operations, however, the parliamentary unit provided technical assistance for more than 70 per cent (278) of all reports noted (394). Users began to have confidence, not just in the efficient professionalism of the unit, but also in its no-strings assurance of editorial independence. The option has always existed for the TV reporter in Strasbourg to do his or her own thing – once accredited, there is no obligation to use in-house staff and facilities, although vastly increased levels of news interest have inevitably led to greater insistence on the pool system, and restrictions on access to the Chamber by outside crews, particularly during big events. And why hang around all day for a 'video bite' of the Member you want to include, when a Parliament copy tape takes the waiting out of wanting?

The presence of a new television facility meant, of course, that broadcasters could obtain pictures without actually being present, and could make use of the EBU's daily news exchange as the basis for a report on events at the session. News items likely to interest any of the thirty-nine stations in thirty-two countries that participate are circulated daily, and the editors of TV news programmes then decide which, if any, of the items they will use. In the case of parliamentary events in Strasbourg, the European affairs editor of the French channel FR3 offers the reports to his EBU colleagues. An analysis of the content of the reports carried by Eurovision shows that the nature of the subject matter began to change halfway through the lifetime of the television operation. Content began to focus on events of a fundamentally parliamentary character, rather than, as in earlier years, the visits of major public figures to the institution.

A further, but significant occasion was the adoption in May 1983 of guidelines prepared by the vice-chairman of the Information Sub-committee, Alasdair Hutton, then Conservative Member for the South of Scotland, and formerly with the BBC. The Hutton guidelines provided a set of formal 'rules of coverage' to govern the television operation. These rules were more generous to broadcasters than the corresponding guidelines governing the cameras in the Commons. The Strasbourg rulebook doesn't exclude reaction shots, insisting only that they should be of substantial reactions which are directly relevant to what is taking place.

Strasbourg is also limited by fewer restrictions concerning shots of the public gallery. The Hutton guidelines allow coverage of 'exceptional matters of official or political relevance' from the public tribune. In practice this amounts to the welcoming of official visitors or delegations by whoever happens to be presiding over the session. Visitors have included, for example, Winnie Mandela and Lothar de Maizière, the former Prime Minister of East Germany. In any case, the celebrity or political significance of whomsoever might be in shot from the Strasbourg visitors' gallery has to be considerable to obtain selection, given the Stygian gloom of the surroundings.

The deployment of cameras in the Strasbourg debating chamber, called, in the manner of continental legislatures, a 'hemicycle', depended on the importance of the event at hand. The guidelines suggested that 'occasions of the highest importance' rated a maximum four cameras. Major debates were allocated three, routine business two. The standard configuration was of three: one permanently on the President, or whichever Vice-President was in the chair; a second offering either a general view of the hemicycle or appropriate cutaway shots; and a third on the Member actually holding the floor.

Speaking time and order are normally very efficiently posted by caption advice; when this works well, cutting smoothly from speaker to speaker in satisfying sequence is no problem. A camera begins to frame up on the next speaker in plenty of time, since information about the Member's seat number is programmed into the van's computer at the beginning of the session. When the floor of the House departs from script, the accumulated experience and the acquired instinct of the camera operators and director ensure that required shots can be found in remarkably short order.

It soon became clear that, besides the elements of technical assistance originally offered to broadcasters in the recording preparation and transmission of reports, producers and journalists away from base in Strasbourg could be helped further by facilities for 'packaging' their reports. TV studio facilities have never been available to the Parliament's technical team. Therefore, to enable interview and 'piece-to-camera' elements to be added to reports from Strasbourg, a live camera point cabled to the OB van was devised. It was installed on the expansive landing outside the Chamber known as the lobby because of its prime-site potential for meetings with European Members.

Such a busy position had the disadvantage of noise and possible distractions for the contributor (with numerous cases of live interruption from curious passers-by) but the compensations of lively and expectant atmosphere are more than adequate. Over the years the sight of contributors and cameras at this busy crossroads of the Parliament building has become commonplace. Discussion programmes – and even national nightly news – have been broadcast from this site as a regular event and have become a popular option with broadcasters. It was evident, however that some broadcasters preferred a more orthodox mechanism for tying a TV package together and, in 1983, the further facility of an ENG crew became a complement to the lobby camera position. Subsequently, demand has proved so considerable that a further mobile crew is now bookable.

Strasbourg perhaps has cause to envy the Westminster operation because of the clear and well-lit images of the Commons that have been seen from the outset. Scenes from the European Parliament appear tenebrous by comparison, particularly if the video material has been copied to provide format compatibility, and even gloomier if transcoded from PAL to SECAM.

The pursuit of an uprated lighting grid for the Strasbourg Chamber is a saga some ten years long – too tedious and complex for recounting here. The principal stumbling block to any lasting solution of the problem has been Parliament's shared and only occasional occupation of its Strasbourg quarters. A number of compromises have been tested through the years – including, at one stage, a combination of searchlights operated by a technician – but the lighting level has remained insufficient and uneven. Given the supreme importance of light to television, it is perhaps not surprising that, for those operating the service, the achievement of a proper level of illumination has become a Grail-like obsession; what is perhaps worth further analysis is the way in which picture take-up has continued to grow regardless. At the time of writing, a definitive solution is at last nigh, and a fiat (*fiat lux*?) has been agreed by all of those required to be involved for the installation of even, adequate and unobtrusive lighting.

THE UNIT AT WORK: THE EUROPEAN PARLIAMENT
ON THE SCREEN

When the service began, lighting was just one problem among many to be solved by the flesh-and-blood personalities who appeared from all over Europe to take up posts that for so long had existed only on paper. The new arrivals were characterized by a kind of pragmatic goodwill as they appraised the considerable detail of their new job, on the ground. The technicians, in particular, regarded the fine tuning of the operation as a crusade of electronic problem-solving. For most of them, it was the first time in their lives that they had ever worked for an organization not primarily concerned with broadcasting, much less a major international institution, with an emphasis on different working values.

The learning curve of the new job became all the steeper as the newcomers began to appreciate that the task of installing a working TV facility could not be separated from the ambitious and highly political multinational institution that had ordained it. Yet the delicacy of the relationship between the institution, as proprietor of the service, and the journalists and broadcasters who were its clients, is self-evident. The broadcast team itself was the intervening variable, frequently requested by customers to give an instant reply to demands for coverage, be it a live feed of a news event or a speedy video copy.

The paramount concern of Parliament itself, as a growing political institution, was to strive after ever more positive contributions to the construction of the European Community. There was clear potential for tension in striving to respect the imperatives of the different parties and member countries. Yet in practice, with the application of a judicious blend of sensible rules and (sometimes grudging) compromise, such tension as there has been has tended to be creative rather than disruptive.

An instinct for balance in the coverage soon emerged. When Ronald Reagan addressed Parliament in May 1985, for example, Left and Green members waved placards protesting against alleged US interference in Nicaragua. Other elements of the House applauded the US President enthusiastically as he paused between passages. In the live presentation of the presidential visit and address to mark the fortieth anniversary of the ending of the Second World War, which was beamed to a worldwide variety of TV companies, cutaways to both these disparate reactions to the Reagan presence were worked in by the director in free but equal measure.

Users of Parliament's pictures could not, of course, justify relaying them without full coverage of events in the Chamber. There could be no qualms, for example, about showing or making available Northern Ireland Member Ian Paisley's interruption of the Pope's address to Parliament in October 1988 – nor his subsequent expulsion from the hemicycle on the instructions of Parliament's then President Lord Plumb. Mr Paisley was responsible for one of Mrs Thatcher's early direct experiences of a televised legislature, before cameras came to the Commons. At the end of Britain's last tenure of the presidency of the Council of Ministers in 1986, the then Prime Minister was reporting to Parliament on the achievements of the British term. Mr Paisley interposed himself between Mrs Thatcher and the cameras in order to brandish a poster summarizing his position on the Anglo-Irish agreement. Perhaps it was an experience which influenced Mrs Thatcher's opposition to televising the Commons.

But, far from playing to the cameras, the usual attitude of European parliamentarians is almost blasé, by British standards. Many had already accommodated themselves to omnipresent television as part of their native political landscape. There has certainly been no special sartorial revolution save for the occasional sloganizing T-shirt. Some Members, like the Danish Conservative MEP, Claus Toksvig, interpreted the laid-back attitude to constant TV attention as evidence of Parliament's essential preoccupation with longer-term objectives of greater power and achievement. 'Stripping away the vaudeville', said this former TV correspondent, would bring a much speedier appreciation of the real issues facing the European Community.

Others were more sceptical. A senior British reporter was not alone in voicing the belief that the only picture coverage anyone would want from Strasbourg would be of knocking stories, full of disruption and international misunderstanding. Initially there was corroborative evidence for the sceptics' case, with huge exposure for incidents such as the disruptive use of a megaphone during a debate. Closer examination identifies a particularly British flavour to both incidents and coverage. Perhaps reflecting its semi-detached relationship with the Community throughout most of the 1980s, Britain by 1984 appeared to be leading Europe in the kind of Parliamentary behaviour guaranteed to make the news bulletins.

But that was also the year in which Green members were elected in significant numbers for the first time. Their resolute informality and outspokenness soon gave them a similarly high media profile.

The potential demand for visual images of the European Parliament was always going to be considerable compared with the demand for pictures of any merely national legislature, even those legislatures whose decisions have routine and international repercussions. Users reveal different editorial criteria, mostly reflecting their distinctive national preoccupations. Even so, while the detailed content might vary in terms of the nationality of those interviewed or the language of the interview, the themes involved may be similar; and the context is automatically that of the European Community. Basic statistics kept to monitor levels of usage show that, in the past eight years, the larger member countries have consistently taken up approximately two-thirds of the facilities on offer: Britain, Germany, France and Italy, together with Spain.

However the contents of reports are impossible to monitor except by a polyglot insomniac. Subjective experience suggests that some countries tend to report general issues raised during session, others specifically excerpt the debates and the decisions arising from the votes that follow. Some reports favour Question Time, as tends to be the case with Westminster; but the Strasbourg version does not appear to dominate reportage in the same way. This is probably because the Government/Opposition adversarial model is absent – a factor which, together with the sheer variety of TV stations involved in Strasbourg coverage, has also tended to keep paranoia among political parties about relative air time at bay.

In fact, journalists attending plenary sessions almost doubled in number between 1982 and 1989, while the number of television reports per session increased more than threefold over the same period. A further, if rather more arbitrary, index – namely the cumulative hours of TV reports transmitted in relation to each session – again reveals a 300 per cent increase (see table 15.1).

The nature and the range of the programmes and their makers has also altered substantially since television facilities were first made available. If the British television landscape altered radically during the 1980s, the entire European broadcast scene developed equally markedly. Initially the parliamentary television unit, within the definition of its operating guidelines, dealt with approximately thirty stations sited in the then ten-strong European Community

Table 15.1   Media coverage of the European Parliament 1980–1989

	Average no. of journalists at sessions	No. of TV reports of sessions	No. of hours of TV reports of sessions
1980	116	347	52
1981	109	216	28
1982	106	182	26
1983	117	392	46
1984	156	394	58
1985	134	413	40
1986	146	488	58
1987	137	576	59
1988	169	656	79
1989	180	770	109

as potential clients. Non-community broadcasters tended to regard the Parliament as having little more than curiosity value. At the beginning of the 1990s, however, the proliferation of TV stations prompted by satellite technology and deregulation means that every Community country except Ireland and Portugal has acquired at least one more television channel. The smallest member state by far, Luxembourg, is at the leading edge of satellite TV production. All are able to receive many more stations than in 1982 – some provided by additional domestic sources, some pan-European or international, some simply the TV channels of a neighbour country available for the first time. Much of this rich multilingual, multicultural mix is relayed by the 'hybrid' satellite-to-cable system so conspicuously absent from the United Kingdom. Taking Brussels as one example of this system's range of products, the viewer there has access to more than twenty channels offering programming in French, Flemish, English, German, Spanish and Italian.

The rapid development of this new plurality in European television, accompanied by growing journalistic and popular acknowledgement of the European Parliament's political role, indicates an ever-increasing demand for pictures and for programme facilities. The institution's higher profile has already resulted in coverage demands from outside the European Community on a much more significant basis.

In 1990 the American public affairs network C-SPAN programmed several hours from the April Strasbourg session, while CNN had begun occasional reports in the previous year. Over the same period, Soviet television began to take up material, some on an extended basis, and culminating in coverage of the visit by the then Foreign Minister Eduard Shevardnadze. During the C-SPAN visit the German networked programme on the session, produced alternately by ARD and ZDF, and the first scheduled, regular transmission to be based on the Parliament's broadcast facilities, went into its sixth year.

Coverage has become less speculative, more a product of an advance commitment to sessions, either in the form of complete programmes or as regular programme strands. At the same time, there is demonstrably a much bigger take-up of Parliamentary news as it breaks. That is certainly a reflection of the much greater media attendance at sessions. Their ever-accumulating expertise in Parliament lore and procedure has also created a more acute awareness of which stories are significant.

Many of the journalists – and indeed much of the debate – travel from Brussels, which now houses a media presence said to be second only to Washington. The parliamentary television team according to the Hutton guidelines, is also there out of sessions 'to enhance coverage of committees'. Less than half the team is currently based permanently in Brussels and, while there is a brisk and challenging traffic in news events, resources are simply not adequate for the systematic coverage of committees. Generally, the OB van remains in Luxembourg, leaving routine coverage of committees to be carried out by a single ENG crew at the request of broadcasters. None the less, it's hard to resist the conclusion that sooner or later the next step will be fuller coverage of the committees – the engine room of this, as any other, democratic legislature – and the public hearings, perhaps after the comprehensive fashion of C-SPAN.

At the time of writing, the distinctive blue-and-gold outside-broadcast van of the European Parliament has entered its tenth year, and has been rigged and derigged for more than a hundred Strasbourg sessions. The nearest parallel in a British political context would be the coverage of a half-century's worth of the two main party conferences – speeded up. By this expedient the European Parliament has secured consistent coverage during a period when it has shrugged off nominal status and secured significantly greater financial and political power.

But fears, similar to those expressed for the Commons, that the presence of TV would bring about a change in the essential character of the Parliament are invalid, because the European Parliament evolved with the cameras already present. The evidence in Brussels, as in Strasbourg and now at Westminster appears, at long last, to be countering John Whale's claim that television was always excluded from any legislature or committee with real decisions to take (Whale 1969: 61). Perhaps some, if not all, of the real business of Parliament has retreated beyond range – as is regularly claimed to have happened in British local politics after journalists were admitted to council meetings. However, as C-SPAN has shown, exposure to the political process twenty-four hours a day can stimulate a powerful curiosity about what is going on. As C-SPAN founder Brian Lamb says, the significant thing is not how many but who is watching – those who are involved (Lamb 1988: xvii).

Perhaps the calm politeness that usually characterizes the public exchanges of MEPs expresses Members' inhibitions brought on by television. That was at one time suggested of the British House of Lords – with the added comment that they could 'afford to be polite – not much power was at issue' (Cameron 1969: 58). In the European Parliament it is more credibly explained by Members need to remain cool and coherent for the interpreters.

The European Parliament is a rare example of a rolling stone which has gathered moss. It's hard not to predict an ever more telling and efficient output, should a single seat ever be decided. Freed from their life of perpetual motion, MEPs would have the luxury of time to consider the finer points of exploiting the TV cameras, such as the American technique of 'doughnutting' colleagues for an impression of greater attendance. Permanently packing away the camp-bed would certainly make for a more substantial interaction with Commission and Council, already solidly rooted in Brussels, if this were to be the chosen home, and could even lead to arguments for a European Community broadcasting service, available to cover the collective work of the institutions.

A decision on the seat would also undoubtedly presage a further spurt in media attention in view of the added coherence and edge this would give to the work of the institutions. For the overall European style of political journalism is drawn to debate – often leading it rather in the American fashion, as opposed to merely reporting it in the British manner. It is intriguing why so many English-language tomes on government and political theory ignore the influence of the fourth estate on the democratic process.

The European debate has become a serious affair, and, as James Cameron once insisted, 'the reporter engaged in serious affairs must be the people's eyes and ears' (Cameron 1969: 72). It must be supposed that those reports will continue to feature images of that debate as it develops in the European Parliament.

References

Almond, G. A. and Verba, S. (1963) *The Civic Culture: Political Attitudes and Democracy in Five Nations*, Princeton: Princeton University Press.

Barth, A. (1985) 'Parlament und Mattscheibe', *Münchener Merkur*, 6 May.

Bawden, J. (1982) 'Is Parliament good television?', *Parliamentary Government* 3(1).

BBC Broadcasting Research Department (1990) *Newsnight*, Special Projects 90/50/046.

Benn, A. W. (1965) 'Televising the Commons', in *The Regeneration of Britain*, London: Gollancz.

Billig, M. (1990) 'Stacking the cards of ideology: the history of the Sun Souvenir Royal Album', *Discourse and Society* 1(1): 17–37.

Black, H. (1981) 'Live Commons broadcasting – how it's rated by Canada's MPs', *Cable Communications* 47(11): 82–7.

Blumler, J. G. (1967) 'Parliament and television', *Encounter* 15: 52–6.

——(1984) 'The sound of Parliament', *Parliamentary Affairs* 37: 263.

Blumler, J. G. and Gurevitch, M. (1981) 'Politicians and the press: an essay on role relationships', in Dan Nimmo and Keith Saunders (eds) *Handbook of Political Communications*, London: Sage, pp. 467–97.

——(1986) 'Journalists' orientations to political institutions: the case of parliamentary broadcasting', in P. Golding, G. Murdock and P. Schlesinger (eds) *Communicating Politics*, Leicester: Leicester University Press.

Bovill, M. and Wober M. (1990) *The House of Commons Experiment: Public Attitudes before and after Three Months*, BBC/IBA Research Report.

Broadcasting (1947) 'Opening of Congress televised: lens falls', 6 January: 86.

Broadcasting (1948) 'Airing of Congress sessions proposed', 1 March: 80.

Bromhead, P. (1963) 'Parliament and the press', *Parliamentary Affairs* 16: 279–92.

Bulletin der Bundesregierung (1955) 'Bonn "lebendig" Übertragen', no. 45, 8 March.

Burnet, A. (1988) 'Open House', *Sunday Times*, 14 February.

Butt, R. (1967) 'The public relations of Parliament', in *The Power of Parliament*, London: Constable.

Cameron, J. (1969) *Point of Departure*, London: Panther.

Clancey, M. (1988) *C-SPAN Survey Results*, November, University of Maryland Survey Research Center.

Cockerell, M. (1988) *Live from Number 10*, London: Faber.

Cumberbatch, G., Brown, B. and Skelton, J. (1990) *The House of Commons Television Experiment: An Evaluation Report*, Aston University mimeograph.

Curran, J. (1990) 'The new revisionism in mass communication research: a reappraisal', *European Journal of Communication* 5(2–3): 134–64.

Darschin, W. and Frank, B. (1989) 'Tendenzen im Zuschauerverhalten', *Media Perspectiven* 3: 168–82.

Davidson, R. H. (1981) *The Impact of Televised Proceedings upon the House of Representatives*, Washington: Congressional Research Service, Library of Congress.

Davies, A. (1980) *Reformed Select Committees: The First Year*, London: Outer Circle Policy Unit.

Day, R. (1963) *The Case for Televising Parliament*, London: Hansard Society.

Deutscher Bundestag (1983) *Datenhandbuch zur Geschichte des Deutschen Bundestages 1949–1982*, Bonn.

Dewar, D. (1966) 'The Select Committee on Televising of Proceedings of the House of Lords 1965–7', *The Table* 35: 58–68.

Downing, J. (1990) 'US media discourse on South Africa: the development of a situation model', *Discourse and Society*. 1(1): 39–60.

Drewry, G. (ed.) (1985) *The New Select Committees – Study of the 1979 Reforms*, Oxford: Clarendon Press.

Dubber, U. (1979) 'Neunzig Prozent ohne Resonanz', *Das Parlament*, 11 August.

Englefield, D. (ed.) (1984) *Commons Select Committees: Catalysts for Progress*, London: Longman.

Ettema, J. S. and Kline, F. G. (1977) 'Deficits, differences and ceilings: contingent conditions for understanding the knowledge gap', *Communications Research* 4: 179–202.

Farr, R. and Moscovici, S. (1984) *Social Representations*, Cambridge: Cambridge University Press.

Faul, E. (1989) 'Die Fernsehprogramme im dualen Rundfunksystem', *Rundfunk und Fernsehen* 1: 25–46.

Flottau, H. (1972) 'Zaungast oder mundiger Burger?', *Süddeutsche Zeitung*, 19 May.

Foucault, M. (1978) *The History of Sexuality*, Harmondsworth: Penguin.

——(1980) *Power/Knowledge*, Brighton: Harvester.

——(1982) 'Afterword: the subject and power', in Hubert Dreyfus and Paul Rabinow (eds) *Michel Foucault: Beyond Structuralism and Hermeneutics*, Chicago: University of Chicago Press.

Franklin, B. (1986) 'A leap in the dark: MPs' objections to televising Parliament', *Parliamentary Affairs* 39: 284–97.

——(1988) 'The television debate', *New Society*, 15 January: 12–14.

——(1989) 'Televising legislatures: the British and American experiences', *Parliamentary Affairs* 42(4): 485–503.

——(1990) 'Parliamentary television in the regions', *Television Week*, October: 10–14.

Fredin, E. S. and Kosicki, G. M. (1989) 'Cognitions and attitudes about community: compensating for media images', *Journalism Quarterly* 66: 570–8.

Fritz, S. (1985) 'Byrd: I'd like to move the Senate into the twentieth century', *Los Angeles Times*, 5 January: 10.

Gale, R. (1988) 'The argument against televising the British House of Commons', *The Parliamentarian*, July: 151–2.

Gallup (1986) *The Gallup International Public Opinion Polls: Great Britain 1937–75*, New York: Random House.

Gaus, G. (1972) 'Werft das Fernsehen aus dem Bundeshaus hinaus!', *Der Spiegel*, 15 May.

Genova, B. K. L. and Greenberg, B. S. (1979) 'Interests in news and the knowledge gap', *Public Opinion Quarterly* 43: 79–91.

Gerhardt, P. (1954) 'Fernsehkamera im Bundeshaus – ja und nein', *Christ und Welt*, 23 September.

Glasgow University Media Group (1976) *Bad News*, London: Routledge & Kegan Paul.

——(1980) *More Bad News*, London: Routledge & Kegan Paul.

——(1982) *Really Bad News*, London: Writers and Readers.

——(1985) *War and Peace News*, Milton Keynes: Open University Press.

Gray, J. (1989) 'Televising the Commons: the reluctant débutante at the media ball', paper presented to the Conference on the Future of Broadcasting, organised by the West Yorkshire Media in Politics Group, York, February.

Green, A. (1986) *Gavel to Gavel: A Guide to the Televised Proceedings of Congress*, Washington: Benton Foundation.

Grisewood, H. (1962) 'The BBC and political broadcasting in Britain', *Parliamentary Affairs* 16: 42–5.

Haley, W. (1949) 'Parliamentary institutions and broadcasting', *Parliamentary Affairs* 2: 108–17.

Hansard Society for Parliamentary Government (1988), Press release concerning televising the proceedings of the House, 8 February.

Hargreaves, R. (1989) 'ITV unhappy with Commons TV plans', *Broadcast*, 31 March: 3.

Harrison, M. (1985) *TV News: Whose Bias?*, Hermitage: Policy Journals.

Harrop, M. (1987) 'Voters', in J. Seaton and B. Pimlott (eds) *The Media in British Politics*, Aldershot: Avebury.

HC Debs [House of Commons Debates] (1959) Vol. 612, 3 November.

——(1965) Vol. 713, cols 1033–133, 28 May. (A motion by T. L. Iremonger to introduce an experiment in television broadcasting.)

——(1966) Vol. 736, cols 1606–732, 24 November. (A motion by Richard Crossman on the first report from the Select Committee on Broadcasting; motion to approve an experiment on closed circuit.)

——(1972) Vol. 843, cols 465–586, 19 October. (Debate on the experiment for the public broadcasting of proceedings by television.)

——(1974a) Vol. 868, cols 445–54, 30 January. (Bill introduced by Dick Leonard to provide public broadcasting by sound and television.)

——(1974b) Vol. 873, cols 223–7, 7 May. (Bill introduced by Phillip Whitehead for experimental period of broadcasting by radio and television.)

——(1978) Vol. 953, cols 245–52, 4 July. (Bill introduced by John Farr to televise the proceedings of the House of Commons.)

——(1980) Vol. 977, cols 1362–71, 30 January. (Bill introduced by Austin Mitchell to establish a parliamentary television unit.)

——(1981) Vol. 15, cols, 166–72, 15 December. (Bill introduced by Jack Ashley to televise proceedings of the House of Commons.)

——(1983a) Vol. 40, cols 805–11, 13 April. (Bill introduced by Austin Mitchell to televise Select Committees.)

——(1983b) Vol. 47, cols 876–8, 2 November. (Bill to televise Parliament introduced by Austin Mitchell.)

——(1985) Vol. 87, cols 277–366, 20 November. (Bill introduced by Miss Janet Fuchs to televise the proceedings of the Commons.)

——(1987) Vol. 123, cols 123–240, 24 November.

——(1988a) Vol. 127, cols 194–288, 9 February. (Bill introduced by Anthony Nelson approving the principle of an experiment in televising proceedings and calling for the establishment of a Select Committee.)

——(1988b) Vol. 135, cols 544–736, 16 June.

——(1989) Vol. 154, cols 607–60, 12 June. (Motion to approve the report of the Select Committee on Televising of Proceedings of the House.)

——(1990) Vol. 176, cols 1223–76, 19 July. (Debate of the report of the Select Committee on Televising of Proceedings of the House approving the committee report and agreeing in principle that televising of the proceedings of the House should now continue indefinitely.)

HC [House of Commons] Select Committee (1988) *First Report of the House of Commons Select Committee on Televising of Proceedings of the House, Session 1987–88*, Cmnd 473.

——(1989) *First Report from the House of Commons Select Committee on Televising of Proceedings of the House, Session 1988–89*, Cmnd 141.

——(1990) *First Report of the House of Commons Select Committee on Televising of Proceedings of the House, Session 1989–90*, Cmnd 265.

——(1991) *First Report from the House of Commons Select Committee on Broadcasting, Session 1990–91*, Cmnd 11.

HL Debs [House of Lords Debates] (1983) Vol. 445, cols 1189–220, 8 December. (Debate to endorse a decision of 15 June to televise for an experimental period the Lords proceedings on closed-circuit television.)

——(1984) Vol. 457, cols 764–860, 27 November. (Debate agreeing to a six months' experimental period of televising of proceedings from January to June 1985.)

——(1985) Vol. 466, cols 991–8, 1004–46, 22 July. (The House approved the continuation of the experimental televising of the proceedings until Christmas.)

——(1986) Vol. 474, cols 963–74, 977–1005, 12 May. (The debate authorized continuation of the televising of proceedings on an indefinite basis.)

HL [House of Lords] Select Committee (1984) *First Report by the Select Committee of the House of Lords on Sound Broadcasting, Session 1983–84*, 25 July.

——(1986) *First Report of the Select Committee of the House of Lords on Televising the Proceedings of the House, Session 1985–86*, 12 March.

——(1990) *First Report by the Select Committee of the House of Lords on Broadcasting, Session 1989–90*, 23 January.

Heath, A. and Topf, R. (1987) 'Political culture', in R. Jowell, S. Witherspoon and L. Brook (eds) *British Social Attitudes: The 1987 Report*, Aldershot: Gower.

Herschede, M. (1989) 'C-SPAN: my personal story', essay submitted on C-SPAN's tenth anniversary.

Hetherington, A. (1986) *News, Newspapers and Television*, London: Macmillan.

——(1989) *News in the Regions*, London: Macmillan.

Hetherington, A., Weaver, K. and Ryle, N. (1990) *Cameras in the Commons*, London: Hansard Society.

Hood, S. (1980) *On Television*, London: Pluto.

Hopen, P. (1987) 'Fensterreden?', *Trend*, 1 March.

Hughes, E. (1966) 'Mumbo jumbo and television', in *Parliament and Mumbo Jumbo*, London: Allen & Unwin, pp. 175–82.

Hughes, R. (1988) *Broadcast*, 5 August.

Ingham, B. (1990) 'Government and media: Co-existence and tension', unpublished lecture delivered at Trinity and All Saints College, Leeds, 22 November.

Johnston, P. (1990) 'MPs detail rules for Commons TV', *Daily Telegraph*, 18 May.

Jowell, R. and Topf, R. (1988) 'Trust in the establishment', in R. Jowell, S. Witherspoon and L. Brook (eds) *British Social Attitudes: The 5th Report*, Aldershot: Gower.

Lamb, B. (1988) *C-SPAN: America's Town Hall*, Washington: Acropolis Books.

Limon, D. W. (1966) 'Broadcasting the proceedings of the House of Commons', *Table* 35: 69–73.

Lindsay, T. F. (1967) 'Press, radio and television,' in *Parliament and the Press Gallery* London: Macmillan, pp. 120–33.

Lueg, E. D. (1980) 'Das Parlament und das Fernsehen', in H. Klatt (ed.) *Der Bundestag im Verfassungsgefüge der BRD*, Bonn.

McQuail, D. (1987) *Mass Communication Theory: An Introduction*, London: Sage.

Maloney, C. (1990) 'Lights, cameras, quorum call: a legislative history of senate television' MA thesis, College of William and Mary, University of Virginia.

Marsh, A. (1977) *Protest and Political Consciousness*, London: Sage.

Menard, P. (1985) 'Parliament and television', *Canadian Parliamentary Review*, Autumn: 20–4.

Mitchell, A. (1988) 'Commons TV', *Guardian*, 27 June.

——(1990) 'Beyond televising Parliament: taking politics to the people', *Parliamentary Affairs*, February.

Nelson, A. (1988) 'The Commons on camera', *Parliamentarian*, July: 148–50.

Norton, P. (ed.) (1985) *Parliament in the 1980s*, Oxford: Blackwell.

O'Neill, T. P. (1984) Interview, 19 March, US House of Representatives, Washington DC.

——(1987) *Man of the House: The Life and Political Memoirs of Speaker Tip O'Neill*, New York: Random House.

Perry, J. N. (1979) 'Dull or not, the televising of action from the House floor is making history,' *Wall Street Journal*, 26 March: 16.

Reumann, K. (1980) 'Machen Journalisten die Politiker lächerlich?' *Frankfurter Allegemeine Zeitung*, 8 July.

Robinson, M. (1981) 'Three faces of congressional media', in R. H. Davidson (ed.) *The Impact of Televising Proceedings upon the House of Representatives*, Washington DC: Congressional Research Service, Library of Congress.

Robinson, M. and Clancey, M. (1985) *The C-SPAN Audience after Five Years*, Washington DC: Media Analysis Project, George Washington University.

Rose, E. (1986) 'Politisches Forum oder Hofberichterstattung', *Das Parlament*, 15 November.

Saarbrücker Zeitung (1963) 'Fotografieren verboten', 16 January.

Schank, R. C. and Abelson, R. P. (1977) *Scripts, Plans, Goals and Understanding: An Enquiry into Human Knowledge Structures*, Hillsdale, NJ: Lawrence Erlbaum Associates.

Schatz, H. et al. (1989) *Strukturen und Inhalte des Rundfunkprogramms der vier Kabelpilotprojekte*, Düsseldorf.

Seaton, J. and Pimlott, B. (1987) *The Media in British Politics*, Aldershot: Avebury.

Segal, A. (1968) 'The case for not televising Parliament', in B. Crick (ed.) *The Reform of Parliament*, London: Weidenfeld & Nicholson, pp. 296–306.

Sennett, R. (1974) *The Fall of Public Man*, New York.

Seymour-Ure, C. (1962) 'The parliamentary press gallery in Ottawa', *Parliamentary Affairs* 16: 35–41.

——(1963) 'Parliamentary privilege and broadcasting', *Parliamentary Affairs* 16: 411–18.

——(1964) 'An examination of the proposal to televise Parliament', *Parliamentary Affairs* 16: 172–81.

——(1974) *The Political Impact of Mass Media*, London: Constable.

Shprintsen, A. (1987) 'The gallery: history and evolution', *Parliamentary Government* 7: 1–2.

Siune, K., McQuail, D. and Blumler, J. G. (1984) 'Broadcasting European elections', in *Electoral Studies*, London: Butterworth.

Social and Community Planning Research (1984) *British Social Attitudes: The 1984 Report* ed. R. Jowell and C. Airey, Aldershot: Gower.

——(1985) *British Social Attitudes: The 1985 Report* ed. R. Jowell and S. Witherspoon, Aldershot: Gower.

——(1986) *British Social Attitudes: The 1986 Report* ed. R. Jowell and S. Witherspoon and L. Brook, Aldershot: Gower.

——(1987) *British Social Attitudes: The 1987 Report* ed. R. Jowell, S. Witherspoon and L. Brook, Aldershot: Gower.

——(1988) *British Social Attitudes: The 5th Report* ed. R. Jowell, and S. Witherspoon, L. Brook, Aldershot: Gower.

Speakes, L. (1988) *Speaking Out*, New York: Scribner.

Speicher, K. (1986) 'C-SPAN's close-up on government', *On Cable*, May.

Stradling, R. (1985) *Monitoring the Televising of the House of Lords: An Interim Report*, London: Hansard Society for Parliamentary Government.

Stradling, R. and Bennett, E. (1986) *Televising the House of Lords*, London: Hansard Society for Parliamentary Government.

Süddeutsche Zeitung (1975) 'Parteien streiten über Funk- und Fernsehprogramm', 29 July.

Van Deerlin (1977) US Congress House Representative Van Deerlin speaking for H. Res. 866, 95th Congress, 1st session, 27 October, *Congressional Record*.

Van Dijk, T. A. (1988) *News as Discourse*, Hillsdale, NJ: Lawrence Erlbawm.

Watson, P. (1983) 'Should the Senate be televised?', *C-SPAN Update*, 31 October: 1.

Wendt, H. (1979) 'Demokratie ist kein Geheimverfahren der Eingeweihten', *Das Parlament*, 17 November.

Whale, J. (1969) *Television: The Half-Shut Eye*, London: Macmillan; repr. Penguin, 1988.

Whitelaw, W. (1985) Robert Fraser Lecture, IBA, 15 November.

Whiteside, T. (1984) 'Onward and upward with the arts: Cable-1', *New Yorker*, 20 May: 45.

Wilson, C. (1969) 'Parliament and the communications media', *Parliamentarian* 50 (2) 106–10.

Wober, J. M. (1985) *The House on the Screen*, IBA Research Paper, London: IBA.

——(1988) *Televising Parliament: Attitudes and Knowledge*, IBA Research Paper, London: IBA.

——(1990) 'Television in the House of Commons: education for democracy', *Parliamentary Affairs* 43(1): 15–26.

Wober, J. M. and McCron, R. (1985) *Television in the House of Lords: Inside Views of the Experiment*, IBA Research Paper, London: IBA.

Woffinden, B. (1988) 'Televising the Commons', *Listener*, 28 January.

Index